AROUND THE
BLOCK

Books by Tom Shachtman

AROUND THE BLOCK

The Business of a Neighborhood

TOM SHACHTMAN

Harcourt Brace & Company

New York   San Diego   London

Requests for permission to make copies of any part of the
work should be mailed to: Permissions Department,
Harcourt Brace & Company, 6277 Sea Harbor Drive,
Orlando, Florida 32887-6777.

Library of Congress Cataloging-in-Publication Data
Shachtman, Tom, 1942–
Around the block: the business of a neighborhood / Tom
Shachtman.—1st ed.
p.   cm.
ISBN 0-15-100077-8
1. Small business—Social aspects—New York (State)—New York—
Case studies. 2. Neighborhood—New York (State)—New York—Case
studies. 3. Chelsea (Manhattan, New York, N.Y.) I. Title.
HD2346.U52N548   1997
338.6'42'097471—dc21   97-16306

Designed by Lydia D'moch
Printed in the United States of America
First edition
A B C D E

*For my nieces, Jennifer and Wendy Ban
and Liza and Erica White*

CONTENTS

SLIPPING INTO
THE STREAM

PREDICTIONS regarding the economic
and social future of cities contain both good news and bad news.
By the year 2000, half the earth's population will live in cities of
more than 100,000 people, and by a quarter century after that, two-
thirds of the population will be urban; the United States of America, well in advance of this global trend, will very shortly have
three-quarters of its population working in metropolitan centers
and living in them or in close proximity to them. Our country's
economic future, then, in the main lies not in the vanishing small
towns of the Midwest or solely in the suburban industrial parks
and malls, but rather in midsize to large cities. Previous worries
that inner cities would collapse after being abandoned have been
supplanted by the belief that big cities will survive. That is cause
for optimism.

At the same time, the predictions are that those cities will be
even further separated into enclaves of rich and poor than they

now are and that the disparity in incomes between the two groups will continue to worsen. More than half the urban population will be desperately poor, and the rich—no more than 10 percent of the citizens—will live and work in luxury, but in guarded areas. The future for the 40 percent in the middle class is uncertain. I view this pattern of income distribution as cause for alarm.

Simultaneous with these trends is a third, the proven ability of the McDonalds's, Wal-Marts, Ace Hardwares, and Hewlett-Packards of the country to squeeze smaller competitors out of existence. If this trend continues unchecked, small businesses may be replaced by big businesses, until consumers are able to obtain goods and services only from a vastly reduced number of providers. This, too, I consider bad news.

Given these trends, what would be the fate of ordinary big-city blocks where today a substantial fraction of the population is employed? In 1993, I decided to find out, for it is in such blocks that two species endangered by the trends—the small business and the middle class—are most regularly found.

I determined to examine closely the workings of the business entities in and around a single block in a big city over the course of a single year and to try and glean from this sample some inkling of what the future might hold. It would have been relatively easy, and reliably upbeat, to track a route to the future in a "hot" block bustling with high-tech enterprises and twenty-something geniuses, but my interest is in learning whether there *is* any future for that substantially larger fraction of America that is not existing on the cutting edge, and for that equally large portion of the workforce that is neither young nor extravagantly skilled.

I didn't want an urban outpost of Silicon Valley, but I wanted to avoid a backwater whose enterprises were obviously behind the times and doomed, and I also wanted to avoid a block filled with businesses about which people might dismissively say, "only in New York," such as blocks in the Broadway Theater District or in the Garment District. What I wanted and needed was an ordinary block in an in-between neighborhood in the biggest city in the country.

On Thursday, April 15, 1993, people walk the Manhattan "square block" defined by Seventh and Eighth Avenues, 17th and 18th Streets, with glazed eyes. Overheard snatches of conversations contain phrases about income taxes being due. White men in suits or blue workmen's overalls, black men in bicycle-messenger spandex outfits, Latina office workers in skirts and blouses, teenagers in denim: they seem to be regular walkers here, for they pay little attention to the sounds and strokes of carpenters, sheet-metal workers, painters, and decorators at their renovation work on a half-dozen storefronts. To a visitor, the sounds and sights around the block are pleasant harbingers of a neighborhood that seems to be emerging from more than the physical winter.

A year has several beginning points: January 1; July 1, when many companies' fiscal calendars start; early September, when schools resume. Income-tax day is also a commencing moment, an occasion for putting the old year and its burdens behind us and for thinking about the new, especially in economic terms. An admittedly arbitrary beginning point, it is a convenient place to slip into a steadily running stream.

The United States spent the turn of the 1990s in the deepest economic doldrums since the Great Depression of the 1930s. Between 1989 and 1992, some 60,000 small businesses closed their doors. In New York City, the downturn resulted in tens of thousands of lost jobs, and uncounted scores of shuttered buildings and empty storefronts. While the country as a whole lost about 1 percent of its jobs, New York lost nearly 7 percent. Technically speaking, recovery began in 1991, but a year later the turnaround was so weak that Bill Clinton's in-house campaign slogan was "It's the economy, stupid." On April 15, 1993, a few months after Clinton took office, while most of the country was considered to have recovered from the recession, New York's economy still lagged.

By the spring of 1997, four years later, when I completed my follow-up interviews—the results are in a postscript at the end of this book—Clinton had been reelected, partially because the economy was considered to be on a steady, modest-growth track that had lasted for a few years and was likely to do so for several more years. Back in 1993, though, the slowness of the recovery was being cited as evidence for the notion that this recession was not a usual trough in the business cycle but a turning point in the transformation of the country's economy. Affected in this basic change were thought to be such fundamental matters as how and where we worked, the tasks we performed, the composition of businesses—even how money was made. I hoped to be able to catch glimpses or echoes of these changes in the microcosm of a single big-city block.

I chose Manhattan as the general site for inquiry because it is a marvel of density; hundreds of business entities within a small geographic area are available for examination. As with many blocks in Manhattan, the one I focused on contains about the same number of businesses as some small and medium-sized towns. My choice was further narrowed by two other specifications: I wanted a block that was both average and disparate.

This particular Chelsea block fit the bill. It was one I'd walked around for a half-dozen years, picking up my son from an after-school program there, visiting its restaurants and shops. I knew it, but I also knew many others; I chose this one principally because of its glorious diversity. It contains the residences of about 2,000 people, but is not entirely residential or even nearly so, not one of those dust-ruffle blocks whose residences are bordered at street level by a few service enterprises. The workplace for about 2,500 people, this block is more commercial than residential, but it is also not one of those all-business areas that roll up their sidewalks at five in the afternoon because they have no permanent residents; this block remains active at virtually every hour of the day and night. In 1992, New York City's 1.9 million employees turned out a gross annual city product of $150 billion. This block's gross product was probably 1 percent of the city total, say $1.5 billion.

That product came from three large companies and more than a hundred small ones—a proportion of large and small businesses that is fairly reflective of the size mix of companies in the United States. We are used to reading and hearing about IBM, AT&T, and General Motors, but 99 percent of American businesses are small, a category defined by the government as having fewer than 500 employees. Even though small companies vastly outnumber larger ones, they employ only 60 percent of the workforce, and on this block the percentage of small-company employees was even lower, below 40 percent.

Nationally, in 1992, the statistics revealed that small companies accounted for only 54 percent of all sales and 50 percent of the gross national product, disparities that most experts attributed to the ability of large companies to make money through economies of size and scale. But in the late 1980s and early 1990s small companies had become the source of a full two-thirds of the initial jobs that people were taking in America and of an equal proportion of the new jobs generated in the economy. The giants had cut back on their workforces: AT&T, IBM, and GM trimmed 300,000 workers between 1990 and 1993. The trend was especially visible in Manhattan: While in 1988, 38 percent of the people employed worked for a big company, by 1993 that figure had dropped to 33 percent. The same number of people were still employed in 1993, the difference having been made up by small companies, including temporary-employment firms. The ability to generate employment was a principal reason I'd become interested in small businesses. But could ordinary, non-high-tech companies continue to generate jobs? Or were the low-tech small fry in the midst of inevitable decline?

Around this block in Chelsea, on income-tax day, 1993, signs of renewal are what first catch the eye. At a storefront on Eighth

Avenue, a hand-lettered sign and workmen removing scaffolding announce that a boarded-up nightclub will shortly reopen; in the next storefront's window, an enlarged postcard against a backdrop of brown paper touts the imminent arrival of a second restaurant. Along Seventh Avenue, there is more construction and renovation in previously vacant storefronts.

As I begin to chat with business owners and employees, I learn that behind the blank facade of the office buildings and street-level depots, spring is bringing difficulties to as many businesses as are undergoing positive renewal. On one floor of the twelve-story office building at 216 West 18th, an Indian-born man waits out a Dickensian lawsuit that has ground his business to a halt; on another, a second-generation Jewish owner worries that his small business is sliding toward bankruptcy. At a street-level plumbing supplies wholesaler, a man whose own enterprise recently failed arrives for his first week of working for someone else; next door in a retail showroom, an interior designer grows restless in her job; in the lumber depot, the young owner faces a life crisis intricately tied to the survival of his father's and grandfather's business; around the corner, a clothing boutique owner wonders whether her enterprise will make it through another year. At a dozen other wholesale, manufacturing, and retail enterprises around this block, owners worry about rent becoming too large a fraction of their overhead, about taxes eating at their dwindling profits, about onrushing technology rendering their equipment—even their ways of doing business—outmoded before they finish paying for the machines.

Like most inner-city neighborhoods throughout the country, Chelsea crystallized in near to its present physical form toward the end of the nineteenth century. This was the moment when the stables and warehouses that supported the department stores of Ladies Mile (along Sixth Avenue to the east), and the piers along the river to the west, with their associated bars and rooming houses, gave way to loft buildings used for the production of construction materials. Later, when the surge of activity in erecting the large office and residential buildings of Manhattan slowed, the lofts and warehouses were converted to serve other types of manufacturing, while the rooming houses were cut up into small apartments. Some buildings from the earlier eras were razed and replaced; most were modified and remain. Zoning laws designed to bunch skyscrapers limited building heights in Chelsea and forbade skyscrapers to be placed on the corners. As a result, the Chelsea blocks today remain relatively low, with plenty of open sky, sunlight, and large interior spaces.

It was on the piers and along the old Ladies Mile that a renaissance of Chelsea seemed to be gathering speed in 1993—a renaissance driven by large, rather than small, businesses. Because of the recession, rents had dropped substantially in some of the big old spaces that used to be department stores. In 1992, Bed Bath & Beyond, a national chain, snapped up the ground floor of one such store at Sixth Avenue and 18th Street, and in the spring of 1993 was completing a first, rather spectacular year of operations. Its success, and the low square-footage rents in similar adjacent buildings, had generated plans by other big chains to open facilities within the year in other of these large old spaces—a men's clothing retailer (Today's Man), a full-service bookstore (Barnes & Noble), an office supply store (Staples). And for the piers between 17th and 23rd Streets, entrepreneurs had announced plans for an $80–$100 million entertainment complex to include an ice-skating rink, indoor golf range, gyms, and other facilities, to open in 1994 or 1995. Would these enterprises, rather than the existing small businesses, control the future of the block? Perhaps a year on the block would provide some hints.

A brief tour around the block, in April of 1993, starts at the intersection of 18th and Seventh Avenue. There are subway entrances on each of the four corners, apartment buildings on three corners, and a Con Edison power station on the fourth. Traffic flows south on Seventh, and we go as traffic flows. We pass a street-level commercial strip containing an upscale restaurant, clothing stores, a laundry, a card store, a bookstore, a kitchen-and-bath-fixtures depot, a children's store, a diner. At the southeast corner of 17th and Seventh is Barneys, one of the city's largest department stores, whose windows cover the whole avenue blockfront down to 16th. The Pressman family, who owns Barneys, also controls a substantial amount of real estate on the block, including two small parking lots. We turn right on 17th, a one-way west-flowing side street.

The major building on 17th near Seventh is Nynex's Art Deco skyscraper, which goes through the block to 18th. A series of drab four-to-ten-story buildings lines both sides of 17th; two are empty, but the magnificent former Siegel-Cooper Dry Goods Store warehouse in midblock, owned by Barneys, contains the block's third large-business entity, Cahners, a magazine-and-newspaper division of the international conglomerate Reed Elsevier. Other buildings house a religious publisher, a business phone system installer, a radiology center, architectural partnerships, graphic designers, and artists. A phalanx of residences on the left is interrupted by the two-story garage of the Eigen plumbing supply depot.

On the corner of 17th and Eighth Avenue, two video rental stores face each other—an independent operation and a unit of the Blockbuster chain on the ground floor of the condominium building. There are also entrances to another subway line. Eighth Avenue seems more densely filled with commercial storefronts than Seventh; traffic careens uptown past low buildings containing a half-dozen restaurants, a pizza shop, clothing boutiques, a hardware store, a newsstand, and a copy shop. The former fish store is empty, but two other storefronts are being renovated. One of the block's three 24-hour deli-groceries is on the northwest corner of 18th and Eighth, and opposite it is the House of Cheers liquor store, in a white shingled building that seems out of place among these brownstones.

On the southeast corner is an old bar currently known as The Pasta Pot, an establishment that seems to be failing. There is also a curious For Sale sign on the red barnlike building of the Chelsea

Day School, on 18th. That one-way eastward-flowing side street has more storefront enterprises than 17th or any other residential block between Seventh and Eighth in the stretch between 14th and 23rd, the two largest streets of the area. They include a dog groomer, an antiques/collectibles store, a clothier of police and firemen, a messenger service, a veterinarian. All the storefronts are occupied. On this stretch of the block, the dominant buildings are the Old Chelsea Post Office and the 216 Building, which contains many printing enterprises. Eighteenth also has Liberty High School, so small that many residents of the block are unaware that it exists, and two supply depots, one for lumber and another, Solco, that is the 18th Street counterpart to the Eigen plumbing supply depot on 17th.

The block is not a perfect microcosm of the American economy. It doesn't have much to do with automobiles, although there is a gas station one block north, on Seventh Avenue. It has only one national franchise operation, Blockbuster—no Burger King or True Value Hardware. It also lacks a supermarket, a shoemaker, a bank, a Laundromat, and a drugstore, although these facilities, too, are available within a short walking distance. Police and fire stations are just a shout away, on 19th. The local hospital with its well-used emergency room is five blocks south. A multiscreen movie complex is five blocks north, and so is a public library.

It is an area that has been undergoing steady, though slow, gentrification. The domiciles around the block run the gamut from rent-controlled and rent-stabilized apartments, mostly studios for which tenants pay several hundred dollars a month, to two- and three-bedroom condominiums in the larger buildings, condos that sell for hundreds of thousands of dollars each. There are a few medium-sized residential buildings and two-dozen brownstones, some more seedy than that name usually implies. The landlord of nine well-kept-up residential buildings on 17th, converted decades ago from rooming houses for seamen and stevedores, says his tenants are singles, young couples, or senior citizens whose children have grown up and moved away.

So, an imperfect specimen, but a block that has its own coherence and is the center of a neighborhood, a block chock-full of people and businesses, multifaceted, quintessentially urban, and thoroughly American. Blocks like this exist in every sizable city in the country, and we usually pass them by without a second thought: No tourist attractions. No exceptionally beautiful architectural gems. Not much notable history. No famous people live here. Last month a neighborhood newspaper, in an article about liquor stores, mentioned some bargains to be bought at House of Cheers, but in an aside dubbed this an "unassuming," sleepy block where very little ever happens.

But things of importance *must* be happening here if the American dream of turning hard work and enterprise into a successful, comfortable life is to survive the great forces of change now roiling the American economy. It is not too far-fetched to contend that as this altogether typical block in the Chelsea district of Manhattan goes, so goes the future of our nation's cities.

Chapter 1

THE BACK OF ONE
IS THE FACE OF ANOTHER

MAN YOHN LEE, the dry cleaner on Eighth Avenue, complains that during the recent downturn, male customers wore shirts two days instead of one before taking them to be cleaned—his weekly intake of shirts dropped from 700 to 500—and female customers tried to get the spots out of their own dresses rather than having them professionally done. The dry cleaner on Seventh Avenue, Lee's competitor, also had problems. To lower expenses, the Seventh Avenue cleaner returned 400 square feet of avenue frontage to the landlord. The decrease in counter space seems not to have adversely affected traffic in this dry-cleaning establishment, but it has shaved his expenses and enabled him to repair the clock on the wall, which had lost its hands, and to fix a sign whose letters had fallen off.

Four hundred square feet is not enough space to accommodate every type of retail business; most clothing and food retailers need more. In this modest-priced location, however, the sale of just a few pairs of eyeglasses each day may prove sufficient to meet the week's overhead for an optician who has just rented the place for a spanking new business.

We used to take for granted that the American ground was so fertile and American capitalist climatological conditions were so favorable that almost any business crop planted was likely to flower. Today's failure rate for new businesses is one in three, and most failures occur in the first year of an enterprise; statistics like these could lead us to the belief that our economic soil has been depleted, compromised, or is at least in need of ever-more-powerful fertilizers, and that the economic weather seems suitable only for certain crops at certain seasons. So a central question for our future becomes whether the American dream of starting a business and becoming self-sufficient through it is not only still possible in the United States, but is also a reasonable expectation for new entrepreneurs. To begin examining the question of whether the American dream can still become a reality on a regular basis, one can look at the half-dozen locations around this block where, in the spring of 1993, something new is replacing something old. The back of one is the face of another, says an Irish proverb. Is there any other relationship between the two?

Sight on Seventh, scheduled to open May 15 on the east side of Seventh Avenue, is the brainchild of a former Long Island science teacher. Myron Michaels retains the studious and inquisitive air of the science classroom, leavened with ebullience and energy. Middle-aged, fleshy, with thinning hair, Michaels wears crisp shirts and, of course, very stylish eyewear. Before signing his lease, he recalls, "I went down to the Bureau of Records at City Hall and worked the computer, calling up demographic data, foot-traffic patterns, that sort of thing." The results of his research excited him: The residents in the area were for the most part middle class, relatively young, but with significant disposable income. To be just a few steps from Barneys, he believes, will mean many potential customers already primed to buy quality, stylish merchandise.

There is competition two blocks south, a branch of a four-unit chain called Myoptics, but Michaels considers it far enough away so as not to detract from his own business. His customer base, he believes, will come from the many apartment buildings and businesses around here. He reminds a listener that the American population is aging and that older people need eyewear and that younger people are also spending more money on eyewear, conceiving of it as a stylish clothing accessory.

Only time will tell whether Michaels's assumptions about his location and the population he can serve are right or wrong, but at the outset of his venture Michaels is upbeat and has a specific reason for optimism: He is on an approved-provider list of the Traveler's, the insurance company that covers many Nynex employees—and a Nynex facility is right across the street.

"You have to have certain minimum spatial requirements to properly measure how the patient reads the letter chart," says Michaels, bounding up to gesture at the dimensions. The smallness of his space has been an intriguing design problem. It's been a challenge to fit in the examining area for the optometrist who will come in one day a week, the display counters, the storage space for frames, and still have enough room so that customers won't feel crowded.

Optical work, with its emphasis on mathematics and precision and the principles of physics, appeals to Michaels. Also, he reasons that if he could deal with teenagers in the classroom, he should certainly be able to satisfy customers for eyewear. His first optical business was as part of an HMO on Long Island, but the organization failed. He then worked for an optician near Eighth Avenue and 23rd Street—as the crow flies, not far from here, but in a part of Chelsea where the clientele (and the merchandise in the shop) was less upscale. At that time, he had wanted his own shop but hadn't been ready. Then "this opportunity came up" in an area that he liked.

As with most entrepreneurs, Michaels is reluctant to divulge to an outsider the precise financial details of his tenancy or his capitalization, but he reports that he has signed a multiyear lease that he finds "comfortable." In New York, most commercial leases contain a clause that permits the renter to stop paying and vacate the space if the business fails, an important comfort to a start-up venture. Most storefronts in this area rent for around $75 per square foot per month, which would put his rent at hypothetical $3,000 per month. Rents have been creeping up, and in the process, changing business assumptions: Whereas in the past, businesses could figure that rent would cost them one-quarter of their gross income, now they must figure it at a third of their gross or more. The hypothetical $3,000-a-month rent will likely require that Michaels sell something like twenty pairs of glasses just to meet it, and twice again that many pairs per month in order to meet his other expenses, pay himself a modest salary, compensate his optometrist for coming in one day a week to conduct exams, and begin to amortize his start-up costs, which neighborhood observers estimate at between $35,000 and $75,000.

The start-up money, Michaels says, came from his own savings and from "people who believe in me"—investors, he points out, not partners. Very few small businesses begin with bank financing or investments from individuals who do not personally know the entrepreneur. But Michaels certainly appears to be a man on whom friends might reasonably bet: He has a business plan and is experienced at his craft, if not completely as an entrepreneur, and he has what is probably the correct philosophy (and budget to match), one that recognizes it will take time to build a client base and that for a while outgo will likely exceed income. Whether his shop will be different enough from the competitor down the avenue to be commercially viable, say, within the year, is a toss-up.

Directly across the avenue, another shop is due to open shortly, and from initial walks by it, it appears it will be a retail clothing store, like the previous two occupants, which sold funky retro clothes.

Recessions expose weaknesses in businesses that good times conceal. The dry cleaner found out that he had more space than he could sustain—a relatively minor weakness—but the women's clothing boutique on the west side of Seventh learned the consequences of a deeper flaw. It had aimed at the wrong sort of customers for this area of the city—a cardinal mistake. Didn't the shop owners have enough sense to recognize the mismatch between the neighborhood and their desired customers before opening up? Many observers of the blocks of this city and the Main Streets of the country have been chagrined to find that new entrepreneurs evidence an inordinate degree of blindness to history. You've seen it, too: People open restaurants in spaces where a string of previous eateries have gone bust or decide that a great place to sell shoes is the location where a hat shop, a foundation-garments shop, and a gloves-and-scarf shop have earlier failed, one after the other. When such new enterprises do not produce enough revenue to stay afloat, the proprietors are invariably puzzled as to why their good ideas are not being embraced by consumers, but they seldom admit their failure to take into account the site's history. Knowing the recent past of this particular site on Seventh, and in light of the knowledge that two clothing boutiques gave up the ghost right here, there is concern among neighborhood observers that a third boutique may be making the same mistake and will suffer a similar demise.

Walking past the site a week later, passersby see a floor-to-ceiling window that features a four-foot-high, black-and-white cartoon of a muscular male lifeguard carrying in his arms another equally muscular and widely grinning male. Within is a boutique not for the usual sort of men's clothing, but for skimpy, formfitting shorts, shirts, slacks.

Manager Tim Cass is an Australian-born architect in his late thirties with a crew cut, an open countenance, and the look of a man who takes very seriously his daily workout in a nearby gym. The shop he has helped design is mostly black, chrome, and mirrors—a sleek and minimal backdrop for the clothing. For the past several years Tim has been allied in a manufacturing enterprise with clothing designer Raymond Dragon. The Dragon line draws on Dragon's expertise with Lycra, a clingy fabric, Cass tells me, and is aimed "mostly at gay males." For the last four years, the

Dragon company has been successfully manufacturing clothing and wholesaling it from a loft in midtown to twenty gay-owned and -operated boutiques around the country—and that, in the midst of a recession. Often, businesses that sail through recession feel so strong that they believe they can easily expand. A year ago Dragon determined that he would like to open a store that sold only his own merchandise. Instead of manufacturing a garment for $12.50 and selling it at wholesale for $25, Dragon will now be able to sell it at retail for $50, a markup of 300 percent.

That neither Tim nor Ray has ever before owned or managed a retail enterprise may not be much of a drawback to operating a store: On this block several other clothing boutique operators entered the business without retail experience. As for location, "We didn't want to be on Christopher Street"—in Greenwich Village, a half mile to the south—"because that's become too touristy." But they did want to be near a gay population center, which Chelsea is, although it has a preponderance of straight residents. They knew the history of the site, but because they were planning to appeal to a different clientele, it did not deter them.

This decision to pioneer rather than to locate in a known gay shopping area seems ingenuous or arrogant. Both qualities are underscored by Tim's tale of discussing the proposed location with Barneys. There have been persistent rumors that when Barneys opens its big uptown department store in the fall of 1994, the flagship location at 17th Street and Seventh Avenue will be downsized—an eventuality that would negatively influence the decision of any clothing boutique to move near the 17th Street store. Barneys executives, Tim reports, told the Raymond Dragon principals that any downsizing would be minimal, and the Dragon partners, believing them, decided to go ahead and open their boutique.

While optician Michaels is betting his life savings and that of his friends on his new shop—a considerable risk—the Raymond Dragon boutique is taking much less of a risk because it is bankrolled from the retained savings of its manufacturing business and the partners are continuing their main line of work while they try operating their own boutique. But Michaels can rely on the drawing power of the Armani and Calvin Klein names and frames he puts in his window, while the Dragon partners don't have big names to do the marketing and advertising for them. They must hope that their particular customers will act as most in-groups do when they make purchases—that is, pass information quickly within the group and patronize merchants known to be sympathetic to the group or to be members of it. Ray Dragon and Tim Cass will sell inexpensive "party clothes" that can be worn once and thrown away, and they hope customers will return often to buy outfits for specific occasions or purposes. To emphasize that notion, the partners plan to change their eye-catching, outrageous window displays every two to three weeks.

One optimistic theory about the future of the American economy, especially relevant to small business, is that this rich culture of ours is going to make possible more and more—and narrower and narrower—niches in which to position an enterprise. But successful niches have usually been defined much more broadly than that containing the relative handful of men who are gay, between the ages of eighteen and forty, and who can afford and who want to squeeze into formfitting "play" rags. If such a narrow-focused niche holder as the Raymond Dragon boutique can prevail where other, more generalized clothing stores have failed, it will be a powerful argument in support of the niche-holding theory of future enterprise.

There's a saw in the restaurant business that anyone who wants to do something other than what he or she is doing opens a dining establishment. That makes for lots of amateurs in the business and for results that are often disastrous. Fifty percent of the restaurants that open in New York shut within three to five years, a failure rate that is even higher than the basic failure rate for businesses. To run a restaurant entails a daily outflow of cash much greater than that of a clothing store, in which the stock is replenished only when items are sold and the owner is the mainstay of the staff.

Moreover, restaurants also have to obtain licenses, pass inspections, and maintain considerably larger staffs. But if a restaurant becomes popular, it can generate profits in the hundreds or thousands of dollars a day, depending on its size. To obtain such intangibles as ingenuity of cuisine and atmosphere, customers of restaurants are used to paying substantial fees.

Behind windows covered by brown paper, in a small, garagelike building on Eighth Avenue, Pat Rogers and Bob Barbero are busily destroying their dream restaurant, Rogers & Barbero, and making way for a new one. About half of all new small businesses are begun by people whose previous small enterprises have not done well but who believe they've learned enough to do better the second time around.

A labor of love that encompassed everything the partners liked in a place to dine, R&B opened in the fall of 1983, when the area was in the first flush of gentrification. Rogers & Barbero was a brave outpost of haute cuisine among bars and delis catering to the working-class poor, a lushly appointed, candlelit, romantic hideaway serving classic French and Continental dishes and featuring a formidable wine list, as well as one of the first computer systems in a restaurant. An article in the *New York Times* then put the cost of construction and start-up at a quarter million dollars; ten years later, Bobby Barbero advises with a shrug that the tab was closer to a half million and included innumerable unpaid man-hours of the partners' own labor.

Theirs was an ingenuous gamble of considerable proportions, but the investment was rather rapidly amortized because, Barbero recalls, "We did very well, at first." He was then thirty, a wiry man who hoped to leave behind his work in real estate forever. Pat Rogers, the computer expert, was a bit older and beefier. Their restaurant drew a sizable dinner crowd, mostly couples: "Everyone ordered at least a bottle of wine." Lunchtime was profitable as well. R&B was close to 111 Eighth Avenue, a large office building that takes up the entire blockfront between 15th and 16th; and, Barbero remembers, "At least 30 percent of the lunch checks were paid for by a Cahners credit card." Their best year was 1987.

The stock-market crash of October 1987 wasn't nearly as devastating as 1929's, and so people beyond Wall Street tended to dismiss it. They hadn't understood the consequences, one of which was that by early 1988 even companies not directly connected with the securities industry were cutting back on discretionary expenses such as lunches at fine restaurants. That hurt R&B, as did the ensuing recession. Here, too, the downturn exposed a weakness: The restaurant was "too pricey for the neighborhood." But this understanding did not dawn on the partners immediately. In 1988–89, R&B still seemed to be riding the crest of a wave, the willingness of corporate managers to spend money on themselves; and so, at first, in reaction to the slowdown in business, the partners looked for an easy and inexpensive way out. Reasoning that the interior was too dark, "We lightened up the place, let the high ceilings take more focus, put in a big window, made the interior more inviting from the street." A few more customers came in because of the cosmetic surgery, but not enough.

Most of the problems renovation couldn't fix. For instance, wine rose considerably in price because of the declining purchasing power of the dollar in international markets, to the point where most restaurants, instead of doubling the wholesale price of a bottle, could only charge customers 60 to 70 percent more than they paid for the bottle or risk the wine being so expensive that diners wouldn't order any. Then, too, when a recession takes its toll on a small entrepreneurial business, Barbero explains, "You still have to pay your suppliers, your floor and kitchen help, your taxes, whatever; the last people to get paid are the owners." By 1992, to stay afloat, the R&B partners were spending most of their time working outside the business, Barbero as a real estate broker and Rogers as a consultant to a company that helps computerize restaurants. They continued to open R&B's doors every evening but knew they couldn't go on losing money much longer. Battlefields often produce survivors who stagger away from combat, apparently in one piece, only to later pitch over from the previously ignored effects of the struggle. In many ways, the Rogers & Barbero restaurant was this sort of casualty of the recession.

Should the partners simply admit defeat and fold their tent? That would waste their most valuable asset, the extensive renovations already made and paid for. But something had to be put in to replace the money-losing R&B. Ten years older than their first time out and "a lot more savvy about the restaurant business," Pat and Bob set about charting their new course. It was then that they acted on the realization that R&B was too pricey for the neighborhood. The final nudge in the precise direction they took, Barbero recalls, came from a friend who casually reported that he and the group of gay young men who had gone out to celebrate his twenty-fifth birthday would have done so at Rogers & Barbero, but it was too expensive. "I realized that young people like to go out several nights a week, and they have some money to spend, but they don't want to spend a lot all at once." This understanding led to agreement among the partners that whatever they did next, it would not be a "tablecloth" restaurant, and that the tab for dining must not be high. The café on the corner, called Eighteenth and Eighth, had recently been using such a formula with good results, and the most successful restaurant in the immediate area, Cola's—almost directly across the avenue from R&B—had also kept its prices relatively low.

Their hard-won experience now permitted Rogers and Barbero to translate their notion of a modest-priced place into a host of secondary decisions. Costs would be pared by having no table covers or linen napkins to launder and by not going overboard on renovations. Potential profits would be raised by junking the extensive wine list, which had been Rogers's joy, and selling mainly beer and margaritas, on which the markup was higher. The risk would be minimized by taking in a third partner as the chef, a man who had originally started as a salaried chef at R&B and had gone on to Café Luxembourg on the Upper West Side. His presence would trim Pat and Bob's potential profit but would also reduce the amount they would have to invest and the weekly salaries they would have to pay. All this would be done in order to price entrées at less than $10, even grilled tuna, for which other restaurants regularly charged $15 and up.

After proposing and rejecting hundreds of suggestions for a name, the partners chose one reflective of the new establishment's stripped-down style. Bob and Pat's first restaurant had been elegant and done for love; Food/Bar, designed strictly for business, would resemble "a nice diner." R&B closed on April 12, and the partners quickly dismantled the interior, brought in chrome and gray Formica tables and plain chairs; Food/Bar opened on April 26.

It was full the first night, and the flood of customers has hardly ebbed since then. At lunchtime Food/Bar draws its customers from the heterosexual population in the various office buildings nearby; in the evenings it becomes a young gay hangout.

The gay community that is the basis of two new enterprises, Food/Bar and Raymond Dragon's boutique, is only one of seven or eight distinct communities that have strong elements on this block. Theorists believe that successful enterprises are increasingly going to be those based within, or that have ties to, specific groupings. Clusters can be based on social factors or strictly economic ones. In this case the gay community and the number of schools create two clusters based on social factors. The "restaurant row" along Eighth Avenue, the printing-related companies in or near the 216 Building, and a cluster of bookstores are grouped along economic lines. An equally vibrant cluster is both social and economic: the one made up of blue-collar enterprises associated with the building trades. In the blocks adjacent to this one are wholesalers of electrical goods, roofing supplies, and tiles, and on this block proper are two plumbing supply depots and a lumber depot. It is within this last cluster, in the last-named enterprise, the lumber depot, that a particularly dramatic renewal is in process in the spring of 1993.

In December of 1992, the proprietor of Maxwell Lumber, Alan Bernstein, committed suicide on the eve of his sixtieth birthday. Notes that he left behind made clear that he had killed himself in order to ensure that his adopted son Marc would be able to purchase, renew, and continue the Maxwell Lumber business.

That rebirth almost did not take place; in the days after Alan's death, Maxwell Lumber was very nearly closed and shuttered. The tale of how it survived takes us into the block's past and into the often brutal interplay between large businesses and small ones. Maxwell Lumber inhabits a drab four-story building on the uptown side of West 18th. Unfinished doors, newel posts, moldings, Sheetrock board, and the like are piled around on the ground floor, as are displays of tools for use with wood. From a cockpit near the front, a clerk deals with customers who pull up their trucks. In an inner office, two women handle the telephones and other office chores. Marc Bernstein is a clean-shaven, freckle-faced man of about thirty, whose earnest look is almost belied by his attire, casual polo shirt and slacks. His office, slightly larger than a cubicle, is adorned with pictures of his adoptive father, Alan, who sports a large, bushy beard, and of Alan's father, Max. "My grandfather started the business in 1935," Marc says, pointing to a plaque on the wall that contains 84¢ in coins and a paper-bag receipt that records Maxwell Lumber's first sale, fourteen board feet of pine. "Today, that amount of lumber would cost almost $50." For thirty years, Maxwell Lumber had three stores in Manhattan, two on 18th and another on 15th. Land values in Chelsea were relatively low then. In the early 1960s, thousands of small enterprises throughout the country moved out of center cities to near suburbs, where rents were lower; in 1963, the Bernsteins closed down two of their stores and opened a warehouse in Long Island City, across the East River, in a factory district. From there, the elder Bernsteins could service the building trades easily and still keep a single store in Manhattan.

"I started working here when I was nine," Marc recalls; that was shortly after Alan had married Marc's mother. "I used to sharpen pencils and take my father's shoes to be repaired." Although Alan had six children, three from the second marriage and three that he had adopted from his wife's first marriage, Marc was the only one that entered the business. He never entertained a thought of doing anything else. After he formally joined the firm in 1985, his father became his tutor, "a wonderful teacher who forced me to do every job here." To master any business, it helps to work through fat years and lean ones, and the late 1980s and early 1990s provided both. The company grew at more than 25 percent each year in the good years of Marc's apprenticeship, until it employed two-dozen people and had an annual gross in the millions of dollars. A fleet of a dozen Maxwell trucks left the warehouse every morning to make deliveries to various construction and renovation sites or to the offices of woodworking companies or department stores and hotels that had their own wood shops. Maxwell Lumber's specialty came to be clear molding, that is, molding without blemishes or knots, made from a single piece of lumber. "If you're going to paint, you can buy cheap molding made from small pieces glued together, since the paint will cover it," Marc explains, "but if you want to stain, you can't buy cheap molding because you want a continuous look to the wood." Marc and Alan bought raw lumber from all over the world and had it shipped to a clear-molding manufacturing mill in North Carolina, which shaped more than three hundred patterns for them to sell to their own customers.

In the fall of 1992, Marc and Alan were noting signs that the company's growth would soon resume. After seven years, Marc was still pleased to be working with Alan, "my best friend" and a tutor in far more than business, a man who started work at 6:00 A.M. each day, worked hard, and exuded an infectious enthusiasm for life.

Out of the blue, a letter arrived from their bank, the branch of Republic National Bank on 14th Street at Eighth Avenue. In the late 1980s the Bernsteins had taken out revolving lines of credit, known as notes on demand. Alan had been doing business with this particular bank branch for decades, since before it had been taken over by Republic. The letter came by regular mail and with no warning: It was a notice that Republic was calling their loan. "We couldn't believe this was happening, so we went to see the bank."

There were rumors that Republic had decided to get out of the small-business-loan game and was calling all loans in that category. The Bernsteins didn't know whether or not this was true; they only knew they were being asked to pay up—immediately.

Although they didn't know it—and would not have been able to act differently even if they had known it—the Bernsteins were on the wrong end of a whip that was being snapped by the bank in reaction to problems encountered by much larger borrowers. In the go-go days of the mid-1980s, banks all over the country had loaned billions to real estate developers; by the early 1990s, many multimillion-dollar loans were in trouble because of a decline in real estate prices throughout the country. New York was especially hard hit because it had been vastly overbuilt in the 1980s; the glut of space made real estate values decline precipitously. In turn, this caused banks to be overextended, especially on their loans to big borrowers, such as developers Donald Trump and Peter Kalikow. The banks had a problem with very big loans because the face amounts exceeded the capacity of borrowers to pay since the property assets pledged for the loans had declined so sharply in value. In the early 1990s it was really anybody's guess whether a big skyscraper in midtown Manhattan was worth the $1.2 billion that the developer had paid for it (with a bank loan of $960 million) or the $800 million he could obtain for it on the open market, since there were no customers for it at the higher price. The banks, unable to collect on their loans on big properties, had to swallow hard and wait for payment on those mortgages until the real estate market recovered. Foreclosure was usually not an option because the banks didn't want to operate the real estate, either. While the banks waited, however, they were under pressure to find money somewhere, and this pressure turned many of them in the direction of their smaller borrowers. The smaller borrowers' properties—warehouses, small loft buildings, mini-malls—were valued in smaller numbers of dollars, but these properties were also more likely to be salable because they were less costly. In fact, the values of the properties put up as collateral for these small loans were usually in excess of the loans' face amounts. So, all over the country, banks called in their small commercial property loans. That such actions could cause immense difficulties for borrowers like the Bernsteins—even to the point of shoving their commercial businesses out of existence—was shrugged off as an inevitable social cost of doing business.

The Bernsteins tried to demonstrate to their branch of Republic that Maxwell Lumber had had a few difficult years but that its loans were being paid off in a timely manner, that the loans were cross-collateralized and secured by four different pieces of wholly owned property worth three times the amount of the loans. When that display did not convince anyone, Alan and Marc pleaded for a few months in which to liquidate the loan, because otherwise, in order to raise the cash, the Bernsteins would have to sell the lumber business and/or their properties at a time when the real estate market was depressed. "But the bank wouldn't work with us," Marc says. "There were no negotiations."

On Thursday, December 17, 1992, it became obvious to the Bernsteins that the bank was going to do something drastic if the money was not turned over immediately. The Bernsteins discussed bankruptcy as a strategy for getting out from under the loan. It would also mean deliberately not paying suppliers or employees. Therefore, though it was a legal option, it was not one that Alan could ethically choose.

"That Friday, there was a big storm in New York that blew down our sign over the building," Marc remembers, believing in retrospect that he should have considered it a bad omen. Alan had flown to Florida for the weekend. The Bernsteins had formed a Florida corporation and had talked about opening up a branch of Maxwell Lumber in Boca Raton, possibly changing the family's lifestyle by moving part of its operations to the resort community.

Marc and his brothers and sisters had plans to meet Alan there on the following Wednesday to celebrate his sixtieth birthday. On Saturday, however, Alan purchased a gun. He was able to pick it up from the gun shop on Tuesday—one day short of the three-day waiting period—and that same day used the gun to kill himself.

The suicide stunned the family because it was completely unexpected; it was especially hard for them to believe that a person who had always seemed so full of life would end his own existence. A funeral service in New York drew 500 people, and another in Florida, almost as many: Marc discovered that Alan had often helped others without seeking or receiving recognition for his assistance. Only in the wake of Alan's death did the stories start coming out. For Marc, they deepened the tragedy.

The special circumstances of the suicide bolstered the Bernsteins' belief that if a proper waiting period had been observed by the gun dealer before Alan was able to pick up the gun, they might have been able to convince him that there was another way out of the difficulties. Incensed at the gun dealer's complicity in getting around Florida's state law in this instance, the Bernsteins became strong advocates for the passage of the Brady bill, being considered by Congress in the early months of 1993.

Alan left notes directing Marc to use certain attorneys and accountants to work out the mess that would follow his death. Reading the notes, it became apparent to Marc that what pushed Alan to suicide was his concern about how to continue to "take care of everybody, as he always had." Some of the advisers suggested that Marc sell Maxwell to competitors who were offering to buy it. Marc also had job offers, but "the more I thought about what my father had done, the more I became convinced I ought to keep Maxwell Lumber going." When an insurance policy has been in force for many years, the insurer is obligated to pay out even if the insured person dies a suicide. So, in January of 1993, Marc was able to use the insurance proceeds to pay off the loans to the bank and to buy Maxwell Lumber from his father's estate. "What happened, in effect, was that by his suicide my father gave me my chance to own my own business."

Maxwell Lumber opened its doors again, and there was little that would have told passersby, or even some regular customers, that the firm had changed hands. The routines didn't change, and that helped preserve continuity. It was not difficult for the employees to accept Marc as the leader because Marc had been with the firm a long time and had steadily taken on more and more responsibilities. In the spring of 1993, though, in the small inner office he had previously shared with his father, Marc experiences an emotion he has never before felt in that place: He is lonely.

Like the Maxwell Lumber building, the one now occupied by the design firm known as Gear Holdings, Inc., on Seventh Avenue, was once a stable—Macy's stable; you can still see a plaster horse head high up on the small building. Gear, too, in April of 1993, is at a moment of large change. But while Maxwell Lumber struggles to maintain an old-line and very straightforward type of business, Gear is struggling to transform something old into something quite new and possibly quite relevant for a future in which manufacturing becomes steadily less important to the U.S. economy.

Gear's future direction is being shaped at this moment, in part, at a site many hundreds of miles from the block, in the display halls of a sales convention in North Carolina. High Point bills itself as the furniture capital of the United States, and at conventions held there in April and October of each year, decisions are made by department store and furniture store executives that will essentially determine what new furniture and furnishings Americans will buy in the coming year or two. At this particular convention, Gear Holdings is introducing a full line of Gear-designed furniture to be manufactured by the Lane Company of Virginia, whose name will also be on the furniture.

During economic downturns, most people (as well as businesses) postpone the buying of durable goods, which are defined as those big-ticket items expected to last for at least three years. The United States is a large producer of big-ticket consumer items—automobiles, home appliances, furniture. One of the problems contributing to the length of the current recession is that it has been accompanied by a sharp rise in the prices of certain materials essential to the making of durable goods. In the furniture business, the most worrisome price rise was in lumber and wood, whose cost went up drastically on all of the world's markets; those raised costs, in turn, translated into a need to have new furniture bear higher price tags than similar pieces manufactured in the past. The need to raise product prices by itself deepened and lengthened the recession: During 1991–92 that need surfaced as a reluctance on the part of designers and manufacturers to go to the expense of bringing out entirely new furniture lines, for fear they might molder, unbought, in warehouses and retail stores. Fewer products manufactured meant layoffs at factories, and less work and pay, too, for truckers transporting the furniture, and so on, down the line.

In the second half of 1992, polls and sales figures began to show that families all across the country were beginning to decide to replace that worn-out bed, to brighten up the living room with a new coffee table, or to buy a new set of chairs for the dining room rather than re-cover the old ones. It is such mundane, individual actions that in the aggregate usually help pull the country out of recession and that have given hope to the spring 1993 convention at High Point.

Gear has high expectations for the Lane line, whose style is American old-fashioned, though the specific details are modern— a conjunction Gear refers to as "fresh traditions." At High Point, representatives of furniture retailers walk through mock rooms furnished with the Gear-designed line of tables, chairs, mirrors, beds, storage chests, armoires, dressers, credenzas, sofas, chaises, and other pieces, trying to decide whether or not to carry the entire line or substantial parts of it, or to pass over this collection in favor of competing lines. Gear's hopes are high not only because popularity of the line will mean substantial income, but also because the line's success will solidify a direction that has involved collective soul-searching within the company. A success will recertify to Gear's principals that they made the right decision in 1990 to move the company entirely out of retail and solely into the design of furniture and furnishings.

A half-dozen years ago, Gear's retail operation occupied a large storefront opposite Barneys. Raymond Waites, Gear's principal designer, and architect James Harb designed an interior that was a delight to browse: a roomy, high-ceilinged, bright place in which Gear's wallpaper, rugs, bedding, and bric-a-brac lined the walls and counters. Children's furniture and furnishings were encased in a walk-in miniature clapboard house toward the back of the space.

Gear Holdings had begun in 1978 as a venture between two friends: Waites, who had worked as a chief designer for Marimekko of Finland, and Bettye Martin Musham, a former marketing executive for Louis Vuitton. A third partner was Bettye's husband, William Musham, then vice-chairman of a multibillion-dollar-a-year electrical products manufacturing firm.

Bettye Martin Musham, the company's CEO, is an energetic and charming middle-aged woman whose hair is kept short, in the style of women who wish to project an air of business. Although she has lived in New York for many years, her voice retains a touch of North Carolina. Gear's first product, she recalls, was a line of luggage. While they marketed luggage, the partners developed the "total home" concept. They wished to design many products that would go together in a room—to have complementary patterns, colors, and looks—so that a retailer could offer the multiple component items for sale in a single display. "It was difficult for any store to buy into the idea," she explains, "because when you put lamps and wall coverings and furnishings into a furniture department, you are mixing departments, mixing salespeople on commission with those on straight salary, causing all sorts of bureaucratic havoc." Bloomingdale's and several other big stores turned down the concept, but in 1980 Macy's tried it. Customers could envision how this wall covering would go with that chair and a particular lamp, throw rug, and pillows; consequently, they bought more items. Macy's was delighted.

By 1983, Gear Holdings had licensed their designs to a dozen manufacturers for products ranging from children's furnishings to shower curtains, made a private-label line for Sears, had a presence in the European Economic Community through an alliance with the Boots Company, and signed an agreement for Isetan, a Japanese department store chain, to carry Gear-designed products. "The Japanese love American country-styled rooms," Bettye marvels.

Gear Holdings had begun life, in part, with a start-up loan from the federal Department of Commerce. It was one of the last such loans to be given out, because the program was an early casualty of the Reagan reforms that sought to get government out of private enterprise. In the mid-1980s, searching for new capital to expand, after paying off this Commerce loan, Gear found it from a private source—the Crowns of Chicago, one of the wealthiest families in the United States. "We're the fly on the backside of the elephant to them." Martin Musham laughs. She believes that the disparity in size is why the Crowns have been content to allow the original Gear partners to maintain day-to-day control of the company's operations. By the mid-1980s, the number of different items for the home designed by Raymond Waites neared a thousand: beddings, textiles, wall coverings, ceramics, and frames, as well as furniture, dhurrie rugs, decorative plates, stationery, and gift wrapping. It was then that Gear Holdings made the decision to open a retail store.

It seemed like a good idea at the time, but as a retail venture the store did only "OK," Bettye recalls. One reason for the store's modest performance may have been the partners' inexperience at retail and lack of passion for it. "Our background and our strength was not in retail," Bettye admits. And since it bore an annual rent of $100,000, the store was a very expensive venture. At lease-renewal time in 1990, Barneys, who owned the storefront, wanted to raise the rent; the Gear Holdings partners decided that this was too high an overhead and closed the retail operation.

It was probably the smartest and luckiest move they could have made, for by the end of 1990 the country was already deep in recession, and continued operation of the retail store would likely have become a serious financial drain on the company. As Gear discovered, the avoidance of potential losses can be as important to a company's financial health as the direct making of profits.

Moreover, the closing of the store reinforced the partners' desire to refine the company toward being "software producers for the big manufacturers." Knowing that their major competitors were manufacturers and retailers as well as designers, Gear determined not to duplicate what Ralph Lauren and Laura Ashley were doing but rather to accelerate in the direction of becoming an all-purpose design firm, with an extra dose of marketing savvy thrown in.

"The role of the home has changed," Bettye Martin Musham explains. "In the '50s, a man's home was his castle; in the '60s, it was a pit stop; in the '70s, it was an investment. Then in the '80s the investment became a showplace, a status symbol. Home in the '90s is still an investment, but rather than being a symbol of status, it's a refuge, a retreat from all the uncertainty that fills our lives." This sort of positional thinking merged with design expertise and sense of style has enabled the company to grow. Although Gear Holdings is not considered a large company, its licensees sold almost a half billion dollars' worth of Gear-designed products in the past year, so its influence and share of market are considerable.

At High Point in April of 1993, the general buzz is that the Gear Collection by Lane is the most exciting entry into the market of the past several seasons. Floor samples of the furniture will not begin to arrive at retail stores until August, though, and another year will have to pass before the figures will reveal whether large enough numbers of consumers are buying it.

In making the choice to become solely a design firm, Gear has seized on a formulation for a business that may be the most effective future model for all purveyors of knowledge-based products and services. Old models of doing business are being rendered obsolete by a tectonic shift in the structure of the economy. Most observers agree that the American economy is heading toward becoming information based and away from straight manufacturing. In this realignment of mountains, valleys, and prairies, new landscapes are created, but it is not always obvious how to colonize them. Gear Holdings, however, has recognized that as a result of this shift, the design component of almost every product or service is likely to assume even more importance in regard to ultimate salability than the manufacturing component. Thus, Gear has shifted into being a "software" designer in the furniture and home furnishings field.

A few months ago, when the telephone in their apartment rang once-too-many times at the wrong moment, and their life seemed overwhelmed with the details of Helen's business from early morning until late into the evening, Niko C. finally put his foot down and insisted that his wife move her fledgling computer-game design enterprise out of their two-bedroom apartment and into an office. "This was part of our New Year's resolutions, actually," Helen recalls. It took her an additional month to convince the landlord of a nearby building on their block to rent to her, on a month-to-month basis—no lease—one of the studio apartments he had been warehousing toward an expected conversion of the building to co-op ownership.

Because of the nature of the rental arrangement, as well as the secrecy that she insists must surround the product line she is developing, Helen does not want her full name used. In most other ways, however, she appears the prototypical IBM engineer—early thirties; eyeglasses with thick frames; rather drab though neat clothing; and an air of distraction about her, as though her mind was elsewhere, perhaps contemplating a design problem even as she converses with a visitor.

Offered a buyout in mid-1992 from what had once been her "dream employer," Helen jumped at the severance package because she had conceived a project that she hoped would make her fortune. If her earlier dream had been to work for the giant in the field, the company on the cutting edge, and thereby make a contribution, after a decade had passed that dream had been overtaken by a new one. As with many people deeply versed in the design and use of hyperspace, she had been impressed by the stories of a few dozen game designers around the world, such as the two American brothers who designed Myst on their own, then sold it and saw their creation go on to make them millions of dollars. After almost a decade at Big Blue, Helen came to believe two things. First, that "the future is in software, not hardware," and second, that "I know as much as anybody about writing programs that fully use a PC's capacities." This knowledge would enable her to "design games that can take full advantage of microswitching capabilities, yet not take up too many kilobytes." Approximately translated into non-geek language and practical terms, Helen's belief was that she could design games that have greater numbers of choice branches resulting from each decision and that would also enable the game character making the decision to have his or her physical and mental attributes changed as a consequence of the decision—make a wrong turn in the maze, for instance, and you are reduced to blindness. Furthermore, her expertise would permit her to fit a complex game on only a disk or two, which would keep the cost low, thereby making the game more affordable to consumers.

Using her severance pay and insider's access to buy equipment and templates, Helen began work in the second bedroom of the family apartment. She very quickly learned that her idea required other sorts of talents beyond her own, so she enlisted those of friends—for which she had to pay in order to retain full ownership of her project. Even more specialized materials and techniques were needed. With Niko's agreement, to pay for these things she began to dip into the money that the couple had been saving toward the purchase of a home they hoped to buy when they had children.

Helen is betting her rainy-day money on her own talents, of course, but also on being in an industry that is itself on a phenomenal rise, most of it a cluster centered in Silicon Alley, the area of Manhattan south of 41st Street on the West Side in which "new media" are being developed. No one is certain of just how many new media companies are in existence, because entities like Helen's not-quite-formed business can't really be counted as yet, but estimates by those trying to track the trend put the number at several thousand, which employ an estimated 10,000 people. By contrast, the long-established book publishing industry employs about 13,000 people.

At the four months' mark, a crisis arose for Helen. She had constructed a rough prototype to the point that a sophisticated outsider might be able to look at it and judge it. Sworn to silence, friends and habitual game players tried it and were enthusiastic. It was good, but rudimentary, and obviously needed a great deal more work. Software giants like Broderbund were known to sometimes look at new products in such rough form, and occasionally to make offers for them in that form, relatively low offers—not enough money to cover the costs already incurred, just a modest advance against a small percentage royalty on future games sold because the product would have to be completed and touched up by the big company's in-house designers. A much better price and a higher royalty schedule was usually paid by a game-marketing company for a designer's completed product, but since the full development costs of such a product can run into the hundreds of thousands of dollars, many first-time game developers cannot wait until they remove the last glitch from their program to offer it for sale. For Helen C., the question became whether to try to sell her game in the rough stage, and possibly never see a cent beyond her initial payment, or hold out for the higher price she could hope to obtain for a completely developed product, and in the meantime keep pouring money and time into the project. Helen and Niko decided that she should continue her development process even though that would eat up the remainder of their savings and send them into credit-card debt. At the very least, they reasoned, even if the game did not sell to a marketer, its ingenuity would most likely net Helen a job offer. In the spring of 1993, Helen feels she is only a few months away from completion of her game—but her savings are almost gone, the credit-card costs are mounting, and she has no income.

Chapter 2

BLUE-COLLAR STROPHE

6:05 A.M. Dawn on an early summer Thursday shows a clear morning with less of the intense overnight heat of the past week—what promises to be a lovely day. On Seventh Avenue, half minutes elapse with no traffic, then one or two trucks cruise by at speeds just fast enough to take all of the timed-sequence lights as they turn green. Eighteenth Street, at other hours a favorite of vehicles coming from the West Side Highway, is also relatively empty. On the northwest corner of 18th and Seventh, the donut cart is open. The two Malaysian-born men inside report that they were dropped off with their cart here at 4:00, but that it takes them ninety minutes to butter the rolls, put sugar in the cardboard cups, brew the coffee, sequence the other supplies for ease of access. There are, indeed, customers at 5:30, they say—from the post office's overnight shift. No other purveyors of "coffee-and" are open at crack of dawn, so the donut cart gets all the available business at this hour.

Parked outside 216, the printing building, is a large truck from

New Jersey; the two sleeping drivers in the cab look as though they've been here for a while, waiting for someone to arrive at the building to accept delivery of their cargo. No one will wake them to ask if they are paid by the load or the hour. People come out of the subway exits at 18th and Seventh, not walking fast, just ambling. When you're due in before 7:00, a minute or two isn't going to matter to the boss. The amblers are office assistants, freight wranglers, supply depot employees, post office mail handlers and carriers, telephone operators: not a suit-and-tie or blouse-and-skirt ensemble on the several dozen people who emerge from the subway depths in the course of ten minutes. Those who must wake in darkness to arrive at work at sunrise are mostly members of minority groups—blacks, Latinos, Asians—who collectively now make up a majority of New York's population.

A clutch of straphangers enters 216 at the freight entrance, the only door open at this hour. Two minutes later, lights go on in an upper floor. There is also activity in the main-floor area of Downtown Offset: Visible through a door propped open because of the day's heat is a yarmulke on a head that also sports long dark sideburns. Since manager Oscar Sabel is white-bearded, the sideburn curls must belong to another man from the Hasidic community in Brooklyn. Their private bus leaves them at the corner of Sixth Avenue at a very early hour. As a "printer's printer," Downtown doesn't serve the public directly but acts as a subcontractor to other printers; not having to deal with the public permits Downtown to open and close early, thereby conforming its work to the dawn-to-dusk rhythm of the workers' religious group.

A few doors to the west, through the shuttered window of the messenger service depot is a view of piled-up bicycles: a lovely and unexpected found-object sculpture.

Yesterday Peter Miceli, the manager at Solco, the plumbing supply depot on 18th, said there are often plumbers' trucks waiting when Solco opens up at seven. None are present at 6:30 today, and the white sheet-metal grating over the depot's entrance is still down. At this hour the most active place on this stretch is the post office, where a dozen people in uniforms, mostly in shorts, languish outside while inside, according to postmaster Ed Risdell, there is the "organized hysteria" of the mail being final-sorted for delivery.

A small, entirely white cat has the run of the exterior of 18th Street, hunting from one side of the street to the other, up and down the stoops. There is the occasional dog walker, but only one intrepid jogger. Farther along toward Eighth Avenue, the New Barber Shop opens. The Latino barber is a natty man; drops of witch hazel glisten on his smooth-shaven chin. No potential customers are going to rise and shine any earlier than he! Who would get a haircut at seven? Only men from the working class, who can't spare any other time for a trim. Opposite the barbershop, a teenager on Rollerblades glides to the door of Liberty High School, brakes, and rolls in.

6:45 A.M. Eighteenth & Eighth, the café on the southwest corner, is shuttered: This is a surprise, because I know they do a big breakfast business. Two South American kitchen helpers begin to open the gate. Opposite, a station wagon pulls up and Man Yohn Lee and his wife and daughter emerge. Mrs. Lee wipes sleep from her eyes as she waits for her husband to raise the gate of their dry-cleaning store; perhaps she has napped in the car. They'll put in their usual long day, not closing their gate until seven tonight.

This block is the early-morning destination of workers from diverse ethnic origins who live elsewhere in the metropolitan area but come here for employment—the Hasidim printers from Crown Heights; the Colombian kitchen help from Washington Heights at the northern end of Manhattan; the Koreans and other Asians (such as those behind the counters of the delis) from Queens; the black and Puerto Rican postal and telephone-company workers from Harlem and Bensonhurst; the older Irish, Polish, and Italian unionized workers in the supply depots from as far away as fifty miles out in New Jersey or on Long Island. With the exception of the laundry owners, these early arrivers are not the block's entrepreneurs but its employees. Although only a few are employed in manufacturing jobs, and so we can't really call them blue-collar, almost all are employed in non-white-collar, nonmanagerial positions. They constitute a group of "soft-collar" workers. Their salaries range from the minimum wage of $4.25 an hour up to about $15 or $20 an hour, placing virtually all of them below the national average annual salary of around $32,000. These are people who, for the most part, come here to work but cannot afford to shop here or even to eat in the restaurants other than the diners or to buy snacks from one of the delis. At a time when many of the area's middle-class residents are still asleep or are just waking up, the soft-collar class that keeps the wheels turning in the area's businesses is already hard at work.

Eighth Avenue is as quiet as Seventh. The restaurants that comprise the bulk of the commercial establishments along this strip are all closed; their days begin near noon and last until midnight, or, as with the bar, Flight 151, until four in the morning.

Two boarders from the St. Francis Residence III, in mid-block on Eighth, sit casually on a stoop; one smokes a cigarette. The early-morning hours look to be very long for such former inmates of asylums for the mentally ill. Although the residents at St. Francis III are no longer institutionalized, all but one or two are unable to hold down jobs and so have nowhere to go and nothing much to do; these men may have woken with the sun or when their medication level receded. One strolls across to the Apollo deli and buys cigarettes. The deli-counter Asians are patient with these customers, who spend a good fraction of their monthly checks at such establishments.

Chelsea Place, next to Food/Bar, is proving to be an enigma. For twenty years it had been a restaurant and nightclub, with the mystique of a quasi-legal destination. The middle rooms were entered through an armoire; a white piano bar dominated one room, while another room was a garden; the front room had shelves from which clothing was sold. The phone number was unlisted, business cards advised patrons to "tell only your best friends," and signs asked members of the media who came to eat or drink not to write about Chelsea Place.

The nightclub closed about a year ago, after several years of what neighbors characterized as severe reverses for GianCarlo Santini, the proprietor. The reverses included the seizure of this and the adjoining building he owned for nonpayment of taxes; the divorce of GianCarlo and his first wife, Joan; and the departure from the business of an accountant who had been an integral part of his management team. However, there is now activity at the site, and these neighbors believe that Santini has recently convinced the new owners of the building, who have not been able to rent the premises to anyone else, to let him reopen the nightclub. In April, signs appeared on the whitewashed window, saying "We're back." An advertisement in the neighborhood paper announced the re-opening of "The only place in Chelsea for the Mature Professional Crowd...featuring the hottest in live music nightly...A Real Speakeasy Experience...Proper attire required." Reading between the lines, one can interpret the ad as implying that Chelsea Place is for heterosexuals above the age of twenty-five and able to pay prices high enough to support live bands.

A chance meeting before the reopening found Santini by the door—a man in his early sixties, short, sallow-complexioned, and bearded, wearing an open shirt and gold chain. What had happened to permit the revival of Chelsea Place?

"Things changed." He shrugged, and didn't offer more.

Chelsea Place opened for an evening or two, then closed again. After that, the signs on the storefront began to change every few days. "Open." "Closed." "Reopening soon." This morning the window displays faux-marble chairs, painted barrettes, tie-dyed and cleverly printed T-shirts, a few cheap-looking cloth scarves. A dead, upturned waterbug mars the effect of the display. Inside, a notice that "the store" will be "close for 3 weeks. People that put money on deposit, can call Ron and Live poun #." Does that mean leave phone number? Are they not to call Santini? Has his alliance with the building owners fallen apart?

The Chelsea Gym on the upper floors of the northeast corner

of Eighth and 17th, above Video Blitz, is active at this before-workday hour. The wraparound, second-story windows reveal many men straining at the machines. A surveillance camera is bolted on the building, focused on the gym entrance; perhaps such a device has been deemed necessary by owner Louis Nelson or by an insurance carrier because merchandise is sold from the counter, a step off the street. The camera doesn't look very useful, though.

An extremely large truck with its motor idling sits in front of the Steiner Factory Building on 17th; it hails from Virginia, and the driver has a weimaraner in the cab. Seventeenth is not wider than 18th, as Peter Miceli contends—they are both thirteen and a half paces from curb to curb—but 17th has considerably less traffic, which permits parking near the Eigen plumbing supply warehouse with more ease than is possible near the Solco depot. Eigen is now open, and their counter display is colorful, large, and replete with point-of-sale advertising. Men in Eigen uniforms load supplies from the warehouse onto their own trucks, to be transported to Eigen's other locations, one on First Avenue at 90th, the other in Brooklyn.

On 18th, Solco is also open, and its own truck is there, though on precisely the opposite mission from that of the Eigen trucks; that is, it's delivering supplies from Solco's Brooklyn warehouse to this retail location. The counter is more drab and has no point-of-sale displays. Peter waves from his upstairs office; he has a ninety-minute commute from Long Island, and awoke before 5:00.

7:12 A.M. The men in the delivery truck in front of 216 are importuning someone from the building so they can unload. They pull the truck onto the sidewalk. The emptying process begins. It is slow going. By 7:20, the workers are just getting the truck's doors open; inside are six-foot-high rolls of paper that will require fork-lifts to move them.

Five people wait patiently in line at the donut cart: a student, a clerical worker, a businessman eager to get on the subway, a man from the Con Ed substation, a postal worker. They are so perfectly diverse, they seem to have come from central casting. Inside the Kap's diner on the next corner, a similar, though less diverse, queue of customers begins to extend.

It's becoming hot. Several 18th Street blue-collar businesses are now open for the day and busy—Solco, Maxwell Lumber next door, and the messenger service. The Martinton parking lot, however, is still quite empty: those who have begun work on the block at this hour have not driven cars into mid-Manhattan and parked them for the day; they have been deterred, most likely, by the high charge for parking here. In front of the two adjoining storefronts of the messenger center, young black men inspect their bikes, testing and reinflating the tires. Two vans pull up: WAY Messenger, from Lancaster, Pennsylvania. Dispatcher Steven Bonfiglio has said that there is an arrangement by which the Pennsylvania guys deliver materials to the 18th Street depot each morning, and Mercury takes them from there to various city destinations. A new sign in the Mercury window features a van and an invitation for people to drive such messenger vehicles: "This could be you," the notice promises. The bike messengers cannot get going until later on, because it is mainly white-collar execs who request messenger service, and they are not in their offices yet. But since every second counts during the workday, the bikers must arrive early and be prepared by the time of their first calls.

In the Raymond Dragon store window is a sign that is a spoof on current ads for *Elle* magazine, a sign that claims Dragon as "A designer of men's clothes that women love to wear." I haven't observed any women in the Dragon boutique yet, but Tim Cass says some do come in. The shuttered store won't open until noon. Similarly, nobody is in yet at Myron Michaels's optical store or the women's athletic gear store, the card store, the bookstore, the children's clothing store, or LeeSam. These retailers cater basically to the middle class—to people whose employment affords them the latitude of waking after the sun rises. It's mostly neighborhood service enterprises such as dry cleaners and diners who feel and meet the need to be available to customers at an early hour. One of the two copy shops recently pushed back its opening time from 8:00 to 9:00 A.M. because it wasn't doing enough business to warrant being open the extra hour.

Posters on streetlamp poles tout a film festival to be held in the Barneys parking lot in back of the upscale restaurant, Le Madri. "Film al Fresco" will feature Italian classics such as *Mediterraneo* and *Oro di Napoli* along with food and drink. Owner Pino Luongo, ever active, has collared as cosponsors AT&T and the Italian coffee company Lavazza.

7:30 A.M. There's "Doc" Nandal of the newsstand on Eighth, announcing his opening by putting out a triangular sidewalk sign offering one-day photo service. The American immigrant dream of rags-to-riches has certainly come true for Pino Luongo but it is stalled at a lower haberdashery level for Chander Nandal, who was a certified veterinarian back in India. In the United States he has been too busy trying to support his wife and small children and so has not had the time to study for recertification as a vet here—an occupation in demand, and one that if practiced would catapault him into the salary range of the upper middle class. He worked as a bank teller and as an employee at another newsstand before buying this one. He scoots across the avenue to the Apollo deli, which has accepted the delivery of the newspapers for him, and retrieves several wrapped bundles. In his own store, he will count the papers to see if the amount matches the number that the deli says it has received; he's often short a few papers and has to argue with the distributor about dimes and quarters owed and lost.

The grate is half up at the tony café, Eighteenth and Eighth, but the restaurant is still quite closed. Aren't they missing the breakfast hour? The diners along Seventh and Eighth have been open for a while. Teenagers are gathering in duos and trios on the sidewalks near Liberty High for a summer session; they have claimed some stoops from the St. Francis III people, who have probably gone inside the residence to breakfast. Business-suited white men and women come out of brownstones on 18th that have nicely placed flowers or gated entrances; these residents look up and down the block and delicately pick their way past bunches of students before walking briskly to the corners to hail cabs.

7:40 A.M. At the entrance of the Nynex building on 17th, a man in a beat-up car waits for a woman operator to finish talking to the very stout female guard. Another car, equally ancient, delivers two other black, middle-aged women; after a moment's chat with the guard, who is not yet in uniform, they go inside to start their shift, which begins at eight. Several smokers linger outside, sitting on the wooden fence parts of the Barneys parking lot, inhaling coffee and cigarettes. A chain keeps unwanted cars out of that lot, so it's still empty, as it has been all night. Unlike most parking lots, its surface is pristine: Barneys really is strict about who can park here and for how long. A truck from an elevator-cab and -door company has pulled into the bay adjoining the building; facilities manager Larry Forella has said that the elevators are in poor condition, so this is likely to be the beginning of their refurbishing. This fall, several hundred additional white-collar workers, sales and managerial employees, will be added to those already at work in the building. How will the presence of several hundred additional white-collar types affect the block?

7:55 A.M. More teenagers loll near the high school. They are spread over an area that extends from the Gascogne Restaurant on Eighth to the residences and storefronts on the north side of the 18th Street block, all of which are currently closed. Two kids are doing some dirty dancing; two others are having a heart-to-heart colloquy of fierce earnestness; many are listening through earphones to their CD- or tape-players; a few study intently. Principal Bruce Schnur says that Liberty deliberately opens earlier than other schools to accommodate its particular student body—teenage immigrants enrolled in an intensive, one-year program to learn English. His kids are vulnerable to being accosted on the subways by bunches of other students who attend the regular city high schools nearby, and so Schnur has arranged a schedule that will move his own students into and out of school at times that will enable them to avoid contact with those who might take advantage of them on the subways.

In the midst of a swarm of Liberty-bound kids near the stoop of 249, a man in his forties sits waiting, neatly posed on an American flag bandanna handkerchief. Moments later, as the school opens, the teenagers depart in unison, and within a minute, there's not a one to be seen anywhere on the block. Now the man on the bandanna and another who arrives from Seventh Avenue open the Towne House pet-grooming place. Proprietor Michael Palmadessa's customers often come early and leave their dogs to be clipped, then return after work to pick them up. The Towne House "Pet Taxi" approaches, with three purebreds collected from customers who prefer door-to-door service. The Pet Taxi has done wonders for Towne House Grooming, Palmadessa says, because this extra service differentiates his grooming salon from others. If he were technical about it, he could say that the taxi defines his niche and widens it, and he could argue that this stratagem has put underused capacity to work.

Next door at Madelyn Simon & Associates, a whitewashed and featureless garage door slides up to reveal a profusion of lush greenery inside. This is an indoor-plants-for-offices firm, and the plants are such a welcome glory in the midst of the city that one can also see why the Simon business is planning to move to larger quarters about a mile from here. It first looked as though the For Sale sign had to do with selling the whole building, whose upper story houses the Chelsea Day School, but only the bottom half is to be sold. Four Madelyn Simon trucks are parked along the street; shortly, they'll be loaded with plants to deliver to offices around the city.

Lights come on in the ground-floor dental offices of the big apartment building on the northwest corner of Seventh; Dr. Schenkel apparently accommodates his schedule to that of his clientele, some of whom need appointments before they go to work.

8:00 A.M. On the dot, the post office opens officially for business, and small vans and trucks pull up, each disgorging a man who goes inside and returns with a bag of mail for his company. Opposite, the paper-roll deliverers are still hard at work unloading. The blue-collar day is at least an hour old for most of the workers, and for some, two to three hours old. In contrast to the previous waves of straphangers, those now emerging from the subways wear better clothing and step more briskly toward Barneys, Cahners, and Nynex, the large employers on the block. These later arrivals are overwhelmingly white and seem mainly to be clerical or sales personnel, rather than managers.

The Eighteenth and Eighth Café opens, and yuppies begin to file in. A couple of muscle-bound guys jaywalk across from the Chelsea Gym, talking about ordering the "pancakes of the day," which are $1.50 more expensive than pancakes at Kap's. Evidently the operators of the café see no reason to open at the crack of dawn because they know their customers, who are neither blue-collar nor early birds.

8:10 A.M. On Seventh and Eighth Avenues, traffic is booming and incessant. What a difference from an hour ago! Eighteenth is entirely clogged now with vans and trucks; there's hardly a parking space empty on the eastern half of the block. The Martinton lot is slowly filling with expensive cars driven by people well-known to the attendant, who greets each by name. Several plumbing trucks hover, wait for others to pull out, and then park at the curbs in order to go to Solco. New York's plumbers generally don't keep a great many supplies on hand because supplies take up a lot of space and in New York space is expensive; so they visit supply depots once or sometimes twice a day to pick up what they need for the morning and afternoon jobs. Among the plumbers calling now at Solco are Ed Cece of Wooster Street and King Diamond of Staten Island. Five minutes later, King Diamond pulls up in front of Eigen; either he didn't find what he was looking for at Solco, or got it and then stopped around the corner for an additional pickup. It is most likely that these two plumbers are working on private residences today, for they will not arrive at their work sites until 8:30 or 9:00; if they were working at construction sites or commercial shops, they would have been knocking on the doors of the block's two supply depots much earlier. A similar pattern is in evidence at Maxwell Lumber, adjacent to Solco: Independent woodworking contractors arrive here early in the day to pick up what they need for their jobs.

Throughout the past half hour, five Nynex installation vans have been accumulating near the building. Now, men and women with belts full of screwdrivers and headsets come out of the bronze doors, get into the vans, and start off down the street; they will fan out to locations all over Chelsea and West Greenwich Village to make installations and service calls. As with the plumbers and carpenters, if the installers showed up earlier to work on a recently rented apartment, they would be unwelcome.

There is activity at the Steiner Building, which houses the Catholic Book Publishing Company. The weimaraner stands guard in the cab as the driver of that Virginia-based truck works with the building employees; they use one forklift to bring down another from inside the truck, and then both machines get started loading pallets of materials whose destinations are all in the Bible Belt.

Eight to nine seems to be distribution hour. Workers from small vans and large parked on Eighth Avenue plop down on the sidewalks boxes of lettuce, cauliflower, and mushrooms for the restaurants, while on 18th, drivers of the messenger vans, plumbing trucks, mail-pickup station wagons, and Madelyn Simon vans take away their various cargoes to be delivered elsewhere. At such moments, this big city reveals itself to be an enormous distribution center, with each transfer of materials a link in a complex chain of human interactions.

Just as we're all becoming designers, we're all becoming distributors of sorts, finding optimal ways of fitting properly into our particular section of a chain. America, land of the middleman. Or maybe it's just cities that fit that bill: It is the presence and capabilities of the Solcos and the Maxwells that make it possible for New York's plumbers and carpenters to operate profitably. Without a depot, plumbers would pay a lot more to warehouse their own supply caches, not to mention having the headaches and paperwork associated with ordering parts directly from the manufacturer.

8:45 A.M. Cahners' two buildings have lots of lights on, now, in the upper floors. The nine-to-fivers' jobs, according to vice president John Beni, can be construed as middleman stuff, too, involving repackaging and distributing information to the public through the medium of the company's myriad publications. The other office buildings are also humming now. Stragglers come from the subways at a more accelerated pace—mostly managers, judging by their clothing, which consists of suits and ensembles, more expensive than that of the previous bunch of straphangers. Can it be that people who are due to arrive at 9:00, and who are paid by the week rather than by the hour, are more in a hurry than those who must punch in at 7:00? One business-suited man comes to the corner of 17th and Seventh, peers into the deli and sees a line at the counter that's eight people long, and chooses to go into the Kap's diner diagonally opposite; his decision is soon vindicated, because he's out again in ninety seconds and hopping through a red light back across the avenue to double-time it toward Cahners. Upheld in this transaction, as well, is the acumen of Teddy and Peter, owners of Kap's, in keeping the "coffee-and" line at their diner moving swiftly.

Around on Eighth Avenue, Chelsea Place's door is now—unexpectedly—open. A twenty-something husband-and-wife team of barrette makers from New Jersey—she designs and paints, he glues—is outside, arranging their wares on two tables. The interior is dark, the barrette makers say, because the owner "had a problem with the electricity," which seems to imply that Con Ed has shut off the power because of nonpayment. The young couple had arranged to lease some of the shelf space inside and sell from there, but because the interior is dark all they can do is offer merchandise from the tables.

9:10 A.M. Now 18th is relatively quiet again, and traffic on the avenues has subsided from a continuous roar to a dull throb. The rumbles from the subways are less frequent, and even the man in the donut cart is sitting down. Fewer people are visible on the street, and these are probably residents or late risers, since most of the people employed around this block are now at work.

Chapter 3

BRAVING THE ELEMENTS

THERE IS NOTHING intrinsically novel about starting an optical goods store, a restaurant, a clothing boutique, a line of furniture, or even a computer-game design business. Such start-ups are regular occurrences in a time of rising optimism after a recession. The strength of Sight on Seventh, the Raymond Dragon boutique, Food/Bar, Gear Holdings' new line, Marc Bernstein's reinvigorated Maxwell Lumber, and Helen C's new game-design enterprise lie in their ability to join a reasonable business concept to a reasonable context, that is, an environment in which the business can have a good expectation of success. The Dragon boutique's context counts on a pool of gay men as customers; Myron Michaels relies on an aging population and a location carefully chosen for foot traffic; the proprietors of Food/Bar know that they will derive some trade simply by virtue of being situated within a restaurant row. Helen C. relies on another reasonable context, the growing appetite for games among the computer literate. Good concept and good context alone, however, do not a sure-fire enterprise make. Case in point: the new Chelsea Place. This nightclub for lower-middle-class heterosexuals, located but a short distance from the tunnels into New York from New Jersey, the home of many of Santini's previous customers, is having difficulty staying open, despite a reasonable concept and context.

In the old way of defining the factors of production, the three elements needed were land, labor, and capital. Land and labor are changing both in definition and in emphasis, and so is capital. The underlying subject of this study is an attempt to evaluate the direction and interplay of those changes in the factors of production. The first change to become apparent is that when considering a small entrepreneurship, land and labor are less important than capital. Looking through guides to starting small enterprises, one finds that the elements considered necessary for starting a business fall into categories that can be labeled *concept, context,* and *capital.* Pretty straightforward and fairly obvious stuff. But the guides do not say much about the configuration of factors that permit a business to continue beyond the critical first two years of existence. Why do some businesses become fixtures of a neighborhood while others come and go? Does success depend on a continually expanding clientele? A low rent? The entrepreneur's frame of mind? Trained and willing employees? Beyond the sprint of the first two years, to achieve success in the middle distances requires some adjustment to the mix of concept, context, and capital. To ascertain whether there is an increased emphasis on one element, while another diminishes in importance, one must look into some of the longer-established entities around the block.

Two long-running retail entities flank Myron Michaels's eyewear emporium. All three storefronts are of virtually identical size and share the same landlord. But while Michaels has signed what he refers to as a multiyear lease—my guess is three years—the Roger Roth & Dave card shop, in existence next door for more than a decade, has a five-year lease that reflects its owners' feeling that they are certain to continue to operate for a long period. Meanwhile Womens Workout Gear, just south of Roger Roth, has just a single-year lease, and we'll see in a moment the reasoning behind that arrangement.

Michaels reports that he opened Sight on Seventh a month behind schedule and has also run into a bit of unexpected difficulty. "I can't carry certain frames that I want," he says, "because the distributor sells Myoptics, which wants exclusivity in this territory." Since that store, two blocks south, is part of a chain of four, its larger volume undoubtedly holds more sway with that distributor. Michaels is not fazed by this rebuff and points out that "I have eight other lines of frames, including Armani, the best-sellers, so I think I've got more variation in price range. And I do a lot of specialized work with the visually impaired, which I doubt Myoptics does, and we carry a special kind of treated sports glasses." In the short time his store has been open, he has done some business and is encouraged, but he admits that "There are days when nobody comes in but the mailman."

Recently, Roger Roth of the card store observed to Paula Shirk of Womens Workout Gear that Michaels's shop was "too Upper East Side" to click with the sort of "funky, casual" people in this neighborhood, and he hoped that the optician would change his style. Paula's belief is that customers will eventually come to Michaels.

Perhaps Shirk is more sympathetic to the optician's start-up difficulties because she still considers every month that Womens Workout Gear stays open to be a victory. "This neighborhood isn't as great as the traffic patterns and other come-ons would have you believe," she advises. A small, athletic-looking woman in her late thirties with dark hair so closely cropped around her head that it looks like a shower cap, she hails originally from Pennsylvania Dutch country. Womens Workout Gear is crowded with workout and running clothes, cover-ups, a collection of sports bras, and a rack of athletic footwear. On one wall are brochures for various gyms, exercise salons, and athletic excursions. Shirk has a handful of employees, one full-time and several part-time.

"Five and a half years ago, in the middle of the night, I vacated a commercial lease on the Upper West Side because the area had become overrun with drug dealers," Shirk says. "I was a bean counter for RCA before going into this business. My worst day here, though, is better than my best day at that job." As with most proprietors of small businesses, Paula feels that the satisfaction of being one's own boss is worth putting up with many aggravations.

Women now make up more than 45 percent of the country's workforce, double that of twenty years ago, and the number of women entrepreneurs in the country is double that of a decade ago. However, they still constitute a smaller percentage of the country's entrepreneurs than men do, and most of their enterprises are one-woman operations. Part reason for this is an aggregate lack of experience in business, since women's participation in business in significant numbers is relatively recent, but there are also structural barriers. Studies show that women are less likely to be able to obtain loans for their ventures and more likely to be asked to pay higher rents. Shirk feels that in addition to overcoming all the usual difficulties that male entrepreneurs must face, women must also brave additional problems specific to them. She points out that while none of the male retail store owners on this stretch of Seventh have been robbed, her store has been hit twice; in one of these robberies, she was tied up and left in the basement. She now keeps a large dog in the store to deter further robbery attempts.

Paula Shirk perseveres in her endeavor because she believes deeply in her basic concept: clothing for women to wear during athletic exercise and to and from workouts. "People told me, 'go unisex,' but that wasn't my concept. I knew that women's needs were not being met and wanted to do an athletic store for women—not unisex, but by and for women. Other athletic stores in this neighborhood have gone belly-up, but we're still here because we're very specifically for women."

She believes that the drawing power of the concept is such that customers come to the store from all over the city, "because they know this is the only store of its kind in New York, one of only a few in the whole country."

Why hasn't this concept been bought or stolen away from her? The reason has to do with the pattern of slow acceptance of innovation that is characteristic of big business in the United States. American commercial history is replete with tales of interesting though relatively obvious concepts that have been overlooked or even deliberately ignored by the big boys because they were being promulgated by small businesses; such concepts are usually dismissed because they are thought to appeal to too narrow an audience—put another way, they are considered to have a faulty context. Paula echoes this history as she recalls that in the early days of her boutique, "Nike wouldn't sell to me because they said a women's athletic goods store wouldn't make it. I kept after them and finally they relented." She needed such big manufacturers when she began; but after a half-dozen years, she has reached a plateau where she can be more critical of the merchandise she carries. "Now I'm thinking about dumping shoes that really don't take women's bodies into account—that are too narrow in the foot for most of my customers. I know that sort of fact because I've had to learn more about running shoes and athletic socks and such than I ever wanted or cared to know."

Concentrating on athletic gear for women has pushed her to study so that she can give "better and more knowledgeable service than you could get at Paragon [a nearby sporting goods store] or at a department store—the sort of service that makes for a good atmosphere. We don't ask a woman her bra or pants size in front of a man, and most often not even in front of another woman. Women who want to work out have to do more than a man does, which is put on a pair of shoes. Women have to be properly outfitted—the right sports bra, for instance—and they have to be emotionally prepared for athletics. Women don't come out of an athletic background and as a result are intimidated or patronized in the usual store." She contends that there is satisfaction in being athletic, and that women have formerly missed out on it because they were socialized not to have that kind of enjoyment. Lack of athletic experience also explains "why women don't know how to evaluate sports clothing or what questions to ask." Her precision about such matters is the key to what makes her shop able to survive tough competition: She creates a cadre of repeat customers whose word-of-mouth recommendations help maintain an adequate year-round sales level.

While she has been able to stay in business here for more than five years, Paula Shirk remains uncertain how long the store will be tenable; the year-to-year lease assuages her fear that the store might fail, or that she might have to move it again somewhere else, on short notice. Her best season is from May to July, but at other times business can be slow. Occasionally she resorts to financing purchases of clothing and other supplies with personal credit. Cash-flow difficulties are one of the major reasons why she prefers a year-to-year lease. Irregular cash flow also pushes her to carefully manage her stock; she maintains that she'd rather buy fewer items, sell them all, and then momentarily regret that she has no more to offer, than buy too much stock and be stuck with excess that she cannot sell or can sell only at a loss.

Her future plans are modest. She'd like to carry more winter sports merchandise, but there is not enough room here and she isn't ready to contemplate moving to a larger space.

While Paula Shirk's store concept is relatively unique in that her competition does not do precisely what she does, two members of the community of blue-collar wholesale building trades enterprises on this block, the Eigen and Solco depots, appear to perform precisely the same function: They both sell plumbing supplies to individual and fleet plumbers.

The head-to-head nature of the Eigen-Solco competition is evident one summer day at noon, as manager Peter Miceli of Solco takes his bag lunch, walks around to 17th Street, and sits to eat at a vantage point from which he can keep the rival Eigen depot in full view. When an observer happens by and teases him about industrial espionage, he responds, with a grin, "Just seeing how they do business."

To an untrained eye, Eigen appears to be the larger of the two enterprises. It is an open, quadruple-width garage, forklifts, huge racks of gleaming metal, men in work overalls or T-shirts that sport sexual puns about the nipples on pipes. There is a separate counter for paper transactions, and an office upstairs for members of the firm, family-owned since the 1920s. Solco—in the building next to Maxwell Lumber on 18th—has less machinery and fewer workers in its five-story, single-width, whitewashed home and appears to have less stock, but that is not so. Since Solco's warehouse is in Brooklyn, the company only brings into the Manhattan depot enough supplies for that day's needs. A small sign hanging above Eigen's depot says that it features American Standard. Solco sells the Kohler line. Virtually every home has porcelain toilets, fixtures, and connecting pipes that come from one of these two American manufacturers, and according to Peter Miceli, there is little difference in quality or price between Kohler and American Standard products; plumbers are able to work with both. In large markets like New York, however, a supply depot must choose which of the two lines to carry. Eigen features one; Solco, the other.

Context takes on another meaning when considering these two rival depots. For some kinds of businesses, proximity between competitors seems to increase traffic for all of them. Customers come to the cluster believing that they will find a greater range of choice in both variety of merchandise and price. The "aggregation factor" operates most visibly in farmers markets, where each stall sells merchandise very like that of the next; in suburban malls where highly similar clothing stores are neighbors; and in one-industry districts in many cities, such as the diamond center on 47th Street in Manhattan—a single block from which several hundred merchants sell jewelry. The same aggregation dynamic helps Eigen and Solco: A plumber can come to this block and be reasonably assured of finding the supplies he needs at one or the other depot, rather than having to visit supply depots at some greater distance from each other. "At one point," recalls Victor Sherman, the CEO of Solco, "we almost bought an open lot just down from Eigen so we could be on the same block." Sherman was outbid, and there is now a small apartment house on the site.

The attempt to move in next door to Eigen reflects Sherman's aggressive style. He is in his sixties, a small, athletic-looking man with a craggy face and silver hair. Family photos in his office on the second floor show him earning his tan in Florida, and cartoons depict him out on the tennis court and the golf course enough to be ribbed about those pastimes.

The narrow entryway of the Solco depot is fouled from trucks that pull up to load and unload, and the rubber covering on the stairs to the offices is worn with age. But a computer system is in use, and so are a multi-telephone paging system and other electronic devices. "It's really very modern. There's no hand writing of tickets for supplies being picked up—it's all done by computer, and the items deducted from inventory before anything walks out of here," Miceli observes. The building, which dates back to the late nineteenth century, had been a stable before it became Sol Shapiro's used plumbing supply store in the 1920s. In 1960 Shapiro sold the business to two of his employees, Murray and Otto. In 1975, they were in their seventies, and wanted to sell. Vic Sherman, who knew the supply business from his earlier work, arrived to look it over.

"They handed me a flashlight and told me I'd need it to look in the bins and check the inventory—it was that primitive. I watched these old goats scampering up and down the five stories of bins and thought that at least I'd live to be as old and spry as they were." The business was used supplies, and the competitors included not only Eigen but LeeSam. "People would come in with those old bathtubs on legs that sat in the kitchens of the Lower East Side tenements. We'd buy them for the going rate, $5 or $10, and we could sell them for $100. We'd get the old steam radiators, pump them full of water, see where they leaked, and patch them up."

It was not an auspicious time to begin—the middle of a slump in construction, when New York City teetered on the brink of default. Yet in Sherman's first year, the gross was a quarter million dollars, two and a half times what it had been under the previous operators.

Aggregation clusters or similar arrangements seem to hold together during the good years without undue tension or internecine warfare thinning the ranks of competitors, but when the bad years arrive, there are often not enough customers for all the firms to survive. That is when some firms go under, while others stay afloat. Survival may be a matter of a firm changing its ways of doing business—in effect, by putting distance between itself and its neighbors in the aggregation cluster so that it is no longer a direct competitor. That's what happened around this block. Before the bad years of the mid-1970s, there had been three competitors in the wholesale plumbing supply business, Solco, Eigen, and LeeSam. But when the crunch came, only one, Eigen, remained in precisely the same business, continuing to sell mainly to individual and fleet plumbers.

It might be supposed that Eigen's survival is evidence that it is the most solid of the three entities, and indeed, Eigen is a vibrant enterprise today, but it must be noted that the others have also survived. LeeSam successfully metamorphosed into a retailer of fixtures, and Solco took another (and eventually more lucrative) route. In Sherman's second year of business, Solco eased out of used supplies and into the sale of new plumbing; then, instead of sitting and waiting for plumbers to arrive at his shop, Sherman went after bigger wholesale customers. He pursued deals with real estate developers, Donald Trump among them, to have Solco's trucks provide plumbing supplies at wholesale prices right to construction sites. Sherman made this shift just in time to hook into what soon became a very strong construction boom in New York, a boom that shortly boosted Solco's annual gross to $2 million a year. He consented to having the entire staff unionized because only Teamster-driven trucks could deliver to construction sites.

In 1983, Sherman decided to "semiretire." Such a decision often produces a crisis in a small business, because renewal of management, or at least the training of successors, is critical to a business's continued existence. It frequently forces a redefinition of the business concept. At Solco, Sherman took in junior partners, one a computer expert, the other an experienced salesman—junior, in that they owned only minority shares—and in 1987, the Solco partners opened a retail showroom next door. "At first, it worked out well," Sherman recalls. "We had the showroom as a selling point for customers building large apartment houses; they could come in and see what the fixtures would look like in the finished version." Eventually, however, the retail venture changed hands; it is now owned by HomeWorks, a Brooklyn-based company.

Sherman does not say why the retail showroom did not work out, but there were several problems. First, as with Gear Holdings, the Solco partners discovered that retail and wholesale require largely different mind-sets. Second, the existence of the retail showroom irked some Solco customers who learned, to their annoyance, that Solco's retail arm was competing with their own re-selling of equipment. Third, there were some union territorial squabbles that Solco had not counted on. To solve all three problems, the company opted out of the retail business.

The major incentive to divest the showroom, though, was the opportunity to apply the company's capital in a more potentially profitable direction, one more compatible with its major thrust. Solco decided to buy and stock a 40,000-square-foot warehouse in Brooklyn. This 1989 purchase expanded the business's capacity. It helped boost the gross from $5 million a year before the warehouse to $15 million a year since the warehouse has been in operation.

Few passersby would guess that this shuttered, nondescript building, and the workaday business of providing toilets and tubing to plumbers, conceals a $15 million-a-year enterprise.

Sherman attributes the company's hundredfold growth since 1975 not solely to his own acumen but mostly to New York's strength as a market. "If I can make it there, I can make it anywhere," goes the refrain in the song "New York, New York." Vic Sherman's understanding suggests that precisely the reverse may be true: One can make it more readily in the big city than else-where because the city's own context is so strong, its population is so large, and its relative wealth is so vast. These factors make feasible and lucrative certain business entities that in any smaller city would likely be marginal. They also make it reasonable to expect that in the future, big cities and relatively small business enterprises will continue to coexist happily and profitably.

A representative of the "new media" community has its tail end on our block, in the 216 Building. The shipping department of Microvideo Learning Systems is there—located conveniently across the street from a large post office—while the company's headquarters is on a nearby stretch of Fifth Avenue, a much tonier address. MLS's concept has been steadily evolving. Begun by people experienced in video as an entity producing training tapes, it has steadily embraced newer and newer media as they emerge, and now produces training materials about new computer software programs on video, disks, and diskettes that are then sold to big companies that are going to install that software. MLS writes, shoots, and otherwise produces approximately one new product each month. Since new "releases" of software come down the pipe quickly, these days, MLS must work with equal speed to master the programs and translate their understanding into instructional materials for nonexperts. The most exciting thing now, an MLS spokesman says, is the challenge of making training materials on CD-ROM. Not only will it have the possibility of being interactive, but by means of that interactivity an employer will be able to test whether employees are really grasping the intricacies and possibilities of the software that the company has purchased.

Businesses based on solid concepts and realistic contexts are often able to get through the start-up years, even though most of them—and almost all small businesses—are undercapitalized when they begin. Initial capital problems have a way of persisting, though, and if not counteracted by a deliberate program of stockpiling money toward future needs, such as that undertaken by Solco, they can turn into nagging, chronic difficulties. Capital problems may stay hidden for a while, only to flare up and threaten to consume a business when times are bad or when the field in which the business operates undergoes extremely rapid change.

Carl Berman, chief officer of Guild Mailing Service, which has been in existence since the mid-1970s, is finding out during the summer of 1993 that the unavailability of new capital is a brick wall and that his enterprise is running smack toward it. Because of his dearth of capital, Berman is facing one of the hardest decisions of his life, a decision precipitated by rapid technological change in his industry and made more urgent by a prolonged recession. Carl is in his forties, a small, wiry, hands-on man who often works alongside his half-dozen employees in a 3,000-square-foot expanse of almost bare warehouse floor space in the 216 Building. Stacks and bins of magazines and brochures wait to be processed alongside post office cartons and bulk boxes; a plastic hanging curtain separates the mailing area from that used by a small printer, who is a subtenant. No high-tech equipment here, no machines that at the push of a button affix labels to envelopes quicker than the eye can follow. Here, labeling is done by handheld, nonelectronic devices.

The lack of highly technologized equipment is not necessarily a minus, according to Berman. He contends that ultramodernized, large bulk mailers—the sort who take full-page advertisements in the Yellow Pages to trumpet completely computerized services and "electronic conversion" of the information on tapes and disks— have to charge high prices for those services, more money than can be afforded by clients who need to mail fewer than 20,000 pieces at a time. Guild charges lower prices because it doesn't offer bells-and-whistles service, although it does have two computers. "We specialize in fast turnovers and in doing runs that are smaller than other companies want to handle. The prices we quote are a function of two things—how many pieces there are and how quickly they have to be delivered."

Berman is not a man who avoids seeing problems; he is a

scrambler who, in order to stay in business, has turned Guild into more than a mailer. "A client seldom needs just printing," he points out. "You need a way to distribute what's been printed. That's where we come in. Sometimes we take everything out of the client's hands, and get all the jobs done—pasteups, printing, and mailing. We give out the printing jobs, mostly to the printers in the building, and then we mail the end product." Because Berman acts as a broker for the printers in the area, they funnel mailing jobs to him in return. His regular clients have been the Museum of Natural History, for a quarterly calendar, and the National Basketball Association, for an insider's newsletter to journalists. His main printer ally, located in this building, is Waldon Press, whose owner is Bill Donat. The association goes back many years: Donat's father, who founded Waldon, often worked in tandem with Carl's father, who founded Guild Mailing.

On a cabinet in Carl's small office are National Rifle Association stickers, and on the desk some photographs of what Carl identifies as Old World lizards. "I'm an amateur herpetologist," he announces. One room of his home has been turned into a climate-controlled jungle with separate niches for lizards from all over the world, many of them quite rare. He is occasionally called by pet-store owners in the vicinity of Kennedy Airport to take charge of rare reptiles that tourists have brought into the country and then discovered that they could not properly care for. He has had some success in raising certain of these animals and corresponds with scientists in museums and zoos about his research.

A mailing service seems an odd venue for a man with such an interest in science, but as with many sons of entrepreneurs, Carl found the family business to be a lure, an obligation, and something to fall back on, all rolled into one. The elder Berman started Guild Mailing Service here in 1974, and shortly thereafter Carl, who had been an indifferent student in high school and so had limited prospects for other employment, joined him. Carl and his father clashed, and the young man left for California and jobs as a millwright and industrial mechanic. Six years later he came back, partly because he was in the process of a divorce, partly because his father was ill and needed his help. Father and son worked side by side through most of the 1980s until the elder Berman was assaulted and robbed of the weekly payroll in the building's elevator.

Carl joined the National Rifle Association and began to carry a gun. The elder Berman's injuries accelerated his retirement, and Carl took over in 1991. That year and 1992 were tough. "The bulk of my business is with nonprofits, and when their contributions dried up, they simply did less mailing." The first eight months of 1993 were also "pathetic," and when the NBA newsletter went on hiatus in June, the summer shaped up as even worse.

"Clients were incredibly slow in paying—not the 15 days net I try to insist on, not even the 30 days I'll stand for, but 60, 90, 120 days. That's killing me." Customers paying bills late is one reason that recessions last so long. And when clients pay late, a small business often must defer the purchase of new stock or equipment, rendering it more vulnerable to marketplace pressures. Carl might have liked to join the ranks of mailers with better equipment, but if clients withhold payment, he has no money to make new purchases.

Business had always picked up each fall, so Carl looked into obtaining a small loan to tide him over the summer. In March of 1993, President Clinton signed a $38 million SBA package to make available to small businesses just the sort of loan Carl needed— but Carl discovered that not a single bank in Chelsea offered these SBA loans. The banks turned him down on regular loans, too, because, in his view, "You have to have money to borrow money." Others might contend that Berman was refused a loan because largely outmoded equipment would not be seen by a bank as good collateral.

Carl owes Waldon Press the most money, but Bill Donat has agreed to wait to be paid. The most pressing of Berman's other back bills was from the IRS, for $10,900. A while ago he sent the IRS $3,000, and they sent a second bill saying that his new tab was

$10,400. "They took $2,500 of my $3,000 for interest and penalties! I said to them, 'Look, you're going to put me out of business, and that'll mean six more people on the unemployment line.' " To his amazement and gratification, the IRS agreed to waive some future interest and penalties. But he still owes $10,000 in back taxes, plus moneys to firms such as Waldon and to other suppliers.

Maybe it was time, he thought, to declare bankruptcy and walk away from the business and its obligations. His only child was nearing her graduation from high school, and he and his wife could go somewhere outside of New York City, perhaps start another sort of business. He was still suffering the aftereffects of an automobile accident that occurred in the summer of '92, which left him with herniated disks in his neck and lower back, and constant pain. "Some days, it takes me an hour to get out of bed. If I'd've laid down and pretended my life was over and I couldn't work, I'd've gotten a million-dollar settlement." Instead, Carl admitted to his lawyer that the exigencies of the business had only permitted him to take a couple of days off to visit doctors. A much lower settlement was offered and accepted.

Perhaps his experience in working through the pain engendered what has become his gritty response to the business crisis. "I asked myself, 'What's the difference if I go bankrupt owing ten grand or a hundred grand?' The answer is 'None.' So I'm maxing out my credit cards—taking the plunge; I'll squeeze out $30,000, and bet that when September rolls around, business will pick up again. And if it doesn't, then we'll all join the unemployment line."

Berman's decision is certainly a gamble, because in the age of computers, customers are usurping many a small supplier's context by buying a computer system that gives them the ability to perform the tasks they once had to parcel out to small jobbers like Guild Mailing Service. The printer of party invitations finds himself displaced by a customer with her own PC and some fancy paper. The accounting service specializing in small businesses finds that it has lost customers to popular software programs that a small entrepreneur can easily install on his or her regular office machine. The messenger service finds customers have diminished their need for its bicyclists because they have bought fax machines. Carl Berman may pride himself on Guild's good, quick service—usually an important factor in building a solid customer base—but the need for his sort of service is diminishing. And in consequence, the amount of capital that once appeared adequate to keep Guild Mailing going on a regular basis is no longer enough to see it through a difficult period and to enable it to purchase the new equipment it needs to compete in its field.

Beyond illustrating the interplay of concept, context, and capital, the stories of Paula Shirk, Vic Sherman, and Carl Berman also bring home the notion that economic matters cannot be untangled from business owners' personal lives. The personal element is often overlooked in texts and statistics about the continued existence of small businesses, perhaps because it is not quantifiable, but it seems in play everywhere on this block, throughout many of the businesses, whether they are retail or wholesale, distribution or manufacturing. Perhaps scholars have not addressed it because the equilibrium between the personal and the professional in the mind and life of the entrepreneur is not only not measurable but is often in the process of changing. This dynamic is most interestingly expressed by Robert Pusilo, co-owner of Authentiques Past & Present, a long-established collectibles shop on 18th Street.

"To me, the history of my business is tied up with the history of my gayness," Pusilo states. A big, solid midwesterner in his early fifties, he prominently sports red plastic glasses and a crucifix on a neck chain. He came to New York thirty years ago to be an actor and singer. "For many years afterwards, I deluded myself by saying that if I found the right woman, I'd get married and have children. This was before I perceived being gay as a positive identity." He attributes the persistence of the old notion to his Midwest, Roman Catholic upbringing and says he still clung to it years after he and Paul Lemma had become a settled couple.

Nineteen years ago, he was working as a costume designer at

a location near here. Walking by this 1930s, three-story building, he liked it and bought it on a whim, for a modest price. The store operates on the ground floor. It is a three-room marvel of density and display: Arrayed in glass cases are hundreds of items, from cut-glass perfume bottles to 1960s souvenir plates, quirky ashtrays, postcards, reproductions of old tin boxes, jewelry, Christmas ornaments, antique clothing, and other collectibles. Most of the merchandise is priced in the tens of dollars. "If I ring up a sale of a single item over $60, that's unusual," Pusilo says. He describes the stock as pop culture stuff—"what my midwestern, working-class mother and father would have had in their house. Often, people come in and say that they had such things in their homes in their youth."

The shop reached its present size, Pusilo recalls, in stages. "In the beginning, it was only a quarter of this size, and we were only open Saturdays and Sundays, because we both had other careers." Robert had assembled a collection of antique clothing, which he rented out in association with his costume-design assignments, and then he bought objects to complement the clothing. Paul, a travel consultant for the Rockefeller Foundation, also purchased things for sale. After Paul retired, over ten years ago, they began to open the shop during the week. As the demand for costume work slowed, Robert tired of traveling to film locations and living out of suitcases and decided to spend more time in the store.

But just about that time he entered a critical period in his life. His parents died, and he tried to return to the Catholic Church, even going so far as to get down on his knees to confess to a priest that he had knowingly "sinned" by having had sex with his lover. Unexpectedly, the priest told him, "There are many things that have been taught in the name of Jesus that are wrong." "This thought had never occurred to me," Pusilo recalls, "and it changed my life." After that he "went back to the faith in my own way," through the gay Catholic group Dignity. Within Dignity there sprang up an activist group called the Cathedral Project. "To express our dissatisfaction with church policy directly to the archdiocese, we sat in St. Patrick's on the first Sunday of every month, and stood up in silent witness and protest when the Cardinal delivered his homily. When we were expelled because of our gayness, we held masses on the street, with us as lay people doing the ceremony, a whole bunch of us for four and a half years—it was wonderful."

During that activist period, "While I spent time at the shop, my mind was elsewhere. Paul did most of the selling, taking people around, helping them choose presents—he's great at that, finds out your budget, who the gift is for. I stayed behind the counter." Internal problems in Dignity, together with the church's adamant refusal to accommodate its members, finally did the group in.

"Mentally, I returned to the shop three to four years ago." Since then, there have been major changes: three expansions in the last two years. These were financed, as with everything the store does, from the resources of the partners. "The first expansion, which doubled the size—making that whole second room—was the key. Now shoppers can go in there and not feel that we're hovering over them. People have time and room to browse, and that has effectively doubled our business." In using their own capital to change the physical dimensions of the store, the partners subtly enhanced their concept and the store's ability to make money.

It still doesn't appear to make very much money, though, and the question remains whether Authentiques, which even after expansion remains a small store, would have an even larger gross if it were in a different location, say on Eighth Avenue, where there is more foot traffic, rather than on a relatively quiet side street. A somewhat similar shop, with less interesting stock, seems to do reasonably well even farther west, on Ninth Avenue, just a block or two from here. But to rent on an avenue now would entail considerably more expense and might compromise the basis on which Authentiques currently exists, which has a good deal to do with Pusilo owning the building in which it is located, as well as with the eclectic tastes of the proprietors. However, the Authentiques owners may soon be forced to do something to augment their income, since Pusilo—as with many of the shop owners on this strip—complains that all sorts of expenses are continuing to rise, such as real estate taxes, electric bills, and the like.

An anomaly characterizing this block is the absence of a residential block association or of any sort of merchants' group. This perhaps derives from the betwixt-and-between nature of the block, neither fully residential nor fully commercial. However, in recognition that commercial neighbors in a small area do have many common concerns, a friendship has sprung up among the storefront operators along the northwestern half of 18th. Those who chat almost daily include Robert Pusilo, Michael Palmadessa of Towne House Grooming, the veterinarian, the Eastern European woodwork restorer, and Joe Hwang of the House of Cheers liquor shop.

"I wash the sidewalks in summer, shovel them in winter, and water the flowers in front of the vet's place, and he gives me a bit of a break when I bring in my dog," says Pusilo. "They all shop here for Christmas presents and the like. We watch out for one another. And we all buy our lottery tickets from Joe."

The changing tides in the interplay of concept, context, capital, and personal life situation exist just below the surface of the House of Cheers liquor store on the northeast corner of 18th Street and Eighth Avenue. For the past fifteen years House of Cheers has been under the ownership of Jung-ok Hwang. Joe, as he encourages everyone to call him, is fifty-five, a slim Korean-born man who wears the steel-framed glasses and displays the courteous manner of an academic. As liquor stores go, House of Cheers is more open and light-filled than most, with wide glass doors and broad windows. Most of the stock in the floor racks is wines from a half-dozen countries, moderately, though not cheaply, priced. Whiskeys form a second tier in back of the wines. Miniatures of hard liquor are locked in a glass cabinet behind the counter, and prominent on the counter is a large Lotto machine. "Lotto is like a religion to some people," Joe says, after ringing up the sale of a ticket to a customer.

Although the United States has frequently been a magnet for the poor, uneducated, and freedom-seeking from other countries, and it has been justly celebrated for its welcome to these huddled masses, it has afforded its most certain economic route to success to immigrants who have brought with them both intellectual savvy and some sort of grubstake. These are the people, perhaps more than any other group, whose positive experience shows why the United States is still viewed as the land of opportunity.

Hwang is typical of this group, though unusual for a retailer in that he holds a university degree in the history of religion, a subject he also taught in Seoul before entering the world of commerce as an international trader. He bought and sold furs in Frankfurt, Oslo, Copenhagen, Montreal, and New York before deciding to emigrate to the West in the mid-1970s. "I hate to live under rule of dictator," he recalls with sudden passion about his reason for wanting to leave his native land, pointing out that most Americans have never understood that South Korea, though our ally, was then under a harsh authoritarian regime. In 1979, when Seoul's economy became moribund, he sold his home to realize capital with which to buy a business in New York and came to the big city alone, leaving his wife and five children behind until he could get established here. Of all the businesses he might have chosen to purchase, he fixed on this small-scale liquor store, then owned by an Italian-born man who had been on this corner for thirty years. It seemed an eminently reasonable thing to do: Purchase an ongoing business located in a stable area that was just becoming gentrified and that sold goods which always seem to be in demand. Such a decision effectively short-circuits the need to dream up a concept and find a suitable context for a start-up. It was a conservative decision, but Joe appears to have felt that with seven people to feed and clothe he ought not to be taking too many risks with his life savings.

The owner, Joe recalls, was "a very good person" who operated the store from 8:00 A.M. until midnight, alternating day and evening shifts with his son. "He didn't want to sell to me," Joe states flatly. "I'm Asian and didn't know anything about wine." Many other people, receiving that sort of rebuff, would have walked away with their capital and looked for another business to buy. Instead, Joe enrolled in wine courses and studied the liquor business, then came back and told the owner what he had done, demonstrating that, as he told the owner then, "I know how to learn." That did the trick. Joe was permitted to buy the business and take over the store in 1980.

Buying into an existing business was a compelling reason for Hwang to keep the store operating as it had in the past, for a while, even though that meant stationing himself there sixteen hours a day. When Joe's Korean friends in New York worried about his health because he kept such exhausting hours, he told them that earlier immigrants to New York "hadn't cared to sleep" while they were building their businesses, and he could do no less. In economic terms, Joe was adding his own labor to his operating capital—something most small-business owners routinely do until their business reaches the point at which they can afford to hire assistance.

Several residential landlords refused to rent to Joe when they learned he would bring five children into an apartment, so when Joe found a space large enough for his family he told the Chinese landlord that he only had four children. Six months after opening the store, he brought the family over from Seoul. He introduced them formally to the landlord, said "Now I must pay penalty," and asked how much extra would be charged for the fifth child. The landlord was "sympathetic" and said that he understood the circumstances and wouldn't charge more for the last child, but Joe insisted thereafter on paying him an additional $50 a month.

As soon as practical, after the family had arrived, Hwang cut back on the store hours, opening at ten in the morning rather than eight. By that time, he had begun to get a feel for the neighborhood, which was undergoing gentrification, and which, he came to believe, would no longer have as much need for a liquor store to be open early in the morning. Simultaneously, he began to shift his stock of goods, reflecting the influx to Chelsea of significant numbers of more affluent consumers, who liked wines. Upscale customers, Joe learned, buy greater quantities of wine than hard liquor.

Of note is that Hwang did not go all the way in this direction and turn House of Cheers into a wine boutique. There are two such wineshops in the neighborhood, both operated by men with European backgrounds. Perhaps Hwang believed he might not be seen as credible if he sold only wines, or perhaps he did not want to risk losing that solid fraction of his existing clientele that still came in to buy hard liquor. Most likely the latter reasoning prevailed, because at about that time he also made a business adjustment to the neighborhood of another kind, doing something that he says many other Korean owners never do: He hired people from the immediate neighborhood (in this instance, Latinos) as his assistants, and not just one man for window dressing, but several, to do real work. Joe is at pains to have a visitor understand that he permits these associates to handle the cash register, even in high-traffic times, a sign of trust that he believes has not been lost on the considerable Latino community that resides in the area and patronizes his store.

Five years ago, Hwang felt so strongly about the solidity of his business and the area that he made a further significant change in the context of his enterprise and the character of his capital: He bought the white clapboard building in which the House of Cheers is situated. It also contains a half-dozen apartments upstairs, and the premises of the barbershop next door. "Chelsea is my second home," he says proudly, although he maintains his own residence in the northern suburbs of New York. Aside from his association with business neighbors, his most important nonfamily ties continue to be with a close-knit community of nineteen Korean American families that own liquor stores in New York City. Every morning, at the time he opens up, a representative of this group offers a prayer for his health and does so again at the time he closes; similar prayers are said for the other owners. Each time a prayer is said, the individual owner puts aside $1 for a general fund; at the end of the year, the approximately $10,000 thus collected is given out in the form of a college scholarship for a young Korean American.

A stream of Latino customers enters the store and makes modest purchases; he greets many of them by name. One man has a few dollar bills but has to hunt in his pockets for the change to make up the rest of the tab and painstakingly counts the coins onto the counter. Joe cursorily glances at the change, then sweeps it up and, with a smile, wishes the man good day. "In the past I inspect every coin, to make sure I am not being robbed, but now is not important whether a quarter off or so. I want everyone to go out of store happy."

As the story of the uncounted coins shows, House of Cheers is now in a steady and reasonably profitable state, something desired by most business owners. In business terms, Joe has a cash flow adequate to cover trough periods, coming from a solid base of repeat customers, and has refined and adjusted his concept to fit comfortably into a niche in the neighborhood. But as with so many businesses here and elsewhere, while the enterprise may be in a steady, well-functioning state, the entrepreneur is in flux. The youngest of his children has now gone off to college—she will be a freshman at MIT—and the others all have college degrees and are in graduate school or working. The emptying of the home nest has occasioned deep reflection.

"You know how, when some autumn leaf falls, you feel a longing? That's how I am now," he confides. The longing that he expresses is for his native South Korea, but beyond the expatriate sentiments are a more complex set of emotions that soon emerge. Joe and his family became citizens ten years ago, but are "still uncomfortable at not being 100 percent American—and not 100 percent Korean, either." There's the rub: He doesn't want to go home again, is an American and proud of it, and wants to be one forever; yet by physiognomy, family, and upbringing he is a Korean, and equally proud of that heritage. In his view, a subtle but pervasive racism keeps him an outsider to certain aspects of American life and culture. And he has discovered that he is also an outsider in the new Korea. "We return there sometimes, but is not the same land we left." Since Joe left, the country has been phenomenally developed and is becoming more democratic. Moreover, the Korean language that he learned in his youth has evolved, so that he no longer speaks the language like a native. Korea's extraordinary economic development has also meant the drying up of the stream of émigrés. Because Hwang's generation has not been followed by other generations in a continual exodus, he and other Korean Americans of his generation are even more isolated in the United States. That is why he and other émigrés of the 1970s today feel "somewhat in limbo" and experience a longing for home and for an old way of life, a yearning impossible for them to slake.

These personal factors are pushing Joe Hwang toward a major change in his business. He says that he is about to put the building on the market and hopes to sell it, perhaps including in the sale the liquor store itself. What he will do then he is not certain, but he believes that at his age, "I must prepare for the rest of life."

Chapter 4

SIGNS OF CAPITAL CHANGES

A FOR SALE NOTICE appears on a shingle over the House of Cheers in August. It is next to the big red neon LIQUORS sign. Having decided on a course of action, Hwang is evidently pursuing it. A week later, the New Barber Shop, Joe Hwang's commercial tenant, tapes a cardboard sign in its window saying that it is moving to Ninth Avenue.

A few steps away, along the north side of 18th, a For Sale sign has been posted for several months in the window of the downstairs portion of the barnlike building on West 18th that houses the Madelyn Simon "plantscaping" concern. In late summer of 1993, the sign is changed so that it advertises the entire building for sale, rather than, as previously indicated, just the downstairs portion.

The reason for this change has to do with financing, according to Jean Rosenberg, the head of the Chelsea Day School, the preschool that occupies the building's upper half. Jean is in her forties, with startling blue-green eyes and earrings that match them. After studying at the well-regarded Bank Street College in New York and working for fifteen years as a teacher in public and private schools, she began Chelsea Day in 1981, with twenty-two children in a rented room at the McBurney YMCA on West 23rd Street. In 1984, she bought this entire two-story building, in association with a parent of one of her students; that parent then sold the downstairs half to Madelyn Simon, while Jean rented the top floor to the nonprofit school. Recently, when the Simon firm wanted to sell its half, Jean sought to buy it and use the space to expand the school.

Jean Rosenberg is still Madelyn Simon's preferred buyer, but Jean is having trouble finding the money with which to buy the other half of the building. She tried to convince a bank to lend it to her, but even though a business plan for the school expansion made clear and likely that there would be enough money to pay future mortgage installments on both halves, the bank argued that she did not have proper collateral for the loan. It insisted that one half of a building could not be put up as collateral in order to buy the other half.

Madelyn Simon looked elsewhere for a buyer, but Jean reports she soon found that selling half of a building was almost impossible. Reluctantly, Jean Rosenberg and Madelyn Simon have now decided to offer the entire building for sale, with the understanding that a potential buyer will have to agree to lease back the upstairs premises to the Chelsea Day School.

While this impasse seems to be a special case, it is nonetheless indicative of the great difficulty most small businesses have in obtaining financing, whether for start-ups, to smooth out general cash flow, or for expansion. It could be argued that Republic Bank's calling in the loans of Maxwell Lumber when they were not in arrears was similarly a special instance, or that a third bank's refusal to help Carl Berman out of a jam by means of a government loan earmarked for such purposes was an equally unique case; but around this block there are almost as many tales of shortsightedness, intransigence, and lack of flexibility by banks and governmental loan sources as there are small businesses. This seems largely due to ignorance on the part of the banking system—ignorance of the true hardiness of these small businesses—and also an inability (or refusal) to understand the direction of the future, which is toward an array of businesses that cater to the growing demand for services and whose purveyors have less-tangible collateral assets than the manufacturers of yesteryear possessed.

For Carl Berman and Guild Mailing, September is a time that will prove the banks wrong. As he expected, the National Basketball Association and the Museum of Natural History are both now resuming publication of their newsletters, and these, together with the resurgence of several union broadsheets that had been mute during the bad days of recession, are generating a glut of materials to be processed and mailed. Carl hires a few temporary workers because he cannot be certain of how long this pace of business can be sustained. "I'm still behind on my back taxes, but instead of six people joining the unemployment line, I got eight people working," he says. "That's better, isn't it?"

As for his own satisfaction, Carl is thinking about getting out of the business altogether. He'd like to write a book on herpetology, but his main objective is to find a venue in which he can make money but not work as hard as in the mailing service business. He is investigating some vacation property upstate, as well as an opportunity to become one of the very few bail bondsmen in the area. His target date for making this transformation: when his teenaged daughter enters college.

Denied bank financing, small businesses have to scramble and seek money elsewhere. Their sources range from the massive accumulation of private wealth of the sort that has bankrolled Gear Holdings, to the middle rank of hardheaded private individuals who demand high annual returns but are willing to invest in likely moneymakers such as Food/Bar, to the first-time or infrequent investors of the "friends who believe in me" type who are sustaining Myron Michaels. The attraction for all is a potentially higher rate of return than can be obtained from dividend-paying stocks, bonds, or certificates of deposit. And small businesses have to offer such returns because they cannot obtain cheaper money from the banks. How much higher a rate do they have to offer? That depends on the circumstances. In the summer of 1993, Helen C. is near the end of her monetary resources—self-financing—and is agonizing over what percentage of her as-yet-unrealized dream she may have to sell to friends and relatives in order to obtain the money to complete her prototype. Venture capital can be very costly: Helen may end up having to reduce her ownership from 100 percent to 50 percent—or less. Will her friends force her to give up that much?

One would hope not, but then the interests of partnerships and friendships are not always the same. In an instance just becoming apparent on the block in the late summer of 1993, a partnership-with-friends is turning an enterprise upside down, threatening to capsize it altogether.

The enterprise is Gascogne, the French restaurant on the Eighth Avenue strip. With the recent closing of Quatorze, on 14th Street, Gascogne became the only French restaurant on the West Side in Chelsea or the northern part of Greenwich Village. It boasts one of the city's loveliest backyard gardens; the interior is decorated as a fine country inn, with vellum menus, good-quality china, candles, and the like. The menu, changed seasonally, features traditional dishes of Gascony, cassoulet, foie gras, and sweetbreads. I had made a first visit to Gascogne the previous spring and spoke with Pascal and Carol Coudouy, who said they were the owners. At the time they were wreathed in smiles owing to a laudatory review in the March 1993 issue of *Gourmet*, which said, among other nice things, that "Mr. Coudouy is, quite probably, the most highly skilled French chef in the city to be found cooking in such a small and personal restaurant."

Pascal Coudouy is in his late thirties, with scraggly brown hair, a fierce-looking mustache, and a mild manner. A son of the Gascony region, he had been a sous-chef for years in Southwest France before coming to New York. His wife, Carol—they met on his previous assignment, at the Ambassador Grill of the United

Nations Plaza hotel—appears younger, lighter-haired, more out-going. Theirs was the traditional pairing in restaurants in France: Monsieur in the kitchen; Madame on the serving floor, welcoming and caring for the guests.

An oversize, mostly white St. Bernard had to be restrained from barking and playing with the visitor; after all, the Coudouys explained, the dog did not expect company at midday since the restaurant was only open in the evenings. When they began Gascogne, they had also served lunch; not enough customers showed up at lunchtimes, so they cut back to dinners only.

The Coudouys said then, in an offhand way, that they owned the restaurant in association with partners who were not present at the moment. Three and a half years earlier, the Coudouys and those potential partners were grumbling about their employers and fantasizing to friends about what sort of restaurant they'd like to own; a few days later, the foursome saw this space and decided to take the plunge.

This past spring, Pascal told stories about the difficulties of having had a "flush run," a term used in the restaurant business to describe a rush of customers that follows an initial good review, which they had had in *New York* magazine when they first opened. During such times, a new restaurant can often become over-whelmed and also victimized by a special sort of waiter who reads the earliest review of a new restaurant and rushes to apply for a job, knowing that the restaurant is probably overrun with custom-ers; the waitperson stays two months, milks the job, is rude enough to customers to make them unlikely to return, and then moves on, leaving the restaurant in the lurch. A second problem came when the glut dwindled, perhaps due to a so-so review in the *New York Times.* "We were going month to month; we didn't know if we could survive." To lure customers, they resorted to another French restaurant tradition, the prix fixe menu: appetizer, main course, dessert, and a small glass of Armagnac chosen from a tray of bottled liqueurs, for $25. That did the trick; their customer base stabilized.

"We do about seventy covers a night," Carol told me. She

implied that she handled the money, while Pascal was the resident artist of the kitchen. The average bill, she said, was $42 per person, including tax but excluding tips, a gross of about $1 million a year.

During the summer, a neighboring store owner said that things had changed at Gascogne—although virtually no sign of the change was visible from the street then, and only one can be seen now. The menu is the same, so are the chalked specials on the windows, done in a European hand. But the review in *Gourmet* is no longer in the window display. A return visit reveals that there has been a palace coup: The Coudouys have been forced out of the restaurant by their once-silent partners. Jennifer Endersby, a tall, thin, and dark-haired woman whose English has a South African accent, says she is now in charge; all she will say directly about the rift with the Coudouys is that "things weren't working out," and that while the Coudouys remain as shareholders in Gascogne, they now no longer exercise day-to-day control over the kitchen or the dining areas. She is working as the manager and hostess, and another chef from Gascony, whose first name also happens to be Pascal, has just been hired. The new chef quite naturally wants his own people in the kitchen, and Jennifer wants the employees waiting on table to be of her own choosing.

A clean sweep is to be expected: If an owner is taking over because he or she has determined the old management to be insufficient, a change in personnel is logical, and new brooms are generally awarded quite a bit of latitude. But the rather complete change in kitchen and dining-room staffs makes it seem likely that either the Coudouys' stake was less than they had at first intimated, certainly less than a controlling interest in the endeavor, or else they have been convinced (or forced) to relinquish control to the "money partners." A friend later says that the Coudouys have taken a vacation and are considering going into a restaurant elsewhere, either in New Jersey or in Zurich, Switzerland.

Jennifer Endersby recounts something of her history and that of the Coudouys. She and her husband are long-term restaurant people. They started Chez Jacqueline in Greenwich Village and, later, Pescadou in SoHo; both are well-regarded, medium-priced, solidly French eating establishments. Pescadou has since been sold to other owners. Four years ago, they began Gascogne with the Coudouys. Eighteen months ago, after they sold Pescadou, Jennifer's husband became ill, and the couple went to France so that he could recover. When Jennifer and her husband returned to New York, they found their other partners complaining and this appears to be what precipitated the change in the Gascogne management. The reason for not also altering the menu and for not advertising that there is a new chef is not discussed, but when you have recently received a laudatory review from *Gourmet*, you don't want to blatantly inform customers about any changes. However, the review did include pictures of the Coudouys and some personal information about them, and perhaps that is why it was taken out of the window.

"Old customers ask about the Coudouys and I tell them things have changed. They say, 'Well, we'll give you a chance,' and they have not been disappointed," Jennifer maintains. The food remains the same, she avows, because the controlling stylistic factor in the restaurant is the cuisine of the region, not the identity of the chef. Will it be edged in the direction of the lighter, brighter nouvelle cuisine? No, she says, "If I want art, I'll go to a museum."

Perhaps the most interesting way capital is acquired and allocated among small businesses around this block is through membership in one of the tight-knit groups in the city which loan money to members' ventures at relatively low cost. Principal among those groups that operate this way are the Korean Americans.

Many of the Korean-owned business entities in the city, including two of the three deli-groceries on our block, obtained start-up credit from already established Korean American enterprises or quasi-fraternal organizations. In the early years of the century, the Hebrew Free Loan Society and other organizations like it in the Italian and Irish communities loaned money to individuals at low cost, money that was often used to seed businesses, but the loans had more of a feeling of charity than of investment. People in the modern-day Korean American immigrant community, however, have carefully and dutifully circulated their money; in many instances, after they have successfully funded a start-up, the community decrees that the money be returned in order to fund a second and a third business, rather than permitting the first to retain it as profits. This spirit of mutual enterprise and an understanding that in order to create the most wealth, capital must constantly be placed where it can do the most good have permitted Korean-owned deli-groceries to spring up all over the city. And when more businesses prosper, the entire Korean American community—rather than only a few individuals—rises rapidly toward the middle class.

Aggregations of friends or like-minded investors can be much looser than the Korean circles. Several professional hockey stars backed the Felixbrod family, some years ago, when they opened the Blue Moon Mexican Café on our block; when that investment proved successful, the hockey players also put money into another Blue Moon, this one on the Upper East Side.

Usually, after a restaurant's initial capitalization has been outrun, it still needs operating capital. However, banks have traditionally been reluctant to meet the particularly egregious need of restaurant owners for financing to regularize their cash flow. Recently, a secondary industry has sprung up to provide that sort of operating credit, and its leading company is Transmedia. Hundreds of restaurants in Manhattan now accept payment via the Transmedia card, though Blue Moon is the only restaurant on our block to do so.

Transmedia, and some restaurateurs who have accepted Transmedia financing, explain its workings in this way: The restaurant obtains a loan of, say, $10,000 and agrees to pay back $20,000, not in cash but in credit-card slips for food and beverages, slips that the restaurant obtains when people pay by means of their Transmedia cards. The customer gets a good deal because he or she is billed for only 75 percent of the total on the bill; in other words the customer obtains a $20 meal for $15. (Taxes and the tips must be paid in full through Transmedia and are not discounted.) As for the restaurant, the slip to Transmedia becomes, in effect, a partial loan repayment. If it takes the restaurant a year to work off the $20,000, so be it, and if the restaurant never obtains enough business from Transmedia card users to pay it back, the restaurant is not liable for the unpaid balance. Although some people in the restaurant business claim that for a restaurant to agree to a Transmedia loan is a sign that it has cash flow problems, other restaurateurs characterize the loan as an acceptable one and as a device for bringing more customers into the restaurant.

Transmedia, which prefers to call the exchanges "advances" rather than loans, believes that it is providing a service and stresses that the repayment is not in cash, which is important to the restaurant. Since a restaurant's food and beverage costs average one-third of a check, a spokesman for Transmedia argues, the restaurant is effectively paying back only $7,000 rather than $20,000 for every $10,000 it borrows. Most of the advances, the company contends, are retired within six months.

One restaurant owner in Lower Manhattan, though not on this block, told me he took out a $10,000 loan, completed the repayment, but then refused to take a second; he charged that when one pays back the "advance" in a reasonable length of time in which to amass double the face amount of the loan in credit-card slips, the actual effective percentage rate is so high that it is tantamount to usury. It's not easy to decide who is correct in their figuring, or what the true loan rate is.

The need for cash-flow financing—or credit for obtaining supplies, which is another way of looking at the entrepreneur's problem—affects all sorts of businesses. Even plumbing, says Peter Micelli, the manager at Solco plumbing supplies.

Peter is in his mid-thirties, with thinning black hair, a broad smile, and an outgoing, cultured manner. "I'm one of the few people in the plumbing business with a college degree," he points out. He has also been an entrepreneur himself. Before joining

Solco, he was the proprietor of a plumbing supply business on Long Island, which he and a partner began after college. A decade of work had brought them up to a gross of $4 million a year before difficulties set in. During the recession, Peter sold his share to his partner, but didn't receive the full amount because the business was shortly declared bankrupt. Peter then answered an ad that turned out to have been placed by Solco, a firm that had tried to recruit him in 1989; back then, he hadn't been interested in working for someone else, but in the spring of 1993, he was. Solco needs him, Peter guesses, because Vic Sherman wants to cut back his own hours, and the partners hope a manager will make the business more efficient and bring in more customers. For Peter, the job means he now has more time to be with his wife and three-year-old. Another plus is the opportunity to learn from a successful enterprise about the New York City end of the supply business.

"Plumbing in New York isn't like plumbing in the suburbs or in a rural area," Peter opines as he begins his roundabout explanation. "The city has the toughest test for plumbers in the country and also requires that all work be done by a licensed plumber. The result is very few guys with licenses, and the ones we have are highly qualified, likely to be more intelligent than your average out-of-town plumber, who doesn't need a license. And because city plumbers' employment is keyed to the scarcity of licenses, it can be very lucrative." However, Peter points out, in the relatively cutthroat construction and repair industry, even a shrewd plumber with a virtual license to coin money can very quickly get in financial trouble. The cause: clients who don't pay their bills on time. The ups and downs of the business, the inherent contradiction between the lucrative possibilities and the realities of being frequently stalled on payments, Peter says, create an opportunity for a supply depot's successful business strategy. "Supplies is all relationships. Plumbers in New York have dozens of places to choose from, and they can be very picky. So it's how you treat the customer that's important. Very often, a guy will get in trouble, and you'll let him slide for a couple of weeks, and then he'll pay.

Because you helped him get by, he'll be your loyal customer from then on. Or you'll get a customer because Eigen kept him waiting in line too long or in the past didn't extend credit to him."

Now we're at the heart of the matter: What Solco does on one level is distribution, but what Solco does on a deeper level, Peter contends, is financial services. And this is the wave of the future. "We pay cash for a product from a manufacturer, and then hand the product to a plumber and extend him credit until he pays for it. The more flexible and savvy we are in giving credit to the plumbers and contractors, the better we do." No overt shingle hanging on the Solco premises announces "We give credit to qualified customers," but that possibility is made known to customers, and some are sophisticated enough to ask about it. The practice is made less risky for the supply depot by an industry association that evaluates individual and fleet plumbers' credit worthiness.

Along with the For Sale signs, reviews disappearing from windows, a tiny medallion of the Transmedia card, and unseen, yet palpable, messages about available credit for plumbers, one last series of signs visible in an establishment on our block in the summer of 1993 speaks to the subject of capital changes. They are in the window of The Pasta Pot. This is an old Irish corner bar with a beautiful interior—its long, wooden floor-to-ceiling bar front is the envy of many restaurateurs in the area. It features a low-priced Italian menu, which is taped to one window, along with a yellowing neighborhood newspaper review, which touts the proprietor's "invention," a pasta dish with a vodka-based sauce. The dining room is usually three-quarters empty, and the place gives off an air of general shabbiness. Recently, hand-lettered cards have also appeared in the window, cards that tout cut-price meals and two-for-one drink specials. These specials are clearly meant to appeal to customers looking for a bargain meal, because these prices are not much above what the diners charge. Rival restaurateurs call these flags of distress, evidence that things are not going well at The Pasta Pot. They believe that its prices have been pushed down so low that margins have become too slim to provide an adequate return on capital to the owners; some ascribe this state of affairs to poor management, others to the confused identity of the place; all predict an early demise.

Like vultures circling a dying animal, several restaurateurs in the area have their eyes on The Pasta Pot, believing they could do well with such a good corner location and well-appointed interior. As soon as its doors are shuttered—and perhaps even sooner— they'll come in for a bite.

Chapter 5

BIG FISH, LITTLE POND

VERY EARLY on what will be a hazy, hot, and humid Monday morning at the end of August 1993, Barneys is about to begin its warehouse sale, a well-known annual event in New York City that will take place on this block in the street-level and basement floors of the building whose upper floors now house Cahners. Of the three big businesses on the block—Nynex, Cahners, and Barneys—the latter is the smallest, with a $250 million gross in 1992, compared to Nynex's $13 billion, but in this little neighborhood, Barneys is the big fish in the pond. The Pressman family that owns the department store is the owner of the two Cahners buildings, Gear Holdings' headquarters, and the Le Madri restaurant building. They also own 106 Seventh Avenue, site of Barneys corporate headquarters, opposite the department store, and control the ground-floor spaces next to that building. In many ways, this is Barneys' neighborhood—another one of the clusters mentioned earlier: the big fish not only owns much of the pond, he influences a great deal of what goes on within the pond.

Around 17th and 18th Streets, the feeling in regard to Barneys as compared to the neighborhood small businesses is an echo of F. Scott Fitzgerald's famous line, "Let me tell you about the very rich. They are different from you and me." Ernest Hemingway deflated Fitzgerald's categorization by retorting, "Yes, they have more money," but in terms of business, Fitzgerald's is the more astute observation. There *is* a gap between big and small businesses, and it comprises more than money. It mainly has to do with the ways in which large businesses are run, which often involve using their size and consequent power. That dynamic can be seen operating in what Barneys has done in the past year or so to completely change the character of the strip of Seventh Avenue opposite its main store; Barneys has done what a smaller retailer would not have the resources to do, that is, convince units of the national chains Pottery Barn, Hold Everything, and Williams-Sonoma to come into the spaces there, spaces that the Pressman family controls. The high-ceilinged large storefront that Gear Holdings had been reluctant to renew for its own retail operation, and which stood empty for some time after Gear vacated it, is now occupied by Williams-Sonoma. The units of the three chains are Barneys' neighbors in the shopping malls across the country where the department store has set up satellite shops and that the overall result of bringing them in has been to turn both sides of Seventh Avenue between 16th and 17th into a replica of a suburban shopping mall, albeit one that, curiously, has traffic running through it.

The malling of America is a phenomenon that has changed the face of how American business is done. The secret of the attraction of malls is integrally related to the aggregation factor mentioned earlier, but isn't the same. The various shops in malls are related by price points—you seldom see a very upscale store in the midst of a dozen lower-priced ones—and also by their contiguity, which produces cross-traffic from one store to another. What Barneys has done on lower Seventh Avenue is to establish a mix of stores that draws on several of these strengths: moderate to upscale pricing, a variety of merchandise all related to upkeep of the home, and the attraction of well-known chains within steps of one another and served by common parking lots, which are free to Barneys shoppers.

Years of advertising and word-of-mouth have convinced many New Yorkers that Barneys' annual sale is the time and place to purchase quality clothing at substantial breaks in price. Some men buy only at this opportunity. The warehouse sale will run for two weeks, but is billed as "first-come, first-serve," so many customers believe they must shop early in order to obtain the best merchandise.

The sale takes place against the backdrop of a rising drumbeat of publicity and some criticism surrounding the imminent opening of Barneys' Madison Avenue store in early September—one of the final steps, and the largest one to date, in the rather rapid expansion that has taken Barneys from an annual gross in the tens of millions to a gross in the hundreds of millions. In terms of square footage, the new emporium will be the biggest department store to open in New York since the early 1930s. But while Barneys' mailings and advertisements stress the forthcoming cornucopia of goods, trade papers report suppliers' complaints of slow payment and poor treatment. Also, the trades' size estimate of the uptown store "gamble" continues to grow, from $100 million to more than double that amount.

At 6:30 A.M. about a hundred people line up on 17th Street, though there is, as yet, no sign to indicate that the unmarked side entrance of a publishing building is the location for the annual clothing sale. Barneys' main warehouses are elsewhere, but two floors here also serve those purposes. Over the last fortnight, passersby have noted trucks pulling up and disgorging racks and boxes of merchandise. Cahners employees have grown tired of the intrusion into "their" space, but seem resigned to riding out the hurricane.

Most of the calmly waiting throng, lined up single file on the sidewalk, are male and white; most wear dress shirts and ties, but no jackets—it is too hot today for excess layers. A young black man wearing sneakers and a warm-up jacket is first in line; he arrived at 5:30, and is proud to be at the head of the throng. A few among the patient have brought folding chairs; many more have purchased newspapers and coffee. Those leaning against the walls are cheerfully oblivious to some foul-smelling garbage nearby.

There are end-of-summer sales at every single one of the block's half-dozen clothing boutiques; some discounts are listed as deep as 50 and 60 percent. Camouflage, the stylish men's store on the corner of Eighth and 17th, is selling shirts for half price, and in the past week has been thronged—evidence, it seems, that the supply-and-demand curves do hold true, that when the price of an item is lowered, that item becomes more desirable to more people. Does the same paradigm apply if, as with Barneys' warehouse sale, an entire store's supply of merchandise is lowered in price?

The relationship between Barneys and the clothing boutiques in the area is complex. Barneys sells Giraudon shoes, which are designed and manufactured by Alain-Guy Giraudon, who also has a small retail store on our block which sells precisely the same shoes that are available at Barneys and his other styles, as well. The proprietors at P. Chanin—next door to Giraudon—say that customers can often buy similar brands, or sometimes the very same brand, of unisex jackets at their store as at Barneys, and there are as many beautiful and expensive ties at Camouflage as at Barneys. Despite the availability of merchandise at these smaller stores, even during Barneys' regular operations, the big store has more customers than all of these small shops combined, customers who don't know or don't care that the same merchandise can be purchased in nearby boutiques for comparable or lower prices.

At 7:00, a phalanx of clerks starts to go in the back entrance of the Cahners building on 18th Street; many look apprehensive. Most are temporary hires and have been trained for only a short period of time. They bunch up at the exit door, blocked by the sign-in process. Soon the employees' line and the line of customers, which is growing ever longer at the 17th Street entrance, will converge in the middle and make seller-buyer transactions. At 7:15, sixteen men in identical blue blazers, gray slacks, white shirts, and rep ties come out of a nearby diner, led by two men in brown suits: the regular security force. Their first task is to put out signs on 17th Street, saying this is the entrance, and on 18th, pointing out the exit, and at the corner parking lot, announcing that the entrance is down the block. The customers' line now numbers three hundred people, some on cellular phones. Pedestrians marvel at the line; residents lean out of windows to stare at it; plumbers hanging around Eigen make fleecing-the-lambs jokes. A car blocks the entrance of a Barneys parking lot, and a New York City tow truck instantly appears to haul it away.

At 8:00, the line has extended beyond the Nynex building and the parking lot, and is forming on Seventh. Maps of the interior of the sale space are handed out to the standees. Men's clothes are in the basement, down a flight of steps; women's and boys' clothes are on the second floor, up a flight. Along with the maps come applications for Barneys charge cards. About one in twenty-five people waiting fills out an application. Near 8:15, the line reaches its greatest length—it stretches beyond the subway entrance at 18th and Eighth, to the second entrance of Nynex. Straphangers emerging from the subway wonder what the commotion is about; they find out, shake their heads, and walk away. Crowd controllers estimate the line at a thousand people at 8:20; just then, to slight cheers, it begins to move. At the warehouse entrance, twenty people are let in every minute. The crowd diminishes quickly. By 8:30, there is no longer anyone waiting on 18th Street or on Seventh Avenue, though the line still reaches all along 17th, and thereafter the line grows steadily smaller.

Inside, the basement is a scene of muffled intensity. Merchandise is stacked to the rafters, leaving very little room for customers to move around. Racks of suits, jackets, and pants, tables full of accessories, stands with shoes, boxes that contain sweaters. There is no attempt at beauty-of-display, just at making the clothing available. The place is politely mobbed, with three-to-four-hundred well-dressed men quietly picking their way through the clogged aisles, saying "Excuse me" and "Pardon me" and "Easy does it" as they shoulder past to get at the rack of $1,000 suits. Does the Fire Department realize just how closely packed this space has become? The air-conditioning is on strong.

This sale has outgrown its original function, which was to empty the shelves of unbought winter, spring, and summer merchandise in order to make room for the fall lines. It has become an opportunity to sell a whole lot of merchandise in a single burst. The area's boutique owners believe Barneys does as much as a fifth to a quarter of the store's annual volume in the two weeks of this warehouse sale; Barneys neither confirms nor denies that assessment, acknowledging only that the sale is a substantial one.

Giving even greater impetus than usual to this year's sale is the approaching opening of the new Barneys on Madison Avenue. Customers there will expect the stock to be brand-new, and it certainly seems here as though things are being cleared out. In this capacious basement is a stupendous array of goods. Bins overflow with offerings. Tags show the original and the sale price. Most of the merchandise is moderately expensive, even though marked down: A $169 sweater is tagged now at $125, about a 25 percent reduction. There *is* value in what is offered for sale here, but these are not bargain-basement prices. Most of the clothing looks as though it has never graced a shelf in the department store but has been stocked especially for this sale; such is the contention of several area merchants. Barneys management, however, unequivocally states that every item offered here has previously been available in the store. Competitors say that while a single item might have once been on a shelf in the main store, large numbers of the same item show up here for the big sale.

What is being demonstrated in this sale goes beyond the intersection of supply and demand curves; it makes clear that the hype surrounding the sale, which is a result of years of expensive advertising of the magnitude that only a large business entity can afford, is as much a factor in the ability to move goods as is the lowering of prices. Pam Chanin and her partner Elizabeth Rosenberg are currently considering whether to sink $10,000 into advertising for their P. Chanin boutique; for them ten grand is a significant sum so the decision is a big one. Barneys probably spends that much each day on newspaper advertisements that serve to keep its name and image continually before the public.

As the sale progresses through the morning, it becomes clear that the publicity has even supplanted something else, the core of personal service that usually characterizes a neighborhood clothing boutique. There is no room and no requirement here for the art or craft of persuasion—which is perhaps the reason that temporary and even inexperienced help can be hired for this event without risk to the big store. The employees on this selling floor act basically as inventory clerks, refolding and rehanging the clothing and only occasionally assisting people in finding the sizes they want or directing them to the shoes and handkerchiefs the customers themselves haven't immediately located. Pleasant traffic cops, the temporary employees are today in the first flush of their work and are being helpful to customers. But will their enthusiasm last the entire two weeks?

An assembly-line procedure akin to that of a supermarket checkout center has been put in place—indeed, it is hard to imagine what this sale must have been like in the era before items were marked with bar codes that pass information on prices and inventory control to waiting computers, a process that also speeds the checkout lines. Arms draped with merchandise, customers form a queue down one entire aisle inside the basement. The sound of credit cards swishing through electronic readers is barely audible, and the registers are positioned so that the dollar totals are hidden from the next person in line. The young black man who was first in the door is among those now checking out. He buys two suits, a handful of ties, and a pair of shoes, for a total of $700, marked down from somewhere between $1,100 and $1,200. Each person in line seems to carry $250 worth of merchandise. During the wait for the checkout, a few pluck an extra tie, handkerchief, or belt from racks conveniently placed in the path of impulse buyers. As customers leave with bagged and wrapped purchases, they are directed through the 18th Street exit. Many seem bewildered to be back out again in the August sunlight.

By 9:15, there is no longer a line outside the entrance though people are still arriving in a steady stream to go into the warehouse.

Barneys' current flagship store is a sprawling though tightly designed retail mansion stretching to 16th on Seventh Avenue, and eastward along 17th Street through a series of smaller buildings. There are a dozen display windows at street level, a doorman at the ready, and phalanxes of well-dressed salespeople. Chrome, marble, mirrors, and dividers separate the inside space into boutiques. The depth of stock in such ordinary merchandise as men's socks is vast, one of the store's strengths, and from its penthouse hair salon to its below-stairs buffet dining room, Barneys exudes a sure sense of style. Some items are moderately priced; many are expensive. A recent survey of department store images, conducted by BBDO advertising agency, found that shoppers considered Barneys innovative, creative, up-to-date, and masculine, as opposed to Macy's, whose qualities were associated with patriotism, family, variety, and thriftiness, and Bergdorf Goodman, which connoted luxury, sophistication, power, and physical attractiveness.

Surrounding this store with an in-city version of a suburban mall is only the latest step in the evolution of the empire that began as a small business remarkably akin to many others, a retail men's store on the corner of 17th and Seventh in 1923, operated by grandfather Barney Pressman. According to family legend, Barney's wife gave him her engagement ring to pawn for $500, with which he rented a few hundred square feet of space and bought forty name-brand suits to sell at discount prices. What grandfather Barney had begun, father Fred expanded in the 1950s and 1960s into a men's store that sold merchandise in many price ranges, including the upper ranges.

Still further changes occurred in the 1970s, when the third

generation of Pressmans, Gene and Bob, the grandsons of Barney, took over. Academic students of family businesses estimate that it takes a new generation of owners about ten years to become comfortable, knowledgeable, and powerful enough to insist on changes in a family business. That paradigm seems to hold for Barneys. Around 1983, after a decade or so in the business, Gene and Bob Pressman decided to transform Barneys into a true department store that would sell clothing for women as well as for men and that would also offer the same sort of additional merchandise—principally home furnishings—that other department stores regularly sold. An enlarged store would require more space, so Barneys leased the smaller buildings along 17th, east of Seventh. For the expanded store to be successful, however, it would have to lure many new customers, and women might refuse to make the trip downtown if they thought their destination was in an area too shabby or run-down. So Barneys decided to do something about the area near the store.

"There was a sense that there was a lot of value in the [surrounding] real estate as the neighborhood shifted from a manufacturing base to a commercial and residential base," recalls Irvin Rosenthal, Barneys' CFO. "We were going to add value to the neighborhood by virtue of what we were doing in the store, [and] there was a lot of vacant and nearly vacant property around that was...underutilized...undervalued, in that it wasn't being used up to the capacity of what was going to happen in the neighborhood."

To support the expansion by sprucing up the neighborhood, and to take advantage of low prices, the Pressmans bought and renovated the 245, 249, and the 230 loft buildings on 17th, as well as the building on the southeast corner of 18th and the old Macy's stable next door to the south, both of which backed onto a Barneys parking lot. Some community residents feared that the fish had become a sea monster that would overwhelm the pond; in the residents' fantasies, customers would jam the streets and real estate values would collapse because the area would become as commercial as the 34th Street transverse dominated by Macy's. To calm the fears, the extension of Barneys into the adjoining buildings was done discreetly: There are no big garish signs outside, and the upper floors of the buildings on 17th look substantially like the brownstone residences that border them.

The fix-up-the-neighborhood scheme worked like a charm. Cahners had originally agreed to take space in 245, "But before the ink was dry on the contract," Rosenthal remembers, "they came back to us and said they needed a lot more space." So 245 and the adjoining 249 building, the old Siegel-Cooper warehouse, which had fallen into almost complete disrepair, were "reconfigured from vertical to horizontal," gutted, and refitted. Similarly, the former printing industry loft building at 230 became a sleek setting for upper-floor offices and a diagnostic radiology center. By the time Cahners, Gear Holdings, and Le Madri had moved into their respective buildings, real estate prices in the area were rising, and this was attributed in part to the brightened appearance near Barneys. The net effect of the purchases was to "stabilize the neighborhood," Rosenthal says, although that hadn't been the primary intent.

That intent was to provide a solid base for an expansion of Barneys that went far beyond adding some square feet to the original store. It was on the basis of its new success at 17th Street, between 1983 and 1988, that Barneys opened two new stores, one on Wall Street and a suburban venture. Its success with three stores then encouraged a partnership with Isetan, a Japanese department store chain that, like Barneys, had been in the hands of a single family for several generations. In 1988, in exchange for what was reported as an initial $250 million investment, Isetan agreed to form an alliance that would include real estate purchases with the Pressmans in the United States and Barneys assisting Isetan in entering the specialty store business in Japan.

From Barneys' point of view, the alliance was a wonderful idea, because unlike American or European investors, the Japanese were not insistent upon immediate return on investment, but were willing to wait to reap the profits. From Isetan's viewpoint, the alliance was a good one because the money would be translated into real estate, which had intrinsic worth, and also into a kind of expertise in merchandising high-priced clothing that was lacking in Japan. Most outside observers heralded the alliance as a natural and one that would be a template for the 1990s—an example of like-minded companies on opposite sides of the globe uniting to pool resources in ways that would benefit both partners and enable them to grow larger in tandem. Unlike other Japanese real estate purchases in the United States in that era, Isetan's seemed more sound because they involved a shared core business, retail department stores. And the money paid by Isetan did not seem to disappear immediately into the pockets of the American owners, as had the purchase prices other Japanese had paid for other American companies. Rather, it was put to work in a Barneys building spree. Less than five years after the Isetan money started to flow, the Barneys empire includes stores in or near eight major U.S. cities, and two in Japan.

In mid-1993 the Barneys-Isetan partnership shifted somewhat when the management of Isetan was taken over by the Mitsubishi Bank after Isetan had skirted close to insolvency and almost defaulted on its loans. The Mitsubishi Bank, one of Isetan's principal lenders, had also held a large bloc of shares in the company. The new managers installed by the bank had a different view of Isetan's relationship to Barneys and a different view of business, since they were bankers and not retailers. However, the international partnership appeared to continue without hesitation on the path to opening the promised new stores—even though the Japanese were said to be unhappy at having to put up more money, perhaps as much as several hundred million dollars, to cover the cost overruns being incurred by the renovation of the building for the uptown store. At the moment, Isetan seems to be worried whether it is throwing good money after bad—and is unable to tell, as yet, whether the first money was a bad investment or just one that is taking longer (and costing more) to bring to the point of profitability.

The uptown store may be the center of the partnership's aspirations, the start of what are hoped to be multiple large-store operations throughout the world—but it is also a gamble. Although Barneys had originally built its reputation and sales, in part, on being not just another presence among the upper midtown crowd of department stores, but serving as the alternative store in an out-of-the-way location, in 1991 Barneys decided that it had finally become sizable enough to compete directly with Bergdorf Goodman, Bloomingdale's, Henri Bendel, Galeries Lafayette, and Saks Fifth Avenue, in their uptown neighborhood. Renovation of the twenty-three-story skyscraper began in September of 1991, with an opening set originally for the spring of 1992. Delays due to the sagging economy pushed back the opening several times. The latest announced opening date is September 1993, and the Pressmans have also committed to opening another sizable store in Beverly Hills in early 1994.

In the spring and summer of 1993, *Women's Wear Daily* reports that Yves St. Laurent, Ralph Lauren, Isaac Mizrahi, Ungaro, and Karl Lagerfeld, who designs under his own name and also for Chanel, are refusing to allow Barneys to sell their wares in the new uptown store. The designers' principal reasons for refusal are that they either have their own stores in the area or that their clothing is already being sold by Bloomingdale's and Bergdorf Goodman and they do not wish to dilute the sales of those customers. Giorgio Armani wanted to refuse as well, but Barneys won in a Swiss court the right to enforce a 1979 contract that permits Barneys to sell Armani's merchandise anywhere in New York. In consequence, the new Barneys will offer Armani suits from a 6,000-square-foot area, the largest devoted to the Italian designer's clothing in the entire world.

Even with Armani in place, the uptown store will be a considerable spin of the roulette wheel. The real estate alone cost $100 million, and both trade and general newspapers report that the tab for renovating the building and opening the Madison Avenue store is running higher than envisioned. Perhaps in consequence of this difficulty, there are also reports that vendors of merchandise and services to Barneys are complaining of not being paid or being paid very late or only in part.

For merchants and residents around our block, Barneys' move uptown is cause for concern in another way: They worry that when the corporate flag is transferred to Madison Avenue—the renovated building will have upper-floor offices for the management and executive cadre—the Pressmans' eyes will no longer be focused as regularly on the area around Seventh Avenue and 17th Street. They believe the Seventh Avenue store will be scaled back, with a commensurate loss of jobs and foot traffic, and they fear that Barneys will never make any further investments in the area.

The concern spreads backward in time and fuels an ongoing community debate about Barneys' real estate purchases and expansion of a decade ago. Did these actions upgrade the neighborhood or had gentrification already begun and the expansion serve only to ensure its success? Merchants such as Roger Roth of the Roger Roth & Dave card store, Robert Chisholm of the Chisholm Prats art gallery, Louis Nelson of the Chelsea Gym, Norman Usiak of the Camouflage boutique, Robert Pusilo of Authentiques, and Joe Hwang of House of Cheers, to cite just a half-dozen examples, were in business on this block well before the 1983 expansion. "The gay men were the real pioneers of this area," contends Nick Accardi of Cola's. "You know the phrase, 'It takes a sissy to make it pretty?' That's what happened here." There are even debaters who assert that Barneys' success with upscale male customers—itself the basis for the store's expansion—can be attributed to its appeal to gay men who were already in Chelsea by the early 1980s. On the other hand, most others acknowledge that the rise in real estate values in the area, which has gladdened property owners and sobered renters, is certainly due, in large measure, to the Pressmans' purchases and renovations.

The question does not resolve. Suffice it to say, however, that so long as there is some Barneys presence at 17th and Seventh, residents and merchants may have no reason to worry about the corporate move uptown because it is unlikely that gentrification could be reversed now even if Barneys did the unthinkable and pulled up its roots.

One of the premier contexts for the growth of small businesses in coming years is as satellites or suppliers to the giant companies. This is readily apparent in one-industry towns (witness the growth of companies serving the motion picture industry in Los Angeles, the automobile industry in Detroit, the federal government in Washington, D.C.) and in situations in which supply routes become firmly established, as they are in department stores, where the clothing designers and manufacturers who sell merchandise to the big stores are the usual small partners. While the relationship between large firms and their smaller partners always seems to be skewed toward the giant, it can and often does take on aspects of symbiosis. In one type of symbiosis, the sponsorship of the larger firm encourages the growth of the smaller firm. That has been the case, Barneys claims, with its relationship to Armani, whose name was not well-known throughout the world before Barneys took him in hand in the United States; today, Armani's name is so well regarded that it can even be used to sell merchandise as far distant from men's suits as eyewear.

The larger firm usually reaps benefits from its sponsorship of the smaller through one or more of three forms of indirect profit: It enjoys the reduced costs that come from buying the smaller business's output at a volume discount; or it benefits from having a more-or-less captive provider of goods or services; or—even more indirectly—it profits from having established an insider's position with a previously unknown company that, due in large measure to the bigger company's exposure of its goods or services, becomes a desirable purveyor. In each form, as the larger firm profits, so does the smaller one.

Two smaller firms around the block, led respectively by restaurateur Pino Luongo and architect James Harb, have evolved through several stages in their relationship to Barneys and are on the verge of changing further. They are interesting to examine because neither fills the traditional position of supplier, and each has been both helped and hampered by its relationship to the big fish.

Architect James Harb, whose offices are in the 230 West 17th Street building that he helped renovate for the Pressmans, has had a long relationship with Barneys and with the Pressman family. Currently, the office of the Rosenblum/Harb architectural partnership is a beehive of activity with seventeen employees, of whom six are licensed architects and another six are in the process of completing their degrees. They are busy designing the executive offices and a gymnasium/spa/salon floor for the Barneys Madison Avenue store, completing work on commercial retail establishments for other clients, and designing freestanding residences, a subsidized housing development, and a child-care facility for the City of New York.

On the walls of partner James Harb's cubicle, a drawing of a home to be erected for a client on a spectacular site in the Catskills shares space with a sketch by Harb's toddler. Harb is a slim, dark-haired man of about forty, born in California, and of Palestinian descent. He dresses in casual, fashion-forward clothes: the artistic businessman. With his neighbor Elliot Rosenblum, Harb started the firm in the early 1980s, after an apprenticeship that included a stint with the celebrated architect Philip Johnson. In the *AIA Guide to New York City*, Rosenblum/Harb is mentioned twice. The guidebook dismisses a series of connected town houses on 104th and 105th Streets as "a reductionist row that pales in comparison to the richly detailed 1888 houses across Manhattan Avenue." Harb points out that architectural students visit the project as a model for urban affordable housing and that the same guide lauds a renovation on Madison Avenue at 84th Street as "A brilliant expansion and recladding of a dull, 2-story taxpayer, turning it from a pumpkin into Cinderella's coach. Through talent, not magic."

The subsidized housing complex was among several residential projects completed in the firm's early years, Harb explains, before "the spigot for that sort of work" shut off during the Reagan years. When there was no more money for housing, "a commission for a new retail store came along. Sure, it wasn't precisely what I'd always wanted to do—everyone wants to do freestanding objects, particularly in the urban environment—but we're realistic and we wanted to stay in business." It was that store project, for Gear Holdings, on Seventh Avenue—the store still fondly remembered in the neighborhood—that led to the "connection to the Pressmans." In other words, Harb had to first establish himself before the Pressmans called; large companies seldom go out on a limb and choose a complete newcomer as an important partner. But equally, large companies are often more eager to work with a promising newcomer—and to pay only a modest sum for the newcomer's services—than they are to hire a well-established talent and pay more for it. Thus, Barneys did not go out and commission Philip Johnson for architectural work, but a Johnson alumnus.

A first Rosenblum/Harb project for the Pressmans "worked out well," according to Harb, and over the next several years the family repeatedly commissioned the firm, to plan the renovations of the 230, 245, and 249 buildings on 17th Street, to design many of the branch Barneys stores around the country, and also to make over several of the family's residences. The Pressmans' patronage turned Rosenblum/Harb from a small architectural partnership to a medium-sized one that has projects going simultaneously in many places around the United States as well as in Japan.

During the intense period of work with Barneys, the architectural firm moved its own offices to the renovated 230 West 17th. "This had been a printing building," Harb remembers. "We found ink stains and heavy machinery imprints on the concrete—impossible to get out. But it made sense for us to be just around the corner from our major client."

Many architects might have chosen to remain at some distance from a major client, in case the patronage disappeared. Indeed, small businesses that supply larger ones often try to maintain a separation from their biggest customers for just this reason. But Rosenblum/Harb decided that exigencies of the situation demanded closeness, and for some time that worked to the firm's advantage. However, when the Barneys expansion surged beyond the phase of creating small specialty stores, the Pressmans awarded the principal architectural work on the newest and much larger stores on Madison Avenue and in Beverly Hills to architectural firms that specialize in large stores, not to Harb's firm. Rosenblum/Harb was given the contract to design the executive floors of the building, a spa, and a gym.

The larger firm pigeonholing the smaller partner as capable of only performing certain tasks, not every task in its field, is a late and often fatal stage in big-small partnerships. Faced with such a prospect, which is usually accompanied by the major client cutting back on its orders, the smaller business that has grown in size to match its workload must find a way to sustain its momentum. Harb had to recognize, once the contracts for Barneys' two big new stores were let, either that his favorite-son status was fading, or at least that Barneys was no longer going to be doing the sort of expansion that called for his services. If Rosenblum/Harb's work had been considered good solely because of royal patronage, the firm's heyday might have been over. But what every small supplier desires to have happen as a consequence of a close big-small relationship had, indeed, occurred in this case: Other retailers who admired the firm's work for Barneys began to commission similar mall units. Calvin Klein, Saks, J. Crew, The Coach Stores, and Perry Ellis became clients. "Diversification is wonderful." Harb smiles about this turn of events. And he doesn't even have to move the offices from 17th Street because the lower Chelsea blocks west of Fifth Avenue have become a hot location for many architectural firms.

Harb sublets a small space on his floor of the 230 building to

Pino Luongo, for whom he designed the Le Madri restaurant, which Luongo owns in conjunction with the Pressmans.

At six on a balmy, clear Sunday evening in August, the back of the Le Madri restaurant—which is the Barneys parking lot that runs from 17th through to 18th Street—has been transformed into a green-carpeted patio bordered by a restrained wrought-iron fence and overhanging trees. After the sun sets, there will be a showing of *Cinema Paradiso* on the outer wall of a warehouse that borders the lot on the other side. This is the third in a series of four Sunday-evening screenings of subtitled Italian classics. Black-gowned women at the entrance take money for tickets, $7 each, and sell scrip with which to buy food. During the summer, Le Madri has a back-porch gazebo, now lined with candlelit lanterns. Owner Pino Luongo's employees have extended serving tables out from that deck from which one can buy small plates of pasta, pizza, salad, and desserts; beer and wine can be bought at another kiosk; popcorn at a third; later, a coffee bar appears. As at a carnival, one always ends up with an unreturnable extra ticket or two and is here inclined to spend it for an ice cream. The logos of the cosponsors—AT&T, Lavazza coffee, Pellegrino bottled water—are everywhere, but the film festival's prime mover is Pino Luongo, who over the past decade has built a restaurant empire that is among the largest in New York.

Luongo is taller than most Italian-born men, with an open, fleshy, Roman face that radiates a certain cocky confidence beneath its careful grooming. His is a modern American immigrant success story. Born to a middle-class family in Italy, Luongo worked in an uncle's restaurant, completed a college degree in history of theater, and had a spotty career as an actor before emigrating to the United States in 1980, motivated in part by a wish to avoid being drafted into the Italian army. He began as a busboy at Da Silvano, an upscale Italian restaurant in Greenwich Village, and soon rose to manager there. In 1983, with two partners, he opened Il Cantinori on East 10th Street. It was one of the first Italian restaurants to feature regional cuisines and subtly flavored dishes rather than plain pasta and tomato sauce. Five years later he sold Il Cantinori to his partners and went on his own to open Sapore di Mare, in the Hamptons. Pino recalls that it was just after that opening that Barneys' principal owner, Fred Pressman, a regular customer at Il Cantinori, asked Pino if he wanted to "do something with me." Pino recalls answering with a qualified yes, because the Pressmans had in mind a luxury restaurant on the corner of 18th Street and Seventh Avenue, and "I wasn't going to make a living out of that location. It would be a total gamble." But Pino did some research, liked what he saw, and with the Pressmans as partners opened Le Madri in the spring of 1989. His flair for the dramatic gesture— he brought over some Italian mothers to cook their own specialties in the kitchen—helped Le Madri garner publicity and acclaim. Working professionals in the lower Fifth Avenue area, a group that included publishers, advertising agency executives, architects, designers, and executives from the garment center, would come to 18th and Seventh for a luxurious lunch and formed the core of a strong dinner crowd. After opening Le Madri, Luongo has gone on to open a half-dozen additional restaurants around the country, some with the Pressmans as partners, some by himself.

In the hour before sunset on this summer evening, couples and foursomes carry their food and drinks to white picnic tables, a few of which are topped by white umbrellas. These form the back of the theater while rows of chairs sit facing a warehouse wall with a temporary screen in front of it. Virtually all of the attendees live in the neighborhood. Although this event has only been minimally advertised, for the most part by means of posters affixed around the area, there is a capacity crowd, a compatible mix of casually dressed young and older people. Some in the audience have seen the film before but are interested in the experience of watching it in this setting; others construe this event as an opportunity to taste Le Madri's food for less than it would cost if they ate a full meal at the restaurant. The food served consists of pizzas, lasagnas, and babas—none of it particularly inexpensive. After a change in chefs, Le Madri was recently rereviewed in the *New York Times*, garnering a rather truculent two-star notice that stressed the restaurant as theater more than as a purveyor of good-tasting food.

What was billed as a Brazilian duo turns out to be a four-man ensemble that performs African rhythm music on a series of drums; during several numbers, the musicians don grass skirts and masks. Pino Luongo wanders around in a black shirt and white linen pants, smoking a cigar, shaking hands with those he knows, and introducing himself to others: the restaurateur as impresario. His own enjoyment of the scene is contagious. This venture will make some money, but its main purpose is an imaginative extension of his niche, broadening what can be done with his restaurant. In the next few months, Pino is scheduled to physically enlarge his empire by opening mad. 61 in the basement of the uptown Barneys store, and a second restaurant, near that new department store, to be called Amarcord. The latter name is the title of a Fellini movie, though not one that is included in the summer film series.

Music and alfresco eating continues until darkness finally falls and the film begins. *Cinema Paradiso* may be the perfect film to show in this setting because it is about the watching of films in a small town, and the biggest scene occurs when one of the main characters, the projectionist, shows a movie on the wall of the town square after the theater has been shuttered for the night. In this New York carpeted parking lot, the shared watching of the film— shared not in an enclosed, dark, anonymous space, but in the open, to the accompaniment of the summer evening, food, drink, and conversation—produces a sense of community among the former strangers who constitute the audience. In Pino's terms, then, a prime task of the evening is accomplished.

It is abundantly clear why the Pressmans picked him as a partner: In many ways, he fits the bill of particulars that a giant company would seek in a junior partner—a man who has already made a success of his own, but who is hungry for more, capable of achieving it, and who needs capital and real estate. Once the partners had successfully completed a project together—Le Madri—both sides could feel comfortable moving on to bigger things. In short order, the partners created modest-priced Piccola Cucina restaurants in association with new Barneys stores as they were erected in Dallas, Houston, and Costa Mesa, and two higher-priced Cocopazzo restaurants on the Upper East Side of Manhattan and in Chicago: six restaurants in five cities in three years.

Is the big-small partnership always essential to the smaller unit's success? Some might argue that Armani might well have gone on to become a household name without Barneys, but others would insist that success on a large scale would only have been made possible by having a partner introduce him to the American buying public. Pino Luongo's detractors point to the fact that during the period of rapid restaurant openings in association with the Pressmans, Pino Luongo also operated without the Pressmans (but with other partners) and did not do well. He opened a second Sapore di Mare on the resort island of Saint Barthélemy, in the French West Indies. That venture later closed. Explanations for its failure range from Luongo's being blocked from buying the hotel in which the restaurant was located, to lack of business due to the recession, to difficulties with his associates. Then, too, the restaurants Luongo opened in association with Barneys' suburban stores have been, by his lights, only moderately profitable. He attributes this more to wrong guesses by himself and the Barneys executives in regards to location than to the nature and presentation of the food, which is what is under his sole control. At lunchtime at a shopping mall, he points out, shoppers are used to cafeteria food and don't have much time to eat, therefore they don't want to go to even a moderately expensive place for a meal that could take an hour or more, while in the evenings most malls close down early, and this is inimical to their restaurants establishing substantial dinner businesses.

Despite these problems, the Luongo restaurants as a group have to be adjudged highly profitable enterprises, as they now gross more than $15 million a year and have made Pino a wealthy man.

He commutes to the city from a restored home in Westchester that he shares with his wife and two children, smokes three Cuban cigars each day, and is well-known in New York for outrageous and often captious appraisals of competing restaurateurs, restaurant and food critics, and the human race. A story he is fond of repeating: He called a customer at home, after midnight, and asked if the man still wanted the table he had reserved for the previous evening. This past spring, gossip columns report Pino changing chefs at Le Madri and trading insults with his former chef at Cocopazzo, who—depending on who was quoted—was either fired or resigned. "Some chefs are ready to come out of the kitchen, some are not." Pino shrugs. "Cooking is not just a self-pleasing job. Food is communication."

"Americans need to learn how to spend money to make life better," he opines, and believes his restaurants are showing the way for people to enjoy themselves. "Americans know about making money, but the essence of life is not the amount of things you buy because you have money, it's the style of life you embrace, the quality of life. Americans don't yet understand what food is about—they don't think about a fruit-and-vegetable stand as being essential to emotional well-being."

Mildly critical of Americans in these regards, Luongo is otherwise unabashedly fond of his adopted country. In the design of the tiles at the bottom of the swimming pool of his Westchester home is the shape of the American flag. It would not have been possible for him to build a comparable restaurant empire in Italy, Pino believes. Most newly wealthy immigrants who hold such views explain that in the old country, capital is less available to upstarts. While not denying this, Luongo believes that it is the emotional climate in the United States that makes this country more amenable to an immigrant's potential climb to commercial achievement. To illustrate what he means, he recalls being alone in New York in the early 1980s, not yet able to speak English, but encouraged by the climate here to become "communicative and frank with myself in a way that was not possible at home," a way that permitted him to conceive and execute big plans. The Italian culture from which he sprang, he explains, is cloistered and age-encrusted; things change slowly. Conversely, in the United States, "People say 'Show us what you can do,' and when you demonstrate that you can do something, they accept you as a doer and don't check to see what is your background, your pedigree." That certainly has been his experience in relation to the Barneys principals. Trying to sum up how American culture sponsors attitudes that are different from those in Italy, he cites what happened to him when, on a whim, he decided to try ice-skating, a sport he had never before attempted. "Back in Italy, I would never have exposed myself as awkward; I would have gone to a rink like that at Rockefeller Center and watched the good skaters and never tried it myself. Here, I just wanted to skate and did it and didn't feel embarrassed about not being good at it right away."

Luongo, too, is reaching what may be the end of his string with the Pressmans and, simultaneously, the end of his period of opening many restaurants. He has just decided to move his offices from 17th Street to a space above the new Amarcord site. This move will bring him closer to what will be his three restaurants on the Upper East Side, but it may also serve another necessary objective, to emphasize his emancipation from Barneys and the Pressmans—although they, too, will be moving uptown, into executive offices in the Madison Avenue store. "After this, no more restaurants," he says quietly. Other plans?

He begins to speak tentatively about moving beyond restaurants altogether. In somewhat the same way that Armani and Ralph Lauren expanded beyond clothing into accessories and home furnishings, Pino wants to move into direct merchandising of food to the public. He plans to capitalize on his name and reputation in the restaurant business by manufacturing and distributing a line of packaged precooked pasta-and-sauce meals, called "Pino Luongo's Cucina Tosca," which will utilize a packaging technique common in Europe but not used widely in the United States, and which will be sold in supermarkets. In the idea and prototype stage are four

Cucina Tosca products, which will range in retail price from $2.59 to $3.09. He hopes sometime soon to manufacture the products in a plant in Canada and then to test them in an upscale supermarket chain outside of New York so he can demonstrate that his name is good other than in his home base.

Though in his battles within the upscale restaurant community in New York, Pino is now a big player, in this new field he is a small player and understands that he is also a neophyte. He has joined up with partners who know retail food distribution. Even so, Pino is uncertain how the enterprise will come out. "The big boys are already coming after me," he avows. "They'll either try to kill the line or to buy me out. Probably both at the same time."

On an early September evening, the uptown Barneys store opens. The invitation-only party at the store draws celebrities from the fashion, entertainment, and political arenas. Guests come from as far away as Paris and Hollywood. Accompanied by waiters with trays of martinis, the guests browse through the main floor, with its aisles of cosmetics and clothing, and admire the exotic fish in tanks that highlight the austere, modern design of the store. Though sales are not the order of the evening, a few purchases are made. After viewing the store, and making appropriately gushing comments to a crush of reporters and television crews, the guests are ushered to the nearby Pierre Hotel, to be entertained at a night club. The very next morning at ten, the store opens its doors to the public.

By this single stroke of adding a new store, Barneys increases the size of its overall business by two-thirds. Accompanying this quantum leap in size, though, are considerable problems. Shortly, trade papers report that in addition to many vendors not being paid in a timely manner, as much as $20 million in building contractor bills are outstanding. Further digging by reporters reveals that while large suppliers are still being treated properly, the smaller among Barneys' seven thousand vendors are being forced to wait. Although it is industry custom to pay designers within the first ten days of the month after an invoice is rendered, a sampling of two-dozen designers finds that none have been paid within thirty days of the due dates of their invoices. Some of these designers have not been paid since May or June, and a few of these report themselves as on the verge of going out of business. Others say they will never sell to Barneys again, but the majority say they will, although they are refusing to ship reorders until the store pays for goods it has already received. The impression conveyed is that the uptown store has cost too much to open and is not doing well.

Barneys executives insist that the new store is doing just fine, thank you, and that the problems are minor, a normal though unfortunate consequence of becoming larger—growing pains. The building contractor problems, they tell reporters, are really disputes among subcontractors, and the vendor payment problems are the result of a shift from one system of accounting to another. They pledge that all problems will be cleared up shortly and point out that they own the Madison Avenue building free and clear and by mortgaging it could easily realize $50 million, enough to wipe out any outstanding contractor debts.

Despite the Barneys corporate denials, industry observers still characterize the opening of the uptown store as fraught with risk, mainly because throughout the retail clothing industry, department stores are continuing to consolidate at a rapid rate. Macy's, which was mired in bankruptcy, is being sought by Federated, a company that owns Bloomingdale's and many other stores, and which itself has only recently emerged from bankruptcy. Moreover, developers of suburban shopping malls have stopped asking department stores to be their anchor tenants in new locations and are instead looking to such retailers as Wal-Mart, Target Stores, or Toys R Us to be their anchors.

In the face of such trends, why would Barneys commit to open a very large New York store and one almost as large in Beverly Hills early next year? The answer, it now appears, has to do with relative size. The doubling of Barneys' business—which these two new stores will accomplish—is expected to provide added heft that will, in effect, protect Barneys (and Isetan) from future attempts by the billions-a-year American retailing giants such as Federated, the May Company, and Dillard to buy Barneys or even to force a price war among stores that would weaken Barneys to the point at which it would have to agree to be acquired. The more massive you are, the harder it is to be swallowed up. To survive when you swim in a larger pond, you must bulk up and become a bigger fish.

Chapter 6

GOING HEAD TO HEAD

FOR SEVERAL YEARS, two video rental stores facing one another on the eastern corners of Eighth Avenue and 17th Street have been involved in head-to-head competition. One is a unit of the giant Blockbuster chain, situated in spacious quarters on the ground floor of the modern Grand Chelsea Apartment Building. The other is Video Blitz, an independently owned business occupying a much smaller space on the ground floor of a three-story converted brownstone. This battle taking place in the video rental field on this one corner of our block reflects similar battles taking place all over the United States between giants and independents in many retail endeavors. The future of American small business is at stake in these confrontations. Can the smaller entities survive at all? On what terms? On the corner of 17th and Eighth, in the fall of 1993, new elements are being introduced into this battle that may decide its outcome.

Video Blitz's frontage is composed entirely of floor-to-ceiling windows, which give it an airy, unrestricted feeling not usually found in an independently owned storefront rental shop. It is open seven days a week, from midmorning until midnight, and its stock is eclectic—collections of foreign films, cult films, musicals, documentaries, and some videos for children, along with a fairly heavy proportion of sex videos, divided into gay, lesbian, bisexual, and heterosexual sections. The general manager reports that Video Blitz rents about a thousand videos each week and asserts that the stock on hand represents two or three times the choices available off the racks at Blockbuster.

The Blockbuster unit is a bigger place, occupying about four times the floor space of its competitor, and is arrayed with the standard glass front, wide aisles, and broadly spaced display racks that have become familiar to millions of Americans since Wayne Huizenga acquired a small Dallas-based chain of video stores in 1987 and expanded the chain to national and international prominence. Blockbuster's rental stock consists mostly of mainstream offerings, quite a few multiples each of the major studio releases of the last two years, and some older films. They also sell popcorn and candy to go with the rentals. "A Blockbuster customer from Topeka would know how to navigate the store on 17th and find the latest Disney release," a neighborhood resident observed. The corporation has recently announced that it will no longer carry tapes made by *Playboy* or *Penthouse*, much less actual pornographic videos, and that it wants to be known as the family entertainment center. By contrast, the manager at Video Blitz points out that "We take satisfaction in providing what other stores can't or won't provide."

That is both literally and figuratively true, and the statement highlights an interesting question. In the future, will Americans be able to choose among the entire variety of products and services that could be available, or will we be limited in our choices because a handful of large companies dominate the landscape and those companies decide they can best make money by limiting our choices rather than through attempting to cater to the entire spectrum of choices? In the fight between very large companies and independents, the matter is not merely whether big or small will prevail; rather, it is what will be the concomitants of surviving the battle.

By any measure, Blockbuster is the biggest player in video rentals. There are 3,000 Blockbuster Video stores across the United States; 40 million people worldwide have Blockbuster cards. New Blockbuster stores are being opened at the rate of one each day, and the company's annual income is measured in the billions of dollars. In recent moves toward a goal of vertical integration— controlling supply—Blockbuster has purchased the television production company Aaron Spelling Productions and the film production studio Republic Pictures. Vertical integration is usually pursued in order to lower costs of supplies, but these purchases, in addition to giving Blockbuster access to large libraries of films and tapes, also provide access to future productions and curtail what products other chains are able to buy. In the service of another vertical integration goal, better control of distribution, Blockbuster also bought the overseas retailers Sound Warehouse, Music Plus, and Virgin MegaStores, each of which have hundreds of units that rent and sell CDs, audiotapes, music videos, and other home entertainment products that complement Blockbuster's videotapes. Blockbuster is moving rapidly in the direction of becoming the largest retailer of home entertainment products in the world.

A large part of the company's enormous growth in the past six years has come at the expense of smaller chains and independent stores. When you are opening stores at the rate of one a day, you have to move very rapidly and rely on shortcuts. Several people in the video rental business have charged that Blockbuster's pattern has been to identify an independent or small-chain store that is doing well—and move in next to it. That certainly appears to be what happened on the corner of 17th and Eighth. The general manager recalls precisely when the giant arrived on his doorstep: three years ago, just days after he had been promoted to general manager. When the signs went up on the ground floor of the Grand Chelsea Apartment Building, he first realized the significance of visits to Video Blitz in previous months from gray-suited men who would ask casually how things were going. "I'd tell them it was none of their business, or that business was great."

At that point, business was indeed very good. Owner Louis Nelson had opened Video Blitz five years earlier, in conjunction with his Chelsea Gym, which occupies the other floors of the corner building. At other locations around Manhattan, when Blockbuster moved in, its smaller competitors had simply shut their doors, unable or unwilling to compete head-to-head with the chain. Video Blitz determined to fight. As an opening tactic, the smaller store began to insist that renters become members. Previously, anyone could walk in and rent a tape for cash, and there had been a significant number of people who kept tapes out until they were long overdue but who could not be readily dunned for back charges. Since Blockbuster asked its customers to become members and to use a card backed up by a member's charge card, Video Blitz did the same. Membership at VB was free, but rentals required a $150 deposit or a credit-card number that would be kept on file. This dissuaded some deadbeats, which helped the store's bottom line.

The second weapon was pricing policy. Video Blitz began flexible pricing programs and midweek discount rentals. Currently, VB offers three-day-two-night rentals for $2.77, and Tuesday and Thursday specials of second-tape rentals for $1 more than the tab for the first tape. Blockbuster's price is $3.99 for a two-night rental of a recent movie, with no break in price for a second rental, although rentals of some older tapes are lower in price. Perhaps more important, the local Blockbuster manager does not have the managerial latitude to alter any aspect of the store's rental price policy.

The third weapon was the staff. Customers at Video Blitz who have tried Blockbuster complain about the larger store's thin selection of tapes and its staff of college students who lack sufficient knowledge about films, to the point that they cannot make adequate alternate suggestions to customers when a desired new movie is temporarily out of stock. The Video Blitz staff is older, more steeped in film lore, and is able to advise customers rather than acting only as clerks at a checkout counter. The general manager attributes Video Blitz customer loyalty to variety of inventory, price flexibility, and staff knowledge. The Video Blitz staff believes that the Blockbuster unit across the street pays a high rent, is operating at a loss, and is just waiting for Video Blitz to give up so Blockbuster can pick up the neighborhood business.

It would be pleasant to report that after three years of going head-to-head, the smaller store's personal service, adaptability to customer base, and depth of stock have enabled it to successfully fend off the giant and to remain in business—but such a conclusion misses certain important points. First of all, though Video Blitz continues to operate, it is still fighting for its life. Of equal relevance is that the competition is not really between two video rental stores, but rather between entities that make money in different ways.

Video Blitz is a straightforward retail rental operation whose edge in its neighborhood and with its eclectic clientele is, indeed, service. But its survival can also be traced to its relatively low overhead. The general manager believes that the store would not be viable if it had to pay rent, and it does not really pay rent because Louis Nelson owns the building.

Blockbuster ostensibly makes money through rentals, but the big corporation more directly shapes its bottom line by acting as a distribution service for the major film and television studios, from whom it buys railroad-car loads of new releases at a very low cost per unit. It is also able to buy at lower cost than Video Blitz does because it buys direct from the manufacturer and thus cuts out the middleman distributor cost that Video Blitz cannot avoid. In these regards, Blockbuster is more similar to chains such as Ace Hardware or Wal-Mart than it is to the independent video rental store. It can make available at a local store a hundred copies of a recent hit release, while a Video Blitz can only afford to buy five or ten (for which VB pays a higher initial per-unit purchase price). The other major way that Blockbuster keeps its costs down is through the strategy alluded to a few pages earlier, that is, by narrowing the range of what it buys. In purchasing only a few products, Blockbuster can bring its size and weight to bear, so that it pays low prices for its inventory. Then the maintenance of a narrow inventory permits the hiring of a staff that does not have to be composed of film buffs, a staff that can be paid lower wages than a more knowledgeable staff is able to command. That also lowers costs. Blockbuster's immense capitalization also allows it to stay in business at such a location as 17th Street even when that store may not be currently profitable, because the company can afford to wait for what it hopes will be the eventual closing of the competing independent store. (In a similar way, Barneys was able to wait out the period during which the former Gear store was empty and not feel the loss of rental income too keenly.) Similar buying patterns, inventory control, low wages, and waiting-out tactics have fueled the spread of the Wal-Marts, the McDonalds's, and the Ace Hardwares across the country, a spread that has killed off smaller competing operations in nearly every location where a larger chain has chosen to open a unit.

The fight between Video Blitz and Blockbuster highlights precisely the appeal of the chains, not to the consumer but to the sort of individual entrepreneur who might consider buying a franchise as an alternative to starting his or her own small business. The chains solve all of the major problems of small businesses: They provide buying power, which lowers the cost of the goods to the store; they provide centralized procurement, which cuts out middlemen and assures continuity of supply; they provide management expertise and experience in their particular retail fields; their concept has been worked out and proved in advance of the store being opened; and they have resources to help individual owners regularize their cash flow. With all of these advantages, it's no wonder that franchising and chain-store ownership is absorbing an ever-higher fraction of would-be small-business entrepreneurs.

That the struggle of Video Blitz with Blockbuster has been carried on for more than three years, with the independent still standing, argues that the devastating impact that the national chains have had on the Main Streets of small towns and suburbs throughout the United States may not be replicated as readily in large cities. In New York and other centers of population, the larger mass of potential customers makes it possible for the independent to maintain its own clientele. It also points to the three most effective ways of doing so: by the independent's differentiating itself from the chain in the provision of service and expertise, by stressing high quality rather than mass merchandise, and by training its customers to respond well to its providing higher quality service and flexibility.

Chain operations suffer as a result of the doctrine that all products must move or be banished from the store, whether that's an out-of-date video, or a spare part that's only asked for once a year, or a blackberry milkshake that doesn't prove instantly popular. Independents can keep a backlist, stock the odd part, keep the blackberry syrup in reserve. And when the independent produces such a part or a milkshake to honor the occasional request or finds the out-of-date video, the independent reaps a long-term repeat customer, the sort of customer that the chain does not have or see as necessary to cultivate. Chains accept that their customers are notoriously fickle and that they shop at the chains mainly to obtain low prices. Chains make their money on volume, not on quality. That is their strength, but it also is their vulnerability.

In the fall of 1993, the balance in the standoff between Video Blitz and Blockbuster is being tilted by a factor that has little to do with the video rental business. Most of the building in which Video Blitz is located is given over to the facilities of the Chelsea Gym; the video store, the gym, and the building itself are all owned by Louis Nelson, and the confabulation of the enterprises is the foundation of the difficulties.

Nelson is a moderate-sized man in his early fifties, with mousy brown hair, a small drooping mustache, and a ring through the right corner of his lower lip. Perhaps he only appears small when compared to the highly muscled and well-developed gym employees who are lugging new rubber flooring into the gym. The Chelsea Gym is for males only and is known as a gay gym; signs on the walls announce that members can have limited-time reciprocal privileges at similarly oriented gyms in Boston, Los Angeles, San Francisco, and Washington. The facility is on five levels: The basement holds showers, sauna, and steam rooms; the ground floor, the entrance, shop, and changing room; the second and third floors have the machines and weights; and on the roof is a green-carpeted expanse used for sunbathing.

Nelson and his lover purchased this building in the summer of 1981, with the express purpose of creating "an all-male gym that would be gay-friendly." At that time the ground floor held a drug-store and the floors above were being used by the Korean owner as a jewelry-making factory. Earlier, the building had served as a brewery, a paint store, and a barbershop. "We didn't open until November of 1982," Nelson says in a soft voice that contains traces of a southern accent, "because it took time to get a variance. The city considers gyms—well, it did then—in the same category as whorehouses."

He and his partner had no experience in running a gym, but they learned by doing, as Nelson appears to have done throughout his life. He had studied chemistry, Russian, and French in college, and came to New York in 1966 and began in the theater as a lighting designer. He did work for producer Joe Papp, then managed an office for opera playwright Robert Wilson and for the New York State Council on the Arts. He lived in the Colonnade Row, a group of old houses opposite Papp's Public Theater, and the owner of the buildings asked him to be the controller on a new building project and to invest in the venture. He made enough money to capitalize the gym. Three years after the gym opened, the partners thought of putting a video store into the ground floor because video stores were hot in 1985, and because the space was not large enough to accommodate many other enterprises.

At that time, Nelson recalls, the Grand Chelsea had not been built, and "We had nude sunbathing on the roof, because there were no tall buildings in the area and we weren't bothering anyone. But then construction started across the street."

That construction had been delayed for several years because community groups had mounted legal and political challenges to the siting of a high-rise apartment building in an area of low-rise brownstones and storefronts. Opponents had charged that the large building would essentially change the character of the neighborhood, raising prices in the area, which would cause the closing of indigenous enterprises and would bring in the sort of merchants who had no roots in the neighborhood and therefore less of a stake in maintaining its viability. Developer Philip Pilevsky eventually won out over those opponents, and began to build in 1989.

At that point, Nelson recalls, the construction workers figured out that his enterprise was a gay gym, and they "started throwing missiles at the guys on the sundeck." The missiles were coffee cups full of excrement. A couple of these hit and injured people on the sidewalk below, and Nelson went into action. He sued the building ownership and the construction company. Today he believes he could have halted the construction entirely, but instead of doing so he agreed to a settlement that included the installation of video cameras on his roof and at ground level for the purpose of recording the scene so that there would be a record if the construction workers did anything else. The cameras remain in place—that is the reason for the one at eye level—even though the Grand Chelsea is completed and occupied. When tenants started moving into the floors of the Grand Chelsea that were well above Nelson's roof and complained about nude sunbathing, he wisely forbade the practice.

Nelson's problems with that building and its occupants continued when Blockbuster moved into the ground floor in 1990. However, the other storefronts of the building, those along Eighth Avenue between 17th and 16th, remained empty at the time, as the original developer defaulted on the building and it was taken over by the lending institutions, two New York–based banks. Part of the reason for the default could be traced to the developer's

having been delayed in the construction by neighborhood opponents and having had to extend himself monetarily during that
period, but most of the difficulties could be attributed to the general decline in the New York real estate market that occurred just
at the time that the Grand Chelsea was opening.

In 1993, the banks sold the Grand Chelsea for a price substantially lower than what it cost the developer to erect the building.
The sale was in two pieces—the residential units in one, and the
retail space of the ground floor and part of the basement in the
other. In the past few months, the owners of the new residential
units have been offering the condos for sale at reduced prices, and
the owners of the retail space have similarly offered storefronts at
deeply discounted rents. It is the latter practice that is now affecting Louis Nelson, for he has recently learned that something called
the American Fitness Centers is to move in to a large chunk of the
ground floor and basement space between 16th and 17th, and that
it is due to open around the first of the coming year.

"I called the phone number they have for information," Nelson
reports, "and their come-on sounds more like it's for American
Airlines than for a gym." Still, the prospect of a much larger gym
opening a stone's throw away from his, a gym that will also offer
facilities for women, has been worrisome. "There is no membership loyalty in gyms," he explains. "Every new gym that opens up,
even some of them that have homophobes working the desk or as
managers, siphons off some of our customers, though they often
return later." He notes that American Fitness is advertising in specifically gay publications, a tactic he believes is aimed at taking
away his customers. Heavy advertising is also a tactic only available
to a well-capitalized enterprise, one that also has the money to buy
entirely new equipment in a field where the "state of the art" is
continually being advanced.

Currently, Nelson's gym is at slightly less than the capacity
1,500 members he had in the late 1980s, and his renewal rate is
down. In 1982, when he opened, the Chelsea Gym was virtually
the only facility in the area. It was strong enough to survive the

shakeout in the industry during the recent recession when many gyms closed their doors—but there are now eight gyms in Chelsea, and four more are to open within the next six months in the area between 14th and 23rd Streets west of Fifth Avenue. Realtors have discovered that gyms are good customers for large volumes of space that have gone begging for years; gyms are also important amenities that apartment-house builders and even office-building developers now feel must be offered in their own buildings. Just as the superstores are taking over the old cavernous spaces on Sixth Avenue, there will soon be supergyms in smaller but still large spaces that were previously retail stores or parking garages or, as in the Grand Chelsea, storefronts that have been empty for years.

Nelson's first reaction to the news of American Fitness was to look for more space for his own gym so he could add facilities for women. The building next to his on 17th Street, the Steiner Building, owned by the Cavalero family that operates the Catholic Book Publishing Company, was mostly vacant, and it just so happened that a passageway could easily be constructed from the Chelsea Gym's second and third floors to one of the huge warehouse floors in it. The two men started negotiations. Recently, however, Robert Cavalero has pulled back from them, preferring to find someone who will buy or lease the entire Steiner Building, rather than just one floor. So Nelson had to scrap his planned expansion. He decided instead to do some upgrading of his facilities—installing the new rubber matting, and so on.

These business difficulties coincide with a tough time for Nelson personally. His longtime lover and original partner in the gym had died in 1987 of AIDS, and recently, another man with whom he had forged a long-term relationship also succumbed to the disease.

In the late summer, Nelson begins to take drastic measures to meet the competition. The first step is to lower his price for membership. His regular list price for a year was $600, and he had been routinely knocking that down to $399 and slightly lower for renewals. American Fitness advertised a $299 annual price to the first one hundred people who sign on as members, and a sale price of $399 for those who sign up by December 1, with the warning that annual fees would be higher than that for people who choose to become members later on. Accordingly, Nelson decides in September to price some new memberships in his gym at $299— a fee comparable to that which American Fitness will offer to its first hundred customers, but a fee that will seriously cut into Nelson's own potential profitability.

In mid-October 1993, Nelson decides that even this price slashing is not enough to keep the Chelsea Gym competitive. And so, on a Friday night, he fires nine of his employees at the gym and at the video store. He does not replace them directly, but apportions out their responsibilities to other employees. Those fired include the general manager of Video Blitz and the manager and the membership director of the gym, all of whom are longtime associates of Nelson's and who had relatively high salaries that reflected their seniority and experience.

The former video store general manager reports that he and the other fired men are "in shock" because even though they knew about the competition from the new gym, they had believed that as long-term employees—and, for some of them, as fellow gay men—they were secure in their jobs. Nelson says that the employees he fired "had gone stale" and were "not pulling their weight."

The firing of nine employees of two linked enterprises has to be considered a serious setback for a small entrepreneurship. No owner fires employees for the heck of it. Proprietors of businesses generally express their profitability by adding employees, and/or by turning a larger fraction of the daily toil over to managers so they can have more leisure time for themselves. Firing employees, then, in addition to being unpleasant, also inevitably means more work for the owner, so that after Louis Nelson has cut back substantially on his supervisory staff, he will now have to be more in the thick of the moment-to-moment managing of both businesses. The firings are also a gamble because Nelson's business is based on service. He is wagering that the firings won't make a difference to his clientele, that a Video Blitz customer won't mind waiting another minute or two at busy hours at the checkout, or a gym member won't complain if the towels aren't replaced as frequently by the attendant who now has several additional tasks to perform.

Even if customers do complain, Nelson realizes that the potential loss of a few customers is outweighed by a large gain in cost reduction. My guess is that nine people removed from the payroll, even if other employees' salaries are slightly raised could save $3,000 to $4,000 a week, or between $150,000 and $200,000 a year—a substantial amount of money for businesses whose combined annual gross appears to be less than $1 million. Did Nelson have alternate choices other than the firings? Realistically, no. There are no other ways of cutting expenses that could result in weekly savings of thousands of dollars. He cannot stop buying new stock for the video store, because that would be certain death; and in the gym, he cannot cut back on supplies like towels or on maintenance of exercise machines, for such cuts would send customers away in droves. He can't stop paying for insurance. Or electricity. Or taxes. Raising prices to boost income is also out of the question, because of the presence of his competitors Blockbuster Video and the American Fitness Centers. Unlike the customers of Carl Berman's mailing service, which are institutions that may be able to absorb a small price rise that can be passed along in diluted form to their ultimate customers, Nelson's customers are individuals and direct purchasers, and they don't have to stand for a price increase but can take their trade to a competing business only a few steps away. In short, Nelson's firing of nine people is the act of a capitalist fiercely defending his investment. "When it comes to protecting the business," Nelson says about the firings, "I become a monster. I do what I have to do. This was the only way to protect the business and the rest of the employees, too."

While Louis Nelson and his enterprises are wrestling with their serious problems with competition, Blockbuster as a corporate entity is in the midst of its own sea change—the sort that generally roils only very large businesses. At the beginning of October 1993, an announcement is made that Blockbuster and Nynex are joining with the cable television and programming company Viacom in its bid to take over one of the largest entities in the home entertainment field, Paramount Communications. This is no David and Goliath story, but a battle between giants. And in this battle, Blockbuster finds itself in danger of being swallowed up, being used as an element in another business entity's vertical integration scheme.

The entry of Blockbuster and Nynex into this battle is interesting in its timing and intent. Paramount had earlier agreed to a merger with Viacom, but the rival QVC cable home shopping network had topped Viacom's original bid, and so Sumner Redstone of Viacom had gone looking for allies with deep pockets. Nynex is to contribute $1.2 billion to the Viacom war chest for the takeover, and Blockbuster, $600 million. For Nynex, the investment is mostly that—an investment—plus the opportunity to learn about making "content" that can later be sent out to consumers over its own transmission lines.

For Blockbuster, the investment means much more. In exchange for Wayne Huizenga and the minority shareowners of Blockbuster obtaining a substantial ownership position in Viacom-Paramount should the takeover be completed, it begins to look as though Blockbuster is agreeing to lose its independence. Whether or not the Paramount deal goes through, Blockbuster is to become a unit of a larger entertainment company—a giant retail distribution arm of a company that will also market its products in theaters and on broadcast and cable television screens.

That outcome is considered desirable for Blockbuster on two counts. First and foremost, it will permit the owners of Blockbuster to make large amounts of money by means of stock swaps and through cash payments forwarded to stockholders as dividends. In this regard, Blockbuster's submersion into Viacom is one more instance of the changed way that most of the big money is being made today in the U.S. economy—today's megamillions are not being made through manufacturing, distribution, or retailing, but through leveraging of stock ownership. It is a peculiar but typically modern fact that Blockbuster as a corporation can make more money in one fell swoop by going out of business as a separate entity and becoming a part of Viacom than it could make in several years of independent operation of its thousands of video rental and other retail stores.

Being swallowed up is also a logical move because, as Blockbuster's top management knows, video stores themselves are on the way to becoming technologically outmoded. Shortly, the means to deliver any of, say, 25,000 titles directly to a customer's home television set in a pay-per-view arrangement will make it unnecessary for customers to rent tapes from a store, any store. When this technology becomes generally available—a time frame estimated at from five to ten years—Blockbuster's current way of making money will vanish. So combining Blockbuster into the larger entity, whether Viacom or Paramount, also makes business sense from the standpoint of the future viability of the Blockbuster enterprise.

Both Nynex and Blockbuster have units on our block, and the attempted takeover of Paramount is the subject of hot speculation among the employees, even though many have been instructed not to comment on it to outsiders. Most employees feel as though they are soldiers who must keep on fighting in the trenches while higher authorities, in a place far removed from the front lines, settle the big issues that will eventually decide the soldiers' fates. The savvy consensus at the Blockbuster store is that the bid for Paramount means that this particular unit and others that are not big money-makers will surely stay open for a while because the corporate entity cannot afford to appear as though any of its units are doing poorly. They seem certain that once the merger and absorption are complete, there will be cutbacks in the workforce when operations are combined. Since very few among the employees make enough money to own stock in Blockbuster, they stand to gain nothing by the merger but the greater likelihood of losing their jobs. Employees always want to feel that what they do is important to the company that employs them, that they are necessary cogs in the wheel. But when the company is making money through a process that seems to have little to do with their own work, through investments and stock rises, employees suffer a sense of futility and superfluity.

Throughout the fall, the battle for Paramount between QVC and its allies—Advance Publications, Cox Enterprises, and Bell South—and Viacom and its allies, Blockbuster and Nynex, continues, with victory not assured for either side, but with the stakes consistently becoming higher and higher.

Louis Nelson, too, has come to understand that his own video business may well become outmoded within the next five to ten years, and this knowledge meshes with his current needs to "hunker down" and "do what I have to do" to permit his other enterprise to survive. Accordingly, he now decides that the time has come to sell Video Blitz and to receive some rental income for the space it occupies. He probably figures he will not be able to sell the business to outsiders, who will also recognize that its days are numbered, but that insiders who know what they are doing may be able to squeeze enough money from it and will be willing to make a deal to take it over. And so, in the late fall, he concludes an arrangement with two long-term employees, Craig and Carlos: As of the first of January 1994, they will own the store. This transfer of ownership is something the three men have been discussing, off and on, for some time. Craig and Carlos will cement the deal with a down payment, and Nelson will give them what in essence will be a loan toward the remainder of the purchase price, and they will pay off that loan monthly, along with their rent payment. The two men will operate the store themselves, which will enable them to cut back further on the number of people they will need to employ. At least two additional jobs will be lost in this transfer of ownership, but the new owners, Carlos and Craig, will have great incentive to convince their customers to rent that extra tape, to consider buying that special favorite movie, to work out ingenious new promotions to boost sales.

Other than to the men who have lost jobs, this is a satisfying transfer that is of help to both sides and to the community. It is the sort of ordinary passing on of ownership that happens often in capitalist societies, but which generally goes unremarked. What makes it worthy of note and perhaps even of celebration is that it goes counter to the trend of the big deals that are absorbing the preponderance of the country's wealth. Small business ownership remains one of the few routes by which the ordinary person can make more money than a weekly salary. The deal between Nelson and his former employees is the sort of transfer that happens most readily in big cities and in modern societies in which sons no longer wish to take over businesses from their fathers. This ownership change elevates two former salaried employees to the status of entrepreneurs and gives them the chance to be their own bosses and to make money from something beyond the sweat of their own brows. As employees in this sort of business, even as middle managers in it, they would be stuck at an income level that would likely keep them just barely above lower-class status. But with a proprietorship in hand, they are very likely to pull themselves solidly into the middle class, and stay there. At the same time, this deal permits Louis Nelson to keep his other and larger enterprise, the gym, open and functioning at a time when competition is cutting into his profitability and also to realize actual rent from his property, which the previous arrangement had kept him from doing. This is a deal in which the goodwill of both sides and the participants' long-standing and intimate working relationship are as important as the amount of money that is changing hands. And the community benefits, too, from having two newly invigorated neighborhood enterprises.

Chapter 7

WHAT'S THAT GOT TO DO WITH THE PRICE OF APPLES?

AROUND THIS one square block are three deli-grocery stores, all open 24 hours a day, and which appear at first glance to carry the same merchandise. There are also a half-dozen restaurants, all ostensibly competing with one another. And for the mornings, there are an additional half-dozen places selling coffee and baked goods. How do multiple entities in the same business in a small geographical area survive? How do they differentiate themselves from one another, or do they bother? An examination of some of their ways of being in the world—business practices seems too narrow a designation—may provide some insight.

The delis, first. Two are corner stores, one on the southwest corner of 17th and Seventh, a second on the northwest corner of 18th and Eighth, and the third is midblock in the restaurant row on Eighth Avenue, wedged between Flight 151 and the hardware store.

The 17th and Seventh store is more take-out diner than grocery. On a shelf near the cashier's station is a cylindrical plastic case that features slowly revolving slices of cakes and pies, and on a counter is a half-carved turkey carcass. Prepared entrées—grilled chicken breast with garlic, cold pasta salad with pesto—are priced at $5 to $10 a pound. So much for the diner aspect; as for the grocery aspects, the long, narrow aisles are barely wide enough for a grown man to pass through without knocking down the merchandise. The brands stocked are upscale: Häagen-Dazs rather than Breyers ice cream, Newman's Own rather than Ragú spaghetti sauce, Samuel Adams rather than Schlitz beer. There are thirty varieties of cat food and almost as many of prepackaged coffee. All packaged items are in the smallest possible portions, giving a hint as to the solitary nature of the clientele. The concentration of Middle Eastern foods seems more a reflection of the background of the management than of customer predilections.

The deli-grocery on the corner of 18th and Eighth is larger, busier, oriented around an enormous salad bar—five feet wide, twenty feet long—and seems to cater mostly to the students at the schools to the west on 18th. Lower shelves, higher ceilings, and wider aisles, as well as a broader selection of grocery items make this a more comfortable place in which to spend a few minutes figuring out what to have. The store features organic and health foods in dazzling array, for instance nine varieties of exotic-flavored "natural" popcorn. Such "healthy" foods are favored by the non-school-age clientele, the manager confirms. But he also displays Breyers ice cream along with Ben & Jerry's, Ronzoni spaghetti next to the higher-priced, gold-and-teal wrapped brands imported from Italy. Prices here are 10 to 15 percent higher than in the deli on Seventh Avenue. Tony, an Hispanic of about forty with a stubbly beard and graying mustache, manages the deli for a family of Koreans who also work in the store but do not converse well in English. The largest problem, he says, is shoplifting. Tony catches people "every day; and not just kids—people in suits." Recently, he persuaded the owners to stop selling french fries because to make them he had to turn his back to the counter, and "kids were stealing while I'm busy making orders for their friends."

The third deli, the Apollo, is almost exclusively a take-out prepared foods emporium; the groceries that it carries are mostly
snacks. It does not have the outdoor display of fruits, vegetables,
and flowers of the other two. The Apollo caters mainly to the soft-
collar workers and is busiest at lunchtime when people who have
only a short break from their jobs, or who wish to spend a bit less
money than they would in a restaurant, line up to buy fried chicken
and other hot selections.

The mostly Korean-owned deli-groceries that started appearing on New York's corners in the late 1970s stopped further
growth of supermarkets in the neighborhoods they began to serve.
Supermarkets already in place were not supplanted, but the steady
increase in the number of supermarkets, which had been going on
since the 1920s, came to a halt as the deli-groceries took hold.
Since the 1970s, as well, waves of renovations and consolidations
have occurred in the supermarket field in New York City. In a
curious twist on history, what the delis now provide are the service-
sector intangibles associated with the sort of stores that existed
before the supermarket era—small-store atmosphere and convenience. However, deli-groceries don't generally provide the per-
sonalized service that a neighborhood shop can render. But then,
most of the owners don't converse easily in English, which makes
it difficult for them to do anything special—that is, personal—for
a customer. What the delis have successfully done is bridged or
blurred old marketing demarcation lines: They carry flowers (flo-
rist), dry goods (market), produce (vegetable man), cigarettes and
newspapers (newsstand), take-out coffee and breakfast rolls (diner),
and salads and sandwiches (lunch counters).

Despite their power in the aggregate, each deli is a small player
and gets pushed around as other small players do. In order to offer
one or two of the best-selling Snapple drinks, for example, they
are forced by the distributor, on whom they depend, to carry the
whole line. In general, they only stock what they can move well
or are forced to provide by their suppliers. They know their
customers—for instance, they carry paper diapers, which a frantic

parent may well pay any price for in the middle of the night, but not baby food, which in an emergency parents can blend at home out of leftovers.

How much more money per item do the delis believe that customers will pay for convenience, given that there are supermarkets within a short walk of the block? At the A & P on Eighth Avenue at 20th, and at the Gristede's Supermarket at 15th and Seventh, milk is 69¢ to 75¢ a quart, Macintosh apples are 99¢ a pound and tangerines are four for $1; at the delis, milk is 99¢, Macintosh apples $1.29 to $1.49 a pound, and the tangerines are three for $1. This means that at our block's three delis, the premium paid for convenience averages about one-third extra per item. The delis also carry fair-trade items, whose prices are supposedly set by the supplier, but even these are often marked higher, $2.69 for an item that is $2.49, the list price, in the supermarkets. The delis only directly match the competing supermarket's price in standard take-out items such as brewed coffee, donuts, cigarettes, Snapple, and other canned or bottled beverages, on which the markup is already high. You won't find deli specials on candy, because the markup is 30 to 40 percent, and no deli owner wants to lose money on impulse-buy items.

But the supermarket isn't selling strawberries at 99¢ a box, while the delis are because the 99¢ strawberries on display in an outside rack serve as a loss leader—a low-markup item whose purpose is to bring people inside with an item already in hand and a greater inclination to add to it other purchases in the store. Deli-groceries are exquisitely sensitive to traffic patterns, and some change prices on certain items during times of high or low traffic, which larger stores like supermarkets do not do. On the weekends, the same deli strawberries will be $1.29—and they'll be snapped up at this higher price, evidently because of increased traffic, which translates into greater demand. The delis must be admired for their flexible pricing policies, which seem more attuned to the "laws" of economics than do the strategies of larger food purveyors, and saluted for understanding that the price of milk is more than a price, that for customers it is a totem or benchmark. Knowing this, the delis keep a quart of milk under a dollar, even if it becomes a loss leader when milk prices rise, as they occasionally do. A price of more than a dollar a quart, the delis must believe, will turn off their customers or send them to the supermarkets. They won't take that risk, but they do gamble that on the weekend the swain going to visit his lady friend will spring for a $5.99 bouquet, even if on a weekday night he won't pay more than $4.29 for the equivalent bunch of flowers. Were this traffic-sensitive price-adjusting system to be carried to its logical extreme, delis would lower prices during the working hours of nine to five, raise them before and after those hours, and double them between ten in the evening and six in the morning, when supermarkets are shuttered. Fortunately for customer sanity, none of these deli-groceries has had the audacity to do that—yet.

A modern definition of a big city is a location with many decent restaurants. Manhattan has more good restaurants than any other city in the United States, and in the aggregate these are the equal, many gourmets avow, of the restaurants of Paris, London, Rome, Rio, or Tokyo. More so than rural folk or suburbanites, city dwellers patronize restaurants, considering them a civilizing factor in daily life and a counterbalance to the stresses and strains of residing in the big city. They are also an expression of a society's wealth because restaurants are luxury goods: Even a meal in an inexpensive diner normally costs three to four times what one would pay to buy, cook, and serve similar food at home, and a meal in what restaurateurs call a tablecloth restaurant can cost ten to twenty times the retail price of the ingredients.

Eighth Avenue between 14th and 23rd Streets has become a restaurant row featuring three-dozen places to sit down and eat, ranging from simple pizza joints to fairly elegant emporiums. The block between 17th and 18th Streets has more restaurants than any other on this strip: The Pasta Pot, Gascogne, Blue Moon, Cola's, Food/Bar, Flight 151, and Eighteenth and Eighth. (There is also Chelsea Place, but it still hasn't reopened.)

Observation on several summer and fall evenings reveals that a couple or a foursome passes by on the sidewalks of this avenue block at the rate of one group every half minute during the hours from six to nine o'clock. Those who have not chosen their dinner site in advance stroll along, glance at the menus and reviews in the windows, peek inside to get a sense of ambience and the characteristics of the diners, and then make their selection.

The restaurants on this block form an interesting constellation of competing eateries, each unit the inhabitant of a niche for which price supplies only one part of the definition. More depends on something hard to measure, the personalities of the entrepreneurs.

In the fall of 1993, the highest-priced and, in many ways, the highest-quality restaurant on the strip is Gascogne; the maintenance of high price and high quality may be another reason why Jennifer Endersby has been making her changes in as quiet and invisible a manner as possible. The Pasta Pot is the lowest-priced restaurant; it has recently cut back its hours, so that it is serving mostly liquor at the bar, rather than food; much of the kitchen and dining-room staff, according to rumor on the block, has been let go.

The remaining restaurants—Blue Moon and Cola's on the east side and Food/Bar, Flight 151, and Eighteenth and Eighth on the west side—are all in about the same moderate price range.

Niccola Accardi, proprietor of Cola's, the other Italian restaurant on the block, is one of those who has his eye on the floundering Pasta Pot. When he rented his own location, six years ago, he found that it, too, like The Pasta Pot, had once been an Irish bar, the details of its earlier existence covered over by the proprietors of the Chinese take-out that had recently occupied the premises. Nick painstakingly restored the patterned tile floor and the glass blocks around the edges of the windows and turned Cola's into a small, spare but romantic restaurant, open only for dinner.

Many of the main courses are priced around $10. Cola's, with just forty seats, is usually jammed from 6:00 P.M. until closing time.

Nick is twenty-nine, well muscled beneath a colorful open shirt, with thinning jet-black hair and the broad smiling face of a man who likes to greet customers by name. He had his first restaurant job at twelve, dropped out of school and opened his own restaurant at nineteen, was a buyer of fish for higher-priced Italian places on the Upper East Side, and apprenticed to their chefs. "I know every job in the business," he says. "I can put my hands right on the meat in the broiler, reach into hot dishes and all the other stuff that comes from a lifetime working in kitchens." He came to understand that he could replicate dishes priced uptown at $18 and $20 and offer them at half that price downtown. With $60,000 of his own, he renovated this space on Eighth Avenue. Word spread about Cola's very quickly, and despite an initial slam in the *Village Voice*, Nick had a successful enterprise. "We don't do advertising," he boasts. "No matches or business cards. Don't take reservations except very early and very late." For the first several years he only accepted cash, but "I got tired of people making a dash for the bank ATMs and of having to hold tables for them while they did; that was the major reason for changing to taking credit cards— we've got to turn those tables over to do 100 to 140 covers a night."

Cola's makes less money on each customer than does Gascogne, then, but serves more customers and provides them with an experience less foreign and luxurious but which is more convivial and takes less time.

Bobby Pereira has also looked at the Pasta Pot space, with thoughts about opening his own restaurant there. He is the manager of the Blue Moon restaurant, which is in the same building as Cola's, separated from it by the entrance to the St. Francis III mission house whose bulk fills the upper floors. Turquoise and black decor, neon signs, and old Mexican-bandit movie posters are the mainstays of Blue Moon, whose windows open out to the street. Customers come to Blue Moon for generous, modestly priced versions of standard Americanized Mexican food, and for the congeniality of its crowd. Open since early 1987, this Blue Moon has spawned two others, one on the Upper East Side and one on the Upper West Side. All three are owned by the Felixbrod family; the restaurants are all on commercial strips in residential districts and all seem to cater to a young, middle-class clientele.

About thirty, and of Portuguese ancestry, manager Bobby Pereira is a dead ringer for a young John Travolta. He grew up in the Fulton Houses projects on Ninth Avenue, just a block away, and at age thirteen went to work for GianCarlo Santini of Chelsea Place. Off and on, despite moving with his family to Queens and taking a degree in graphic design at FIT (Fashion Institute of Technology), Bob spent ten years working with Santini and speaks of him fondly. When Chelsea Place closed, Bob was hired by the Felixbrod family to manage this Blue Moon—in essence, to replace the father of the family, who was retiring. Bob has used his graphics and construction skills to redo the menus and remodel the restaurant, moving the bar from the back to the side and installing those front windows to "open up the place." At lunch, Blue Moon serves office people from the big buildings. A larger yuppie crowd begins to file in at happy hour for margaritas and salsa and tortilla chips. Many who come for cocktails stay for dinner. "Most evenings, the tables are always full, but there's a good turnover, so nobody has to wait long to be seated."

This past summer, Bobby Pereira married a gemologist for Macy's. He invited both Howie Felixbrod and his former boss, GianCarlo Santini, to attend the wedding. For Pereira, the marriage was a rite of passage in more than one way because he had been waiting until this event was concluded before he seriously contemplated another big step. His older brother, Cliff, who had once worked in the kitchen at Le Madri and was currently the chef at an intimate, well-regarded restaurant in Greenwich Village, was going to become the executive chef at Metronome, a much larger new restaurant, on the corner of Broadway and 21st Street, which was currently being readied for a late-fall opening. It would have room for several hundred seats, and the owners, a doctor and a lawyer, neither of whom had ever been in the restaurant business, wanted experienced people to run it. According to Bob, the owners had appointed someone to oversee the renovations and manage the restaurant, but the renovations were not going smoothly, and Cliff has just about persuaded the owners that Bob will be the best possible choice to take over the refurbishing and then to manage the place.

Bob's formal offer hasn't arrived yet, but he knows the time has come for him to move on to bigger things. Though still young, he is now a veteran in the business. "I looked at the old fish store across Eighth Avenue for a restaurant of my own, but I don't like the setup—the elevator shaft is right in the front of what would be the dining area. But I'll do something, soon. And it won't be small." Perhaps this wasn't the moment to go out on his own. The Pasta Pot space was not yet available, and he could use some experience at a higher management level. His leaving the Blue Moon will have an impact on the Felixbrods, he knows, but Bob believes they do understand that it is an opportunity he ought not to refuse.

Across on the west side of Eighth Avenue is Food/Bar, which, according to a delighted Bob Barbero, has been "full since the night we opened—on schedule." Even in late afternoon, many of the diner-type tables are occupied, and there is a genial hubbub in the place. In contrast to the smaller quarters of Blue Moon and Cola's, Food/Bar is high-ceilinged and open, with seats for eighty people, twice as many as at Cola's, and lots of room between tables. The view of the kitchen at the back of the restaurant is inviting, part of the theater of the eating experience. This particular gamble seems to be paying off. The partners have left off their outside jobs, and once a week the three men go out looking for locations where they might make an additional restaurant using the strategies that are already successful here.

It is difficult to decide whether the "nice diner" concept has made Food/Bar successful or whether it has more to do with its serving in the evening as a gay gathering place and singles bar. Eighth Avenue in Chelsea is becoming known as "gay Broadway," and to be in the midst of that strip and openly hospitable to a gay crowd may be reason enough for a restaurant's financial success.

Next door to Food/Bar is Flight 151. A decade ago, under another name, 151 Eighth Avenue was a dark den of a bar whose clientele was primarily Spanish-speaking and poor. Today, the front wall has been replaced by windows that are often removed so that the inviting old wooden interior is open to the street, and the clientele is better-heeled and more mainstream. Those attributes are reflected in the decor: 1940s propeller-driven planes, signs about aviation, and a menu that tells of a "legend" about a Flight 151 during World War II—a plane carrying a secret recipe for chili that had to be protected from Nazi raiders by American flyboys. Pinball machines are a big draw. In the men's room, when the door closes, an audiotape plays a message that mimics an airline stewardess informing passengers that they are free to move around the cabin, "especially if you've had a Killian's," a draft beer. Hamburgers, french fries, and Buffalo chicken wings are the usual accompaniments to the beer. Flight 151 shares with Blue Moon a predominantly heterosexual crowd, but Flight 151, whose bar is much larger, serves as the block's principal straight singles meeting place.

At the corner, there is Eighteenth and Eighth, a small coffee shop that has become a café. Inside, tables abut one another and the walls are decorated with dazzling dried flowers and a collection of quaint, kitschy teapots. As a restaurant, this is perhaps the most surprising entity on the strip, offering tasty Californian versions of American food, priced somewhat higher than the burgers of Flight 151 and more on par with the offerings at Food/Bar, with whom it shares the distinction, in the evenings, of catering mainly to a gay crowd. It does not sell beer, wine, or liquor, and it does a considerable breakfast business, as well as lunch and dinner.

Since the least expensive place, The Pasta Pot, is often mostly empty while several other restaurants are frequently full, it is evident that price is only one among a combination of factors that are assessed by diners when they make their choice for dinner. Each restaurant has found a way to distinguish itself from its adjacent competitors, to provide a mix of style, atmosphere, price, and comfort level that its patrons perceive as something of value.

On any given night, potential customers who prefer a quiet, intimate meal will likely choose Cola's; those who yearn for a gourmet experience may sample the prix fixe at Gascogne; those who want mildly spicy food as accompaniment to their margaritas will head for Blue Moon; and those who seek principally a bar experience will bend elbows at Flight 151. Customers like to eat in a place where diners are already in evidence, so popularity and crowd density are also elements in a customer's choice. The customer's age enters into the decision: Most of Gascogne's patrons, for instance, are older than those of nearby restaurants. Although gays and lesbians dine in all the restaurants of the area on every evening, on this block, at night, Food/Bar and Eighteenth and Eighth have become specifically gay gathering places, while Cola's and Gascogne usually attract both gay and straight couples. The end result of this fine-tuned specialization is that the group of competitors have also become complementary entities, which helps the whole of the restaurant row to be greater than the sum of its individual parts.

A few hundred yards from the block, along the commercial strip of 14th Street, you can buy three New York souvenir T-shirts for $10. At Roger Roth & Dave's card store on Seventh, or in Pam Chanin's boutique on Eighth there are similar though somewhat-higher-quality New York souvenir type T-shirts for sale, and the price may be as high as $18 or $20 per shirt. The lower-priced ones are what are known in the garment trade as "knockoffs," which replicate the designs of higher-priced merchandise, but still, the price differential between the high and low is quite large.

Off on the other side of the scale, the shoes in one boutique bear price tags in the hundreds of dollars, with nothing below $99, while those in the Giraudon boutique next door to P. Chanin go as high as $200 and as low as $39 a pair.

What seems to guide the pricing decisions of Giraudon, P. Chanin, Roger Roth & Dave, and other retailers in these instances is not the underlying cost of the merchandise nor a policy in which the markup is set at a certain multiple of the wholesale price. Rather, it is the retailers' perception of what their particular customers will be willing to pay for the merchandise. Joe Hwang, for another instance, although he carries more than a hundred different wines ranging in price from a few dollars a bottle to about $20, has decided not to carry wines which would have to bear price tags of $50 or more because he knows that there will be very few customers who will agree to spend that kind of money for wine in his store. Those who might buy a $50 bottle, he seems to presume, will prefer to do so elsewhere.

Perhaps the ultimate understanding of pricing your products at what the customer can be convinced to pay is provided by what is happening this summer at the recently opened Taylor's Prepared Foods and Bakery in midblock on 18th Street, in regard to the scramble for customers of weekday morning "coffee-and."

Back in May, reconstruction had been going on at a long-closed Spanish American take-out joint in midblock on West 18th to ready the space to be occupied by a new branch of the Taylor's bakery on Hudson Street. The new Taylor's on 18th, the carpenter said, would have the same "rustic, casual, inviting" look and foods as the one on Hudson.

Cindi Taylor, the proprietor, had been itching to expand for some time, but until that May had felt hostage to the enormous upset of the street construction that had been tearing up Hudson for the previous two years, and which had almost compromised the financial integrity of her emporium there. Once the construction moved past her block of Hudson and her weekly grosses began to soar again, Cindi and her family had looked for a new location and found the vacant storefront on West 18th.

A diminutive, animated woman in her thirties, with flaming red hair and blue eyes, Cindi was trained as a pastry chef and worked in that capacity for years at a gourmet store and at several of the city's major caterers. Three and a half years ago she went into business for herself, buying and expanding what had been a small gourmet take-out place. "What we make is 'Mommy food' or 'comfort food,' " pastries that aspire more to bountifulness than to elegance. A chocolate mousse panettone is high and tilts like a Leaning Tower of Pisa but is obviously luscious; a fruit pie at first glance looks like something you might concoct in your own kitchen, and at second seems much better than home baked. The prices at Taylor's are relatively high—$2 for a huge cookie that is almost a meal in itself—but people have shown themselves willing to pay such prices, Cindi asserts.

Whether that willingness can provide a basis for expansion, or how far it can be stretched, is still in question. But Cindi is bent on expansion. At Thanksgiving of 1992, she recalls, even though Taylor's prepared 600 pumpkin, apple, and mince pies, "I couldn't fill all the orders we had for them" because she could not exceed the capacity of the ovens. Her current goal is "to bake a thousand pumpkin pies this coming Thanksgiving."

Toward that desired end, Cindi wanted more space for baking. But to rent on Hudson for such a purpose would be foolish since storefront space there was quite expensive and the ovens required adequate room, proper ventilation, and plumbing rather than storefront visibility. She thought of putting in a café at the closed antique furniture store next to the Hudson Street Taylor's, but for oven space she looked elsewhere and found what she considers an excellent new location on the ground floor of a wide tenement on the south side of 18th Street, fairly near her new loft. In the back and downstairs is plenty of room for ovens, and the front provides room for a retail operation. The rent is low, especially when compared to rents on Hudson, and the taxes are less than the $10,000 a year she pays to the city for the other storefront. These low rates have combined to make possible a new enterprise that might otherwise have located in another part of the city or that might not have happened at all. "We figure if the bakery counter breaks even, that's good enough," since the cost of the relatively cheap space can be absorbed as part of the regular expense of supplying the Hudson Street store. Cindi is considering having the growth of Taylor's follow the mold set by Dean & DeLuca, Cindi's former employer and a successful gourmet foods operation that now also runs a string of cafés, but she isn't certain whether expansion ought to be limited to selling prepared foods and catering or should go all the way to retail cafés. The strength or lack of strength of the 18th Street store's bakery-counter receipts will help determine the future of the Taylor's enterprises.

By summer's end, Taylor's has opened on 18th and is competing for "coffee-and" business. Between the hours of seven and ten in the morning, hundreds of people on the way to offices on this block buy a breakfast or snack to eat at their workplaces. Prior to the opening of Taylor's, they bought their repasts at one of a half-dozen locations: a donut cart positioned on the northwest corner of 18th and Seventh, the three deli-groceries, the Eighteenth and Eighth café, or the Kap's diner. Prices range from the cart's $1 for a coffee and a donut or a buttered bagel, to $1.50 for similar goods at the delis or at Kap's, up to about $2 for a similarly filled brown bag at Eighteenth and Eighth, where the quality of the coffee and baked goods is higher than that of the diner, delis, or donut cart. Proximity to the office is always a factor in where someone buys his or her eye-opener, but price is important, too, or else the donut cart, which offers the least-attractive items at the lowest prices, would have no appeal.

Now there is Cindi Taylor's bakery, with "coffee-and" starting at $1.50 for a regular with bagel and quickly escalating to $2.50 to $3.00 if the caffeine accompaniment is a muffin, the choice of most customers. The quality of the baked goods is the best on the block—the coffee may not be better than that of the café, but the muffins at Taylor's are larger and appear more freshly baked and delectable. Within weeks of opening, Taylor's has so many morning customers that to approach the counter to buy entails a wait of a couple of minutes. None of those in line seems to mind, however; their patience is tied to their respect for the bakery and its products. At least while waiting they can smell the goodies; near the donut cart, you smell car and truck exhaust. Heidi, the assistant bookkeeper at Solco, who used to work at the White Horse Tavern on Hudson Street near Taylor's other location, moans that they have come to this block especially to break her diet. Tim Cass, manager of the Raymond Dragon boutique, is already hooked on Taylor's tuna sandwiches for lunch. A bike messenger from next door, a dollar in hand, wanders into the new bakery; in a few moments, he comes out again, suffering from sticker shock and stuffing the dollar back in his pocket because he can't get very much for that amount of money at this upscale emporium.

Taylor's bake shop's customers used to patronize other establishments but are now evidently willing to break old habits, switch allegiances, and to pay more than they once did for their morning's repast. Instanter, those customers have developed a taste for something they might not have known they liked before—they have been hauled upscale. That is testimony to the power of a better mousetrap called quality. How high would Taylor's have to price its victuals before customers might stop buying morning "coffee-and" there and slink back to their old suppliers?

Chapter 8

PUBLIC GOODS

"SEPTEMBER IS our Christmas," postmaster Edward M. Risdell explains during an early morning visit on Wednesday, September 1, to what he calls the "organized hysteria" of the Old Chelsea Postal Service on 18th. It certainly doesn't feel like Christmas, as this is a hot day and many of the postal employees are wearing shorts. The Old Chelsea building and institution is in many ways the center of this block and of zipcode 10011, an area that stretches from 26th down to 10th Street in Greenwich Village, and from Fifth Avenue west to the Hudson River, and is about half residential, half business. This installation of the United States Postal Service is housed in a sprawling depression-era building that features marble floors and bronze friezes of woodland animals over the entrance to the large lobby. The premises, comfortable and a bit august, summon up associations with the benign government of the past.

Fifteen hundred board feet of mail has arrived—more than

750,000 pieces of mail, twice the daily amount that this post office delivers during other seasons. While for the big department stores the six weeks before Christmas are the busiest of the year, for many other merchants the crunch comes earlier. September is busier than December for the Postal Service because of the extra large volume of catalogs and flyers intended for families returning from vacation and preparing to send children back to school.

The main working area is a very long and open room, perhaps double the size of the large lobby below since it also runs above the quadruple loading docks. It is divided into wooden bays each with cubbyholes labeled to denote individual apartments or offices. In each bay two to four men and women, surrounded by crates, boxes, cartons, and rolling mail carts, are working at a fairly rapid pace. "As long as their hands are moving, I'm happy," Ed Risdell says.

This is the season when, more than at any other time of year, by providing its "public good" the Postal Service works hardest at being an integral partner to private enterprise.

The concept of the public good, which has come down to us in the United States filtered through the mind of Alexander Hamilton, is that there are certain services essential to the defense of the country, or to the conduct of the country's affairs in other ways, that must be provided by or through the government, regardless of whether or not the provision of them is profitable. Presumed unprofitability is one reason that these "goods" were originally construed as beyond the province of private enterprise; they were also considered too important to the country to be handed over to the influence of any private individual or group. The concept of public good was first applied to the national defense, then to the provision of postal services, then to schooling. When telegraphs, telephones, and electric power came into general use, the concept was changed so that the right to provide communications services, while awarded to a privately owned monopoly, was heavily regulated so that in return for reaping profits the monopoly was obligated to provide service to all who required it and could pay minimum rates, even when providing service to some customers was unprofitable for the monopoly.

As the most vociferous champion of private property among the Founding Fathers, Hamilton would no doubt have been pleased by one of the most significant yet relatively unheralded shifts of modern times, by which the provision of public goods is coming more and more into the realm of private enterprise. In this chapter, I'm going to look at that healthy chunk of our block's economy given over, one way or another, to the providing of public goods. There is a full spectrum of entities in that business on the block, and they range from the fully public, such as the schools, through the middle ground of the Postal Service and the privately owned but quasi-public monopolies of Con Ed and Nynex, to enterprises and institutions that are fully private but which have taken over functions that were formerly the public-goods province of the state.

When we think of our economy, we usually don't take into account the portion that has to do with government spending. But out of an annual GDP of $6.1 trillion, government spending (including salaries) accounts for $1.1 trillion. Add to that what the states pay—New York State spends an additional $75 billion a year, a good deal of it on education and teachers' salaries—and the percentage is even higher. There are more teachers in the country than almost any other category of employee, and public administrators outnumber those in private companies. Two more locally relevant facts: Federal, state, and city governments provide a larger proportion of the jobs in New York City, an estimated 350,000 to 400,000 of them, than they do in the rest of the country. The 250 full-time employees at the Old Chelsea Postal Service rank this public-goods provider among the block's largest employers.

Privatized to an increasing degree in the past decade, the Postal Service is no longer what it was prior to 1971, an arm of the government. It still has the obligation to provide service to all, but it no longer receives subsidies from the federal budget to do so and is under a mandate to at least break even and, if possible, to turn a profit. In the past few years it has been in the black and has actually been giving some of its surplus earnings to the Treasury.

The need for profitability is one reason why Ed Risdell objects to the popular idea that much of the mail these days is junk. "Please don't call it 'junk mail'—it's third class, and we make a lot of money from it." Even so, the Postal Service is tough with bulk mailers, who must now advise the local station of the timing and desired "window of opportunity" for delivery of their mailings so that the appropriate number of temporary workers can be hired to assist with the load. One batch of pallets containing catalogs brought up from the basement pleads for the contents to be delivered between September 1 and 4; since the batch arrived five working days before that, and the window is reasonable, Risdell says, it will be accorded the desired treatment. Pallets of shrink-wrapped catalogs from the basement are regularly brought up to this second story, where they are broken down and sorted.

Mail is sorted by destinations or "ends." Eighty-two ends are served by this post office, divided into thirty-one different carrier routes. Yesterday afternoon and last night this mail was worked on by other shifts and by "night routers" who come to work at one in the morning. More than half the pieces this post office delivers each day are machinable, that is, they can be sorted automatically. This includes almost all the third-class mail, which accounts for 41 percent, and some first class. That still leaves 100,000 pieces or so to be sorted by hand, though. By the time the mail reaches this floor, it has already been put in bunches identified by color-coded cards that say WEDNESDAY or DELIVER BY FRIDAY. The mail is being final-sorted "in walk sequence," that is, mail for the first stop is placed on top of mail for the second stop, so the carrier won't have to root around in the bag to find what he or she needs next. The regular carriers' familiarity with the recipients makes the carriers the logical ones to do this final sorting, the most likely to understand that the John Smith of 13 Main Street is different from the J. A. Smith of 18 Main, and to avoid mix-ups in the residents' mail.

As the final sorting proceeds at an orderly pace, Risdell limps about the room, having rebroken a joint that was injured earlier in an automobile accident. Miming a golf swing, he jokes, "Missed the ball and hit the foot." Risdell arrived at Old Chelsea six months ago to take over from a management team that had been entrenched here for as long as area residents can remember. Ed is in his late forties, a Staten Islander with a high gray pompadour and a silver mustache. He worked in a knitting mill and as a building contractor, then walked a beat delivering mail for fifteen years before entering post office management a decade ago. "When I first started as a supervisor," Ed recalls, "I was going to change the entire Postal Service. That was too vast. Then I said to myself, 'I'll change New York.' Still too big. But I *can* change my corner of the world, and that's what I'm trying to do." In this instance, changing meant cleaning house. On arrival, he found that the postmaster's office door had usually been kept closed and had a No Admittance sign and a note advising all employees, even supervisors, that they must have an appointment in order to see the boss. Risdell put the sign in a closet, propped his door open during business hours, and endured the curious who kept peeking in and apologizing because they'd never before seen the interior. Risdell also found that the first-class mail was not being sent out promptly—something he has vowed to correct—the employees were at loggerheads with the supervisory staff and the institution's relationship with the community had deteriorated. Ed's goal for the Old Chelsea supervisory staff is to "get more with the times," which in his lingo means dealing properly with a younger generation "that wants to know why they should do a task, not just to do it because a supervisor says so," and to administer in a way that is properly sensitive to the various ethnic groups represented in the workforce. "I can talk to anybody, from the president of the United States to the janitor because I respect the work that person is doing—but I also demand that they respect what I'm doing."

That postmaster's job, Risdell says, has many facets. "I'm the head cork because I'm always plugging holes." He is also a referee between employees and supervisors, and a father confessor. "One employee recently told me he has AIDS. That sort of information can't be committed to paper and has to be kept confidential." And he acts as "Macy's Complaint Department" for everyone from irate customers at the lobby service windows to vice presidents of big mailers or receivers of mail who have problems with deliveries.

Risdell emphasizes the personal in his battle to reinvigorate his local post office, but what he is really doing is introducing the gospel (and laws) of private enterprise to previously alien territory—effecting the transition of the Postal Service from a governmental backwater to a semiprivate provider of a still-essential public good—in one of the largest privatization efforts ever undertaken. For nearly two centuries, the Postal Service was unchallenged in its provision of mail services. Volume has steadily increased, nearly tripling in the years since 1971. In recent years, however, its monopoly in certain areas has been vigorously attacked by private providers, as consumers required and became willing to pay for more individualized versions of "essential" services. The Postal Service has lost ground to such private concerns as Federal Express, DHL, and UPS. This has been particularly true in the lucrative overnight delivery business. Indeed, an important part of the growth in the American economy in the last decade has come from the upsurge of these competing service companies, which stemmed from the Postal Service's reluctance or inability to keep up with the needs of business. Today, however, as Risdell points out, the Postal Service offers overnight delivery services virtually identical to those of the private companies and at equivalent rates. Nonetheless, the Postal Service is having a hard time winning back business customers from the private carriers. Another blow to the Postal Service's utility to businesses has come from the fax revolution, which enables many documents previously sent through the mails to be transmitted instantaneously over telephone lines. There is now a third challenge to the Postal Service from "electronic mail," sent from computer to computer, also over telephone lines. It is entirely symptomatic of the Postal Service's modern

dilemma that adherents of E-mail call what the Postal Service delivers "snail mail." More so than most private businesses, then, this
particular purveyor of public-good services is losing ground to its
newfound competition, losses that make it increasingly vulnerable
to change.

The increasing private-industry-type pressure on the Postal
Service to keep costs under control comes to the surface during a
discussion of the salary structure of the post office. "We need to
schedule things very closely so we don't need too many transition-
als," Risdell says. Transitional employees, he explains, are those
not on the permanent payroll. Rookie carriers earn $22,000 a year,
and with seniority the positions pay $30,000 plus benefits. These
figures are close to the national wage average for all employed
people who are members of unions. "It's not a great job, but it's
steady—most people take it for the benefits," Risdell believes.
However, it is no longer a guaranteed lifetime job, and for the past
decade or so, postal employees (as with most unionized employees
in private industry) have been asked to pay for part of their health
insurance.

Very few Old Chelsea employees live in Manhattan, Risdell
believes. "On their salaries, they can't." Compensation ranges for
mail handlers and clerks are similar to those of the carriers. A
carrier's working day consists of two and a half hours in the building, readying the mail, and five and a half on the streets, delivering
it. That is going to change because the Postal Service's goal is to
have the mail "presorted in walk sequence," which will be accomplished by having so much separating done by machinery that final
hand-sorting time will be reduced to one hour; as a result, carriers
will be able to spend the other seven hours of their shift delivering
mail. When achieved, this change will mean fewer clerks and carriers, since each carrier will have more hours available than they
now do in which to deliver more pieces of mail. Such full automation will take hold "When I'm on the golf course, either playing
the back nine or as plant food," Risdell opines.

As Risdell indicates, full automation is likely to be decades away

In the early 1980s, the third-generation owners of Barneys bought a half-dozen buildings on the block, hoping to stabilize the neighborhood and support the department store's move into upscale retailing.

The west side of Eighth Avenue, with Seventeenth Street at left and Eighteenth Street at right.

Jung-ok Hwang has operated the House of Cheers liquor store for almost two decades and owns the building in which the store is located, but he still feels that he is "not 100 percent American—and not 100 percent Korean either."

A recent family tragedy enabled the Maxwell Lumber Company, on Eighteenth Street, to remain in business. Proprietor Marc Bernstein's office is filled with snapshots of the previous owners, his father and his grandfather.

The window displays of the Raymond Dragon boutique have often occasioned controversy—and brought in customers.

The east side of Eighth Avenue, with Eighteenth Street at left and Seventeenth Street at right.

Each successful restaurant along Eighth Avenue's row found a niche—some for the straight crowd, some for gays, some for those seeking an inexpensive meal.

As the year on the block began, optician Myron Michaels, a former high school physics teacher, started Sight on Seventh with his own savings and capital of private investors who, he says, "believe in me."

Under pressure from larger and better-financed competitors in the fitness and video rental fields, Chelsea Gym and Video Blitz owner Louis Nelson decided to take drastic action.

Video Blitz

Alan Gross (left) owns the brownstone in which Eighteenth Street News is located and often helps out his friend, the shop owner, Chandler Nandal. It's in Gross's interest, he says, to have his tenant continue in place and viable.

Postmaster Edward M. Risdell came to The Old Chelsea Post Office with a mandate to clean house and improve service, he says during a visit to see what he calls the "organized hysteria" of final-sorting the mail for delivery to thousands of area businesses.

Taylor's, with the highest-priced, highest-quality "coffee-and" on the block, quickly became a neighborhood favorite. But how high could Taylor's raise prices before the new customers think about going back to their old haunts?

Jean Rosenberg, director of the Chelsea Day School for children aged two to five, is also the school's landlord. When the owner of the other half of the building wanted to sell it, problems arose for the school and for Rosenberg.

"The history of my business is tied up with the history of my gayness," says Robert Pusillo, co-owner of Authentiques Past and Present, seen here (right) with his partner, Paul Lemma.

because a huge amount of hand labor is still required in the final sorting. Even pieces that have been sorted by the mailer to a particular carrier route—by markings such as CAR-RT-6—still must be further "broken down" to go to the correct individual apartments and offices. However, the Postal Service is committed to considerable change. In the fall of 1992, Postmaster General Marvin Runyon initiated a vast restructuring that eliminated through voluntary retirement 100,000 of 750,000 post office jobs nationally. In New York City alone, Risdell recalls, 100 managerial positions disappeared. Now, employees who leave are not replaced, and further cuts are in the works.

Risdell is adamant that service has not appreciably suffered because of this downsizing. "What error rate would you settle for? In private business, you're happy if it's 2 or 3 percent. In the Postal Service, if I have one-half of 1 percent, that's way too high. We work to keep it even lower. And we're self-supporting, too. Congress doesn't give us subsidies anymore, the money all comes from sales. So these days, when somebody complaining about service yells at me, 'You do what I say because I pay your salary,' I can at least tell them—politely—that that isn't so."

Aside from the national defense, the most conspicuous and in dollar terms one of the largest public-good functions of the state is the provision of basic education through the maintenance of "free" public schools. In terms of the allocation of tax monies, schools are one of government's greatest expenses—employing more people than auto factories in Detroit, computer factories in Silicon Valley, and all national cigarette producers combined. In the vicinity of our block, schools are quite a significant presence, since on the square block adjacent and directly west of the one under study there is a large junior high and a high school, two smaller public schools, as well as the headquarters of the school district and the office that oversees the city's "alternative" high schools.

Perhaps the most unusual educational institution in the area, though, is the one on our block, the small Liberty High, which is not actually a high school but a yearlong program of immersion in English for immigrant children of high-school age who have never before attended a New York City school. Liberty's principal, Bruce Schnur, says that he is precluded by law from asking whether applicants for Liberty High are in this country legally or otherwise. "We don't turn anybody down so long as they meet the basic requirements." Principal Schnur appears to be in his late forties, with a high forehead and glasses, a lifelong New Yorker who spent two decades teaching social studies before becoming an administrator. The goal is for students who "graduate" Liberty to go on to other city high schools and finish their education; to accomplish that they need to be able to hold a conversation in English and to make their way around the city. "We don't have bells at Liberty," says Schnur, "and when the building is renovated and they put in bells, I won't use them. We're not a factory."

The principal is fortunate that his charges have learned anything, this fall of 1993, because the opening of a great many New York City public schools was delayed by the discovery that they had unencapsulated asbestos leaking out of damaged ceilings and walls. Liberty passed inspection and opened on time, though. It probably escaped the asbestos problems because its physical plant is not as old as those of other schools. For many years, the building was a commercial enterprise, the Royal Business School. When it went bankrupt, a private investor bought it and shortly sold it to the Board of Education. Liberty High had begun in 1986 in the old Performing Arts building in midtown. After fire razed that building in 1988, the school system seemed willing to let the Liberty concept die, but a consortium of students, faculty, and parents successfully petitioned Chancellor Richard Green to reopen Liberty in another facility.

The commencing of this school year has also occasioned a hot debate across the United States on the precise limits of the public good in regard to education—specifically, whether there are too many illegal immigrants in the United States, clogging such facilities as public schools, and whether immigration to this country should be more tightly controlled. A study by the New York City Planning Department, just released in early September of 1993, estimates that there are 400,000 illegal immigrants in New York City and an equal number of legal ones. The illegals tend to be Italian, Polish, and Ecuadorian, rather than exclusively, as many in the public have imagined, Dominicans and Chinese. About one-third of all students in city public schools come from non-English-speaking families.

Partisans on both sides of the debate ought to have a peek at Liberty High. Children born in forty countries are represented here; more than half of the 600 students are Hispanic, and one-fifth are Chinese. This year's student government president is from Taiwan, the vice president from Somalia, the treasurer from Poland, the secretary from Yemen. Liberty has compiled a consistently good track record of graduating students with high attendance records and good work habits; a recent class's "adjustment" rates to the public high schools were very good, between 88 and 96 percent. The school is evidence both of the need for educational facilities for the foreign-born and of the possibility of transmuting by education those who might be potential burdens to society into those well able to take their places in the mainstream.

Economic and social matters are of as great concern at the school as strictly educational ones. For instance, the Liberty day begins early, at 8:00, includes mandatory lunch inside the building, and ends early, at 2:17 in the afternoon. "By getting our kids out twenty minutes before the dismissal of the other places down the block, we protect them from crowds of tougher kids from those schools," Schnur maintains. When the school first moved to this building, the Liberty students encountered trouble at the 18th Street subway stop: Roving gangs regularly took advantage of their immigrant vulnerability. Schnur and other school-system officials conferred with the Metropolitan Transit Authority, which agreed to limit the opening and closing hours of the station and to have special guards on the trains after Liberty ends its day; that effectively stymied the gangs. Lunch served to what Schnur calls "a captive audience" has a similar purpose: to keep the students in the building because "they don't have money to afford lunch in the neighborhood, and they might get into difficulties if they tried to buy food." The early dismissal also funnels the students out so that they can work; many of the Liberty boys, and some of the girls, have paying jobs after school. The Chinese children, Schnur knows, put in very long hours, and the Dominicans toil as delivery boys for restaurants in Washington Heights.

Another sore subject in public discussions this year is bilingual education. According to state law, on a high-school level, bilingual courses must be offered for groups over twenty in number, which at Liberty means Spanish and Chinese. These groups study math and social studies in their native language, but are taught all other subjects in English, and that means the bulk of the students' everyday courses. Each student has two hours a day of ESL (English as a Second Language), plus an English course. Schnur estimates that one-quarter to one-third of his students are illiterate in their native languages.

Because a Board of Education formula precisely governs the student-to-teacher ratio, Liberty has forty-five teachers; many were immigrants themselves, and for quite a few, this is their first teaching job. "They had the specialized skills I needed," Schnur says. Those skills included knowledge of Mandarin Chinese and the ability to teach mathematics in Spanish. "Besides," he adds, "I prefer to take them young, because the older ones are too set in their ways."

His diatribe amuses coordinator Carol Yankay, a redheaded former advertising executive whose office wall is papered with photographs of herself in exotic foreign countries. She speaks six languages and has been with Liberty since 1986. "This is teacher heaven. I was ready to retire until this opportunity came along," Yankay confides when Schnur is occupied with a phone call. "Teachers who find their way here don't ever want to transfer. The kids need you a lot and appreciate you a lot, and you can see what a difference you can make in their lives in a short span of time. In fact, the kids have possibilities at Liberty that they don't have on the streets of their own communities." These include safety while in classes and the formation of strong cross-cultural friendships. "It's hard to survive...in my neighborhood," a Dominican boy writes in a school paper. "Here at Liberty though, there are no colors, just people."

Last spring, Schnur attended an educational conference on East 96th Street and at lunchtime wandered toward the city's newest and largest mosque, which is nearby. Schnur, who is Jewish, usually trades greetings daily with his Islamic students—"I say *shalom aleichem* to them, and they say *salaam aleikin* to me"—and they had made him aware that it was the Ramadan period. As Schnur approached the mosque he encountered an overflow crowd attending services. Curious, he pressed in closer and became part of the crowd for a while, then went back to his conference.

That evening—and unbeknownst to the administrators, Carol Yankay recalls—the telephones of the Islamic community heated up with word of what had happened. "Mr. Bruce came to our mosque." "Mr. Bruce attended Ramadan services." "Mr. Bruce came to pray at our mosque during the holiest festival." Next morning, the school was abuzz with the principal's feat. Students from Arabic countries were excited and proud, and the staff began to mentally cross its fingers in the hope that this serendipitous event would help them over a hurdle. Families in the Islamic community had historically been reluctant to send their daughters to the city's schools. Perhaps now that Schnur had demonstrated his sensitivity to Ramadan, next semester, in addition to the cadre of Islamic boys, their sisters might arrive for classes at Liberty.

Regularly, at Liberty, whole classes go on walking tours of the city, visit museums, attend theatrical performances, and have meals at various ethnic restaurants when Yankay is able to make low-priced arrangements—in short, they are introduced to the city and to American life. To send children here is a big decision for immigrant families, and the Liberty staff tries to cultivate the families' participation in the schooling by holding city orientation sessions for the parents every Saturday morning and weeknight adult ESL classes. "Our back-to-school night is the best," Schnur insists. "The food is out of this world."

Diagonally across 18th Street from Liberty High is the small, red barnlike building whose first floor houses the Madelyn Simon indoor-plants business and whose second floor is home to the private school known as the Chelsea Day School. Nationally, about one and a half times as many preschool children attend private institutions as public ones; in New York City, the figure is three times as many children in private schools for the very young.

This is evidence that in New York the public good of education is not being adequately provided by state-run institutions and that parents feel that in order to obtain better education for their children they have no real choice but to pay for private schooling. Many parents contend that if schools like Chelsea Day did not exist, to obtain better education they, too, would join the exodus to the suburbs that in the past forty years has absorbed more than a million middle-class New York families.

The alternative-to-public-education character of Chelsea Day can be seen in many facets, for instance, in its flexible scheduling, which cannot be obtained from the public school system, but which parents are willing to pay for because it permits mothers to resume working when their children are not yet old enough to be enrolled in a primary school.

The Chelsea Day School's focus is immediately apparent when a visitor enters through the outside door: In a niche near the stairs are many folded-up strollers. Upstairs are three classrooms, two large and one small. About thirty-five children under the age of five are wholly engrossed in activities with toys, games, blocks, reading materials, and cages with turtles and gerbils. Halloween is fast approaching, and the children are making costumes and decorations for this favorite holiday, supervised by an almost equal number of teachers, visiting student-teachers, and a fair complement of parents. Most, though not all, of the students are white and live within a half mile of the school. It is still early in the school year, and some of the children have not yet become comfortable with being out of the sight of their mothers, fathers, or caregivers; the extraneous adults will leave shortly, though. Beyond the classrooms is a large, well-appointed rooftop playground centered around a tree house and jungle gym structure. The outdoor area effectively doubles the space available for the children. Since the roof has a high fence around it and the surrounding buildings are taller, the playground feels as safe as if it were at ground level.

"At two, three, and four, children first need physical safety, then emotional safety. Academics follows, but only if a child is ready for it," Jean Rosenberg says of her philosophy and practice at Chelsea Day. She points out that "The Board of Health is our guardian, not the Board of Education." The head teachers for each age-group of children are certified, as all teachers in public schools must be, but Chelsea Day's other employees are not required to have teaching certification. "An elementary school on 15th Street had just closed, and some of the parents urged me to start one. There was enough of a group to make it practical. I also needed a place for my own son, who was a toddler." An entrepreneur of sorts, Jean does not consider herself as such; rather, she functions as the director of a nonprofit operation. As an individual, though, she bought this two-story building in 1984 in association with one of the parents; that person then sold the downstairs half to Madelyn Simon while Jean rented the top half to the school. To become the director of an entirely new nonprofit private school was a "natural evolution of my growth as an educator. Besides, I like to administer and I love talking with children and parents. I even like sweeping the floors now and then, and while I'm at it, to fantasize about building the school up to six stories."

The school's philosophy was inspired by the work of British educator A. S. Neill, which stresses individual development. In accordance with that philosophy, the school is structured so that not all the children come for the whole day, every day, and tuition is computed on the amount of time used. For a child of two and a half, who can tolerate and benefit from only a few mornings of school per week, the charge is less than it is for a four-year-old who comes every morning plus three afternoons. Currently the enrollment is fifty-seven children from fifty-five families. The student-to-teacher ratio is five to one: five full-time employees and five part-time, including a handful of specialists. About half of the graduates go on to private schools, while the rest attend public schools, including PS 3 and PS 41, which serve Greenwich Village.

Another reason why parents are willing to pay for a public good in the form of a private school is readily apparent at Chelsea Day, where the tuition buys three things that most public schools are no longer able to provide: a plethora of materials, a very low student-to-teacher ratio, and well-kept premises. The tab is steep: Tuition at Chelsea Day ranges from $7,050 for five full days to $2,200 for two half days each week. These fees are similar to those charged by the other private kindergartens in the area. Nonetheless, Rosenberg contends, the fees are barely enough to pay the school's expenses, allow for modest salaries, and buy supplies; for instance, the school is unable to provide health-care benefits for all employees—"A real goal, but not economically feasible right now." Nor can the school afford to offer any scholarships. During a cash-flow crisis a few years ago, Jean's board of directors recommended that the school institute a bond program. "I was against it because I thought this would place the school out of the financial range of many households in the community." However, she recognized the operating necessity and reluctantly agreed to the measure. Now a family must post a $750 bond before a child enters the school; the money is returned, without interest, the October after the child leaves. The cash-flow crisis eased, and since then, the school has been on an even financial keel and at full capacity. Chelsea Day now has more applicants than it can accept. "I'm selective in that I try to take as many boys as girls, to balance the age groups—not too many who are two years six months as opposed to two years nine months, for instance. And I try to give priority to cultural and racial diversity, when possible. We're not 'first come, first served.' "

Because Chelsea Day is at capacity, Rosenberg would like to expand. More students, if they could be accommodated in a space contiguous to her current area, would bring in more money but entail only a relatively small added cost. That she is a director and not entirely an entrepreneur is revealed in her attitude concerning a trade-off that might come with larger size: loss of very close touch with the parents. "Being responsive to fifty-five families stretches me; I don't know what having more families would permit." She has dreamed, though, of establishing an early childhood learning center that would teach parenting skills—a community service, with courses offered for modest fees. Expansion of the classrooms and establishment of a parenting center would be feasible in the downstairs half of the building, but, as mentioned earlier, Jean is having difficulty getting a bank to agree to giving her a mortgage on that half. Madelyn Simon has another buyer waiting in the wings and needs to move by January of 1994, so there is a sense that the window of opportunity for Chelsea Day's expansion is a narrow one.

Jean's idea for a parenting center highlights an intriguing gray area. Such a center would be construed as providing a public good and applauded as a positive service to the community: Why couldn't a public school offer it? Has the conception of what we expect to obtain from government in terms of public goods been diminished, or is it that we understand that in an age of belt-tightening for governments, there is little likelihood that a state-supported school system would find a way to offer such a service, except if it were to be funded by a private foundation? More likely, such an additional service that the community might well benefit from will have to be provided for by private enterprise—or not exist at all.

The Chelsea Day School empties out at three in the afternoon. Very shortly thereafter, a small parade of two- to three-dozen elementary-school-age children, two adult men, and a few teen-agers can be seen and occasionally heard singing while wending their way through the streets from the vicinity of PS 41 on 11th Street to the red barn door on 18th. There the children of Allan's Afterschool claim places on Chelsea Day's rooftop playground un-til six o'clock, when they are picked up after work by their parents.

The group's Pied Piper is Allan Margolies, a substitute teacher in the city public school system. Allan is in his forties, but even though his hair—today in a ponytail—is becoming flecked with gray, he conveys the sense of being perpetually young, perhaps because of his continual association with children.

Allan's after-school-care enterprise, in its relationships to Chel-sea Day and to the public schools of the area, is the educational equivalent of Pino Luongo and Jim Harb in their complicated part-nerships with Barneys. In business terms, Allan is a small-niche marketer whose enterprise fills a need that neither Chelsea Day nor PS 41 had been willing to meet.

Here's how it evolved: Twenty years ago, after completing his master's degree in English, Allan returned to New York City and took a temporary position teaching a kindergarten and first-grade class at PS 41, which was quite near his apartment. "I discovered that I liked teaching children of that age and was good at it," he recalls. His family had run a summer day camp for many years, and Allan had worked as head counselor there, which also contrib-uted to his ability to work with the children. He was ready to work at PS 41 for a second year, but because of the seniority system he was bumped from the job by another teacher who wanted it. "Then some of the parents at the school asked me if instead of teaching I could care for their children after classes." Agreeing to do so, he established the after-school program in the apartment he and his wife, Mary Ann, shared and ran it from there for ten years. Then their son, Avi, was born—making the apartment more crowded—and Jean Rosenberg moved the Chelsea Day School to its current location. Allan began renting space from Chelsea Day, an associ-ation that has proved mutually beneficial and pleasant.

The niche has grown steadily, and today Allan is seconded at the Afterschool by Kevin Zilber, a younger kindergarten teacher who has also been a K–1 sub and teacher at PS 41; by his son, Avi; and by a handful of teenagers who were once clients and are now paid assistants. "They like to hang around, and I like to have them around," Allan says. "I love watching them grow up. And because they've been here so long, they're really great with the younger kids." Virtually all of the children in the group attend public schools. In one classroom, some are doing supervised homework; in a second, another bunch are working on the activity-of-the-day, dance/movement; and in the largest inside space, more are playing games. Still others are making good use of the playground. At five o'clock it will be hot-chocolate time, with extra servings available for those children who help out by cleaning up or doing other chores, such assistance not to be too narrowly defined.

Allan's charge is $65 a week if a child comes all five days; the fees go up slightly per day if fewer days are used. "It's basically a service for working parents," he points out. "It allows them to have a full day of work and not to worry because they know that their children are OK." Extra charges are added for special activities like karate, for which trained experts are available. His service is insured, and Allan also offers it on school holidays, when he takes the children bowling, to museums, or on other outings.

"Today's kids are more undisciplined," Allan notes. "They do a lot of acting out in school and have less ability to concentrate than they used to. I try to make an environment that's calm, that allows each child some independence but also some structure. We seldom have any fights, but if we do, we talk to each kid separately and thoroughly. That can't always happen in school. And here, also, the kids get to use their imagination and to make their own choices." He likens what happens in the after-school sessions to group therapy, in which there is "lots of verbalizing needs and feelings." The nurturing environment is one reason parents and children adore Allan. Another is that he has more males than females working for him—a feature also uncommon in the early grades.

There is one troubling cloud on Allan's horizon. A new principal has taken over at PS 41 and has instituted an after-hours program there that seems almost to be modeled on Allan's. This competing plan uses regular schoolteachers, is obviously convenient for the parents, and charges less per day than Allan can. "After all, they don't have to pay rent and insurance," Margolies points out. He doesn't know how many children are being lured away from his service to the public-school program, but he is pleased that the rival has made one cardinal mistake: Not understanding the clientele or the nature of the service to be provided, the school has insisted that the parents pay for the entire semester's child-minding costs in advance. "That's simply not possible or practical for many of the parents," he says. "Besides, here, if a kid doesn't show up one day, I don't feel comfortable charging the parents for that day, even if they told me beforehand that they were going to use it. Most parents will continue to prefer my pay-as-your-child-goes program. I hope."

Two entities that like the Postal Service are in the middle of the spectrum of public-goods providers and must provide service to all who request it and can pay certain minimal charges are the privately owned Consolidated Edison and Nynex, both of which have installations on this block. At one time these companies or their predecessors were government-sanctioned monopolies. Con Ed is still pretty much in that category, as it has no real competitors within the geographical area that it serves, but Nynex, as merely the local successor to AT&T, has competitors aplenty these days.

The Con Ed substation on the block is a place that non-employees look at but do not enter, a fenced-in open-air sculpture of wires, transformers, and machinery in enclosed buildings, with danger signs all about. This substation is one of many focal points in the city where power generated elsewhere, mostly north and west of New York, some from as far away as Canada, is received, stepped down, and redistributed through underground lines to the buildings of the surrounding area. In a few other geographical regions of the country, state-regulated power monopolies are now beginning to be challenged by smaller providers, but not in New York City, even though New York's residents and businesses pay some of the highest electric power rates in the country. Critics insist that the cost to consumers of this particular public good, electric power, could be lowered by competition here.

In the early 1970s, the New York Telephone division of AT&T—a company that was then a countrywide monopoly—expanded rapidly in response to the growth of the financial services industry in Manhattan, which required lots of new telephone lines. That expansion was accompanied by an expansion of AT&T's managerial cadre; thousands of managers chose to work for the phone company then, in part because they believed their jobs would be secure for life. What few of them foresaw was a landmark event in 1983, the court-mandated breakup of the parent company, AT&T. This action to open up competition for long-distance services established seven regional "Baby Bells," each of which was expected to be financially viable. Nynex now serves New York and New England, grosses approximately $13 billion a year, and with 80,000 employees is the largest private employer in New York State, second only in total employees to the state government.

The Nynex facility on our block, the Art Deco skyscraper that stretches between 17th and 18th Streets just west of Seventh Avenue, was built in 1931; today, ten years after Nynex was formed, there is turmoil among the employees in the building, and it is due to technological advances and to the sort of competition that was never dreamed about when the building opened in 1931. That people still have a hard time thinking about it is evidenced by the now-outmoded insignia of Ma Bell that still graces the marble facade and the ornate bronze doors, and by the New York Tel logos that accompany the Nynex ones on the repair and service vans that line 17th Street in the early mornings and are dispatched from an office here. This skyscraper is half empty, and why that is so will be explored in a later chapter about the consequences of technological innovations for businesses on this block. One element in the mix is the difficulties for Nynex that stem from still being mandated by the government to provide basic residential telephone services—part of any definition of public goods in relation to phone service—while its new competitors are not required to do so.

It is November; on Seventh Avenue, the ginkgo trees are dropping their sour fruit on the sidewalks, where passersby mash them into a fragrant paste. Along Eighth, the spindly trees are bare, though the weather seems too warm for winter. The Pasta Pot restaurant on the southeast corner of 18th and Eighth is similarly betwixt and between, half open and half closed. The iron grate is down on a Sunday, a day on which they used to do a good brunch business, and on other days displays notices that the kitchen is shut for renovations but that the bar is open for happy hour. Above the restaurant is a drab three-story tenement that has at various times been a grocery store, a leather bar, and a church. It is now occupied by the Special Events fund-raising unit of the nonprofit Gay Men's Health Crisis (GMHC).

Manhattan is a center for charitable organizations, among other reasons because the concentration of wealth in the city provides a substantial donor base. GMHC was formed eleven years ago in response to the flood of early reported cases of AIDS in the homosexual male population, a flood that the founders believed was not being met by adequate responses from the appropriate public-goods providers, the hospitals and other elements of the health-care system. This building was GMHC's second home, which it quickly outgrew. Today, with an annual budget of $25 million, a paid staff of 250, and 3,600 registered clients, GMHC is the leading private agency caring for people with AIDS; from a handful of different buildings in Chelsea, including this one, it offers telephone or in-person counseling and legal services, it hands out AIDS prevention information, and it provides meals and other assistance at a day treatment center. No longer treating only gay males, GMHC also offers services to those who have contracted AIDS through infected needles, blood transfusions, or heterosexual sex; 10 percent of the clients are now women. The HIV-infected population of New York is estimated at 235,000 people. According to the New York City Department of Health, 40,000 people have died of AIDS-related causes in New York City, 9,000 in the past year.

Although you won't find many people in this neighborhood objecting to GMHC—even the "straight" merchants carry its posters in their windows so they won't be considered anti-gay— there is some belief in the wider population that GMHC has perhaps been too effective. The cause of stopping AIDS has enjoyed wide publicity and considerable charitable support, in large part due to GMHC's efforts. Critics argue that the emphasis on AIDS in our society is out of proportion to the toll the disease is taking on the population; other diseases, they point out, affect greater numbers of people but do not generate the level of concern and donations that have been attracted to the AIDS cause.

Eighty-six percent of the GMHC budget comes from private donors, while 14 percent comes from government sources. Of the private funds, 51 percent is realized from special events. A portion of that money is donated by corporate event sponsors, more by thousands of individuals who make contributions, and a substantial amount is the result of the work of phone callers and envelope stuffers at the facility on the corner of 18th and Eighth. At the entrance on ground level, GMHC Special Events looks as if it might be a scene shop, but the second floor is a partitioned, modern office space whose whitewashed walls are decorated with slogan-filled posters. On the third floor are banks of telephones and an open cupboard with an inordinate amount of sodas and snacks. Patricia Evert, the Director of Special Events, says these are for the volunteers: "We want to make them feel welcome while they're donating their time." In this building, the charity's large fundraising events are organized: the annual Walkathon, Danceathon,

Radiothon, and art auction. Evert and three other people are on staff, and event coordinators are hired on a project basis. "We draw from a pool of 4,000 volunteers and get from thirty to fifty people here each evening between 6:30 and 9:30. The calls taken by the counseling volunteers at headquarters require a lot of training. We're more flexible. Right now we're focused on the Danceathon. Things get more hectic as the event date gets closer. The last week is frantic. Now that the disease has affected a wider population, the marketing must, too," Evert adds.

The volunteers are men and women of all ages and backgrounds, straight and gay alike. Volunteers receive instruction before starting to make calls. "For instance," Patricia says, "we never leave a message, even on an answering machine, because you never know who in the person's family or circle might not know that the person called is involved with AIDS fund-raising. Our goal last year was $7.2 million, and we made over nine," Patricia sighs, "but unfortunately that's still not enough."

Way back on the evening of January 7, 1985, under cover of darkness, demolition crews using a crane with a saw-toothed scoop bucket ripped into four dilapidated buildings on 44th Street near Broadway and within a short time leveled them. Gas, electricity, and water lines had not been shut off, nor had a demolition permit been obtained; it was just good luck, experts later agreed, that there had been no explosion. Shortly, it was learned that the developer Harry Macklowe had ordered the buildings torn down to make way for a hotel that would bear his name. A hue and cry followed, in part because one demolished building was an SRO, a single-room-occupancy hotel, and the city was in the process of making certain that no further SROs would be torn down, since they were being used to house welfare clients who could not afford regular housing. Macklowe was ordered to pay a $2 million fine so the city could buy and renovate an SRO to replace the one he'd illegally demolished.

It turned out that at the same time the city was ordering Macklowe to pay $2 million in restitution, the brothers of the St. Francis of Assisi monastery were looking for a third facility in the city to house the chronically mentally ill, and the result was the mission on our block.

Since the Franciscans were chartered in the thirteenth century, the order has been caring for the poor who arrived on their doorsteps. In response to a Vatican II broadening of that mandate, twenty years ago Father John McVean arrived at the New York monastery, charged with doing more to help the poor. As translated by the Franciscans in Manhattan, that "more" really has to do with providing a public good, specifically a public good that state-run facilities have been mandated to stop providing, at least in the quantities that once were common.

McVean and John Felice are both solidly built, quietly intense men in their fifties, with iron-gray crew cuts—on the street, you might mistake them for policemen or firemen and would surely think they were blood brothers. In them compassion is not worn on the sleeve but seems to be a deep-flowing inner stream. In the early 1970s, looking for poor to assist, McVean found a focus. Near the monastery was an SRO hotel on 32nd Street whose occupants had been recently released from mental institutions. In an economy move around that time, New York State had emptied its mental institutions of long-term residents who so long as they took their medication were considered harmless and stable. McVean recalls that these former patients "were swinging from the rafters, not taking their medication properly, and needing lots of help to avoid becoming homeless." Galvanized to take care of this poor population on their doorstep, the Franciscans opened a first permanent residence for them in 1980, a second in 1983, and were looking for a third in 1985 when the Macklowe story hit the front pages of every newspaper in town.

The developer would have been only too happy to give the money directly and publicly to the Franciscans, but the city mid-level bureaucracy wanted to take charge of it. A fracas ensued. The Franciscans were told that they had a hundred days in which to find a suitable building. SRO owners began to call them, offering buildings that just happened to have $2 million price tags. The one they settled on, decrepit but functional, was on Eighth Avenue between 17th and 18th. The owner wanted $3 million, and they compromised at $1.92 million and the leasing back to the owner at $1 a year for twenty years the two commercial spaces that now house the Blue Moon and Cola's restaurants. (You can bet that the owner re-rents the space for a lot more than $1 a year each.) Then municipal officials started to renege and to delay the process past the hundred days; they also assessed the property at $1.2 million and said the city wouldn't pay more. An editorial in the *New York Times* exposed the tangle, the Astor Fund and other charitable organizations stepped in, and the building was bought and renovated. At the opening of the St. Francis Residence III in 1987, Governor Mario Cuomo and Mayor Ed Koch made big fusses over the Franciscans and gave them proclamations suitable for framing. "After that," Felice says, "the public officials pretty much ignored us."

The Franciscans later invited Macklowe to a function, and in return he invited them to his office, where the tenor of the conversation among his aides was how magnanimous Macklowe had been in donating the money to buy the building. "I opened my mouth and said something about Macklowe having been fined and got some dirty looks," McVean confides. In fact, Macklowe got all his money back from the city in the form of additional tax abatements, so it really cost him very little except the short-term interest on the $2 million. The residence is still on the developer's mailing list, though, and circulars for the opening of new buildings and charitable events arrive occasionally in the mail, sandwiched between flyers on special deals for hypodermic needles and bulk rates for mattresses.

If GMHC is everywhere visible in the neighborhood because of its counter displays and facilities, the St. Francis Residence III is almost invisible; many nearby residents do not know of its existence, even though its tenants regularly roam the neighborhood. Advocacy for AIDS patients has resulted in widespread knowledge about the disease and its victims; in contrast, the public knows very little about the chronically mentally ill among us, who have been turned out of state mental hospitals. Not incidentally, the two categories of unfortunates—AIDS victims and the mentally ill—make up a large fraction of those who are homeless in New York City.

The wide six-story St. Francis III building is neat and sightly, the bricks steam-cleaned, the wooden door shellacked, its glass panels clear. At the end of the entrance hallway is a manager's office with slots for mail. The winding stairwell of stone, wood, and steel is the building's glory, open in the center but with light grillwork between floors to deter suicides and the sort of tumbling-down accidents that people on heavy medication often suffer. Some of the eighty residents walk about, displaying the damped-down, shuffling demeanor of the continually medicated and chronically mentally ill. One office has a MetPath pickup box attached to its door. In another, two staff members separate out blue, yellow, and orange pills for the nurse to dispense, while a third disburses some money to residents for their daily activities.

This is actually a private-public partnership, in that the city, the state, and local hospitals cooperate in the work of the residence. The staff includes three part-time psychiatrists, a full-time city social worker and recreation therapists whose entire clientele is on-site, and a psychiatric nurse. Funding for these professionals comes from a variety of public and private sources.

"Shelter is a dirty word around here," McVean advises, because that word is associated with temporary residences that are subject to many abuses. This is the permanent residence of eighty chronically ill people who have passed a screening process to obtain entry; usually referred by social service agencies, applicants must be long-term residents of the city, over the age of twenty-five, not considered dangerous, and not current alcohol or drug abusers. "Once someone is with us, we assume they'll be here for the rest of their lives," Felice explains. The residents are not considered sick enough to be hospitalized, but are clearly not well enough to hold down a job or have an independent life. Long too ill to be cared for properly by their families, they have become permanent wards of the state. "If they weren't here, they'd be homeless; many of them have been."

Critics of the Franciscans' effort say that the residences are not really attacking the overall problems of the homeless or mentally ill because the Franciscans take the cream of the crop and refuse to accept as residents the most difficult and recalcitrant among the homeless and mentally ill population. "Our people were as severely at risk as any others on the outside," McVean points out. The residents may be a small fraction of the state's estimated 95,000 mentally ill, but they are a larger proportion of the estimated 8,500 mentally ill thought to be homeless. "At least here, they have a chance for a life." The Franciscans provide a room for seven days a week, along with breakfast, lunch, and dinner from Monday through Friday. No meals on the weekends is a way of encouraging the tenants' independence, so that the residence does not become just another mental hospital for them. "The point is to permit these people to have lives in the community," McVean says. Whereas it costs upward of $20,000 a year to keep a person in a mental hospital, here it costs $20 a day, or around $7,000 a year. Virtually everyone at St. Francis III is on SSI, the government's program for the permanently disabled; the current SSI payment is $520 a month. Rent is pegged at $225 a month and is deducted from the residents' monthly government checks.

"We joke that our clients are like rent-controlled tenants," Felice says. Like rent-controlled private apartment dwellers, the residents seldom leave voluntarily, they can't be readily evicted, and their housing costs are subsidized. Food and upkeep of the facilities costs more than the $225 per person per month the Franciscans charge, and the order makes up the difference with contributions. "At our last end-of-the-fiscal-year meeting, I pointed out that the overhead could be met by a $15-a-month-per-bed increase in the rent, but this was dismissed as not feasible because it would leave the residents with too little daily money."

Vacancies arise at the Franciscan residences because there has been a death—usually, a resident's body is found in a room during a routine morning check. "They smoke too much, don't eat right, but those aren't the sole causes of death," Felice says. "Most of them have had hard lives, many health problems, and they just have heart attacks or fatal strokes and die in their beds—not the worst way to go."

"Recently the *Times* published a series of articles on the problem of homelessness in the city," McVean observed. "At the end, the experts all come to the conclusion that what's needed to solve the problem is a series of small, in-community residences which provide support services"—a virtual description of what the St. Francis residences have been providing to the chronically mentally ill for more than a decade. "We had a good laugh over that."

After deductions for room and board, residents have about $300 a month left to spend. They can bank the money, and some do, but most aren't very regular about husbanding it and often overspend in the first few days after cashing their checks, and then they have nothing left for later in the month. Accordingly, the staff has a program that permits the residents to bank with them; each day, a staff member doles out one-thirtieth of a resident's monthly remainder. Residents can also earn a bit of extra money by taking their own clothes and bedding to a nearby Laundromat once a week, something the friars encourage because it is an independent action. One or two residents manage to find and keep part-time jobs in the community; Kenny, a long-termer, regularly does some tasks for the newsstand. On the weekends, residents have to find and pay for their own meals, so they buy sandwiches at the delis and patronize the supermarkets, where, according to the friars, they mostly purchase junk food. Through such purchases, a great deal of the money paid to the residents via SSI goes fairly directly to the retail businesses of this neighborhood—on the order of $25,000 a month.

The fall of 1993 is a moment in time when the need for and the size of government transfer payments is being more closely questioned than ever before, so it is important to note that most of what are considered transfer payments from the federal, state, and local governments to organizations such as GMHC and to the residents of St. Francis III remains in the community—14 percent of the GMHC budget ($3.5 million a year) and most of the SSI money ($500,000 a year) that goes to St. Francis III residents.

December 1, 1993, has been designated World AIDS Awareness Day. An AIDS awareness stamp is to be issued by the Postal Service, and in a political coup of some magnitude, it has been arranged that Postmaster General Marvin Runyon will lead the ceremonies as the first such stamp to go on sale in the country does so at noon—on our block, at the Old Chelsea Post Office on 18th Street. Prominent among the arrangers is the Gay Men's Health Crisis organization. Since mid-November, the lobby of the Old Chelsea has featured in one corner of the marble interior the GMHC's Wall of Remembrance for AIDS victims—large placards and bulletin boards, containing photos and mementos of those who have succumbed. Postmaster Ed Risdell has permitted the display as part of his outreach to the community.

As noon approaches on the first of December, outside the Old Chelsea are many Postal Service cars, some from the Postal Service's police force, as well as a handful of vans from various television stations and networks. There are also sacks of mail addressed to Governor Mario Cuomo in Albany. On the east side of the lobby, near the Wall of Remembrance, tables have been set up on which community groups have displays of information and pamphlets. On the west side of the lobby is another table to be used for first-day cancellations. Postal employees in their neatest uniforms roam the floor along with a large contingent of GMHC workers and a few delegates from other community organizations. The GMHC people have prepared postcards to mail to Governor Cuomo. Onlookers are encouraged to sign these so that they can be added to the thousands already collected that are sitting in the mail sacks outside the building.

Most visitors had expected this to be a dignified and somewhat solemn event. There would be a short speech by Postmaster General Runyon to accompany the ceremonious unveiling of an enlarged version of the stamp, with its design of a red ribbon curled into a loop, and the affair might well provoke tears for the victims of the disease. The Postal Service seemed to have done this one right: For instance, it has arranged the copyright of the stamp's design so that nonprofit organizations can use it freely to make ancillary products—T-shirts, posters, and the like—from which they can profit. It seems like a lovely arrangement: dissimilar, previously unlinked organizations working in concert on a public-goods project.

Many people with press passes are in the room. Now television camera crews enter, with their profusion of cables; all must step gingerly to avoid tripping on them. Several local stations are represented, and there is also a crew from CNN, accompanied by the most recognizable newsman in the room, former CBS correspondent Bruce Morton. A perfectly coiffed, silver-haired and dark-suited postmaster general and a beaming Ed Risdell emerge from the back work areas of the lobby. An appreciative audience of a few dozen pamphleteers begins to take their seats and the television cameras and crews turn their lenses and attention to the two men. They are about to do the honors—when ACT-UP hits.

A phalanx of angry-faced men and women in ACT-UP T-shirts and bearing placards condemning the issuance of the stamp storm through the open doors of the post office and into the lobby. The AIDS Coalition To Unleash Power calls itself a group of urban guerrillas who believe that not enough is being done to counter AIDS and that any step currently being taken by private or public entities must be protested as inadequate. The television cameras and lights turn toward the ACT-UP group and jostle for better position to record their actions. The group knocks over the few chairs, corners Runyon and Risdell, and shouts "We need a cure, not a stamp" and "Lick AIDS, not stamps." Their placards castigate President Bill Clinton for not fulfilling his campaign promise of a "Manhattan Project" to make an all-out attack on AIDS.

Everyone is standing, now, as if at some outlandish cocktail party. The presentation is a shambles. ACT-UP has its own postcards, which the protesters throw around like confetti; these advocate Congressional passage of a bill that asks for vastly increased funding for the anti-AIDS effort.

The rather helpless GMHC workers look dismayed while Runyon and Risdell try to maintain their dignity, and the few Postal Service police who are in front of them prepare to defend them against physical attack. It is clear that the officials did not expect this demonstration and are chagrined by it; had they expected it, there might have been more police. Negotiations with the protesters finally permit Runyon to give a shortened version of his prepared speech, but then the protesters shout him into silence and take camera and audio focus. After two minutes of the screaming, the post office police decide to make their move and form a cordon behind which Runyon, Risdell, and the other officials can reach the entrance to the enclosed back areas of the post office.

Since there is no one to demonstrate against, ACT-UP now winds down; the protesters form into a line and march out the front door. Some camera crews follow. Almost immediately, rival bunches of public relations people from ACT-UP and GMHC circulate among the reporters, telling them that this or that prominent spokesperson is available for an interview. Denny Lee of ACT-UP tells Angela C. Allen of the *New York Post* that the AIDS stamp is a "useless symbol . . . a joke . . . a smokescreen" to hide the lack of real government action. "The stamp does not wipe out AIDS," echoes ACT-UP's Kevin Jennings to reporters from the *New York Daily News*. Patricia Evert and the GMHC people, whose neat tables with informative material are in the midst of all this, look around with tight lips, as if trying to figure out what they can salvage from this fracas. GMHC promises reporters a "mail-in" of all the cards being sent to Cuomo, many of which were inscribed at GMHC's big dance held ten days ago. A straggling camera crew decides to see if they can get a sound bite from a local politician. The other camera crews leave. A few awareness volunteers hug one another, then also exit the post office.

The lobby is a mess. Maintenance employees emerge, to right and fold the knocked-over chairs, then begin to sweep up. They are inordinately careful not to pick up with their bare hands anything that someone with AIDS might have touched—evidence that AIDS awareness has a long way to go. A few remaining GMHC people confer; though shocked that one AIDS-fighting group would disrupt the event of another, especially an event like this, which was considered a breakthrough to national understanding, they say they should have expected that the radical and perpetually unsatisfied ACT-UP group would disrupt the proceedings. Now that quiet has resumed, Ed Risdell pokes his head out of the back area. As the sweepup continues, two women postal employees sit at a table and very carefully stamp "First day of issue" and "AIDS Awareness Station" cancellation marks on a few customers' newly bought red-ribbon stamps affixed to postcards and envelopes. They make sure that only a small portion of the stamp is covered by ink, so that the stamp is fully visible and therefore of value to collectors.

Later that evening, footage from the demonstration proves unexpectedly absent from television reports of AIDS awareness day. ACT-UP's antics, and even the unveiling of the stamp by Runyon, are overshadowed by other protests, principally one that took place as President Clinton was speaking in Washington but also by images of Liza Minnelli singing on behalf of another AIDS research organization, AMFAR, and so on. The incident at the old Chelsea Post Office barely rates a mention in the next day's *Post* and *Daily News*, and none at all in the *New York Times*.

Chapter 9

TECHNOLOGICAL INNOVATION

THE TECHNOLOGICAL revolution imposed by the need to cut costs and spearheaded by the computer is in the process of changing virtually every enterprise on the block. It has, for instance, made obsolete the cliché "no tickee, no laundry." The two dry cleaners no longer have to rely on tickets alone as a way to match up customers and their clothing: Ticketing keyed into the computer with the customer's name works even when a customer has mislaid his or her copy of a receipt. In one cleaners, a motorized chain belt carrying cleaned clothes is now also computer-controlled, saving steps for the owner and resulting in customers spending less time in the shop.

The efficiency of the staff at Food/Bar at its busiest hours is now far greater than it would have been only a few years ago, because computerized ordering by the waitpersons has outmoded paper writing of tickets here, as it has at Solco Plumbing Supplies. At Food/Bar, at Solco, at the Chelsea Day School, at the Chisholm Prats Gallery, similar tracking innovations provide the entrepreneurs with precise information. Such information is helpful in controlling inventory, making it easier to tell how many half days Little Susie attended school in a particular month, or catering to the gallery customers' preferences in collectible posters.

It is difficult to say whether the improvements represented by this handful of examples is resulting in the loss of jobs, as occurred so palpably in the ravages that automation wrought on the American blue-collar manufacturing workplace in the '50s, '60s, and '70s. But if job losses come, they will take the form of "silent firings" that occur when for one reason or another the jobholder moves on and no one is hired to fill the position. In the fall of 1993, one silent firing of sorts is in process at Solco as manager Peter Miceli voluntarily leaves the firm (where he has worked for about six months) to go out on his own—not as a competitor, but as a customer. Peter had only joined Solco in the spring after his own business had gone sour; back then he had been happy to work for someone else and not endure the headaches of being the boss. Now he is once again paying attention to a siren call.

"Maybe the taste of being out on your own isn't something you really ever lose," he suggests, and explains that after six months of exposure to the peculiar exigencies of the plumbing business in New York City, he has made a decision. "In the wholesale and distribution ends, margins are getting slimmer all the time. But if you do it retail—have a plumber's license—you can make good money." One close friend has just obtained such a license, another expects to get it on the next go-around, and Peter believes that the three of them will make a good team. Adding to his readiness to go out on his own is his wife's new status. "She passed her exam and is now putting in the two years of work for a public accounting firm" required for obtaining a full CPA license. With one partner in the family bringing in a stable income, the other can now afford to start a business. Peter told Sherman that he would be leaving, and did it properly, giving enough notice. It would have been discourteous to leave in any other fashion—and besides, he wants his new company to be able to obtain supplies on credit from Solco.

As a manager at a supply depot, Peter had been surrounded by forests of pipes and fixtures; at Capmor Plumbing, he's in a small, rather bare office whose main fixture is a telephone. Peter seems exhilarated to once again be an entrepreneur. His worries at the new office are about receiving payment for work the firm has already done and about getting Capmor onto the lists for competitive bidding. There are small City of New York jobs to be sought as well as some work for New York University and bids to make for contract work for other large landlords. He and his partners have some money set aside from their own funds to "grow the business" and so are less subject to cash-flow problems than other newly minted plumbers might be. "It'll probably take about two years to get to the point where all three of us are bringing home good incomes." By that time, Peter expects to be ready to pass the New York City plumber's exam himself. He's not interested in company growth for its own sake and wants to keep the enterprise at a level manageable by himself and his partners, maybe a half-dozen trucks and three times that many people; currently, they have three trucks.

As for the silent firing, the partners at Solco made their own decision. Hiring a manager had been somewhat of an experiment, a way to relieve the pressure on Vic Sherman and to generate new business. But the salesmen are the largest business getters, and the partners decide that because of this, and of their computerized setup, they no longer need a manager, so they divide up what had been Miceli's duties between two long-term employees. This enables those two employees to obtain raises, and the firm to have what had been the managerial functions filled without high additional cost.

Looked at in the terms of corporate America, the transition at Solco occasioned by Peter Miceli's departure is the elimination of a middle manager. On a much larger scale—some would even call it catastrophic—that is what has been happening at Nynex.

We tend to think of technological advances as having the greatest impact on blue-collar jobs, but computerization is taking an almost equal toll on the white-collar managerial force as big companies try to produce more with fewer employees. In 1990, the corporate chiefs of Nynex decided that 20 percent of its managers had to go within three years. Several thousand midlevel managers left Nynex in 1990–92, but these severances were accomplished through attrition and early retirements. In mid-1993, however, the belief among Nynex employees is that the benign measures have already absorbed all who wished to go and that in order to reach the 20 percent goal, within the next few months several more thousand managers will receive actual termination notices—the first real firings in the company's history. Moreover, since the chieftains have broadened their edict to shrinking the entire workforce, not just managers but installers, switching board workers, and assistance operators at 18th Street are also uncertain whether or not their next paycheck will contain a pink slip or a not-to-be-refused invitation to retire.

Automation of any sort seeks efficiencies so the company can compete better. At Nynex, it is being driven by the fact that the giant company has increasingly been encountering serious competitors in the provision of local phone services and that because of declining margins in its core business, upper management has been looking to new fields to produce revenues. Currently, 86 percent of Nynex's revenues comes from services rendered to local customers—what this book has called "the provision of public goods," and Nynex calls "providing universal service"—but the company believes that only headaches and reduced revenues lie ahead in that core business.

Nynex chairman William Ferguson has recently tried to find investments that would take the company away from merely providing hardware and lines and into furnishing the content that will be carried on those lines. The backing of the Viacom bid for Paramount is one of these. Others are an attempt to increase the company's income from cellular service, which is expected to be quite lucrative in the future; from cable television service in Great Britain, where Nynex is the largest supplier; from new telephone systems it is building for Thailand and other Southeast Asian countries; from new fiber optic cables under the Atlantic and the Pacific; and from services such as stock quotes and other "nonvoice" information. Nynex would like to do more, but federal regulations still prohibit companies that offer local telephone service from also selling cable television service in the areas they serve; Nynex and the other Baby Bells find these regulations unduly restrictive and are lobbying for permission to enter the lucrative cable market.

Simultaneously, Nynex is scrambling to retain local service dollars that it once took for granted, fighting competitors less hampered by restrictions and regulations, such as MFS (Metropolitan Fiber Systems) of Omaha and Teleport of Staten Island. Recently, MFS took a $1 million-a-year customer away from Nynex, and Teleport beat out Nynex for a $6.3 million contract to provide pay phones at the two New York City airports, the bus terminal, and the World Trade Center. The reasons why upstarts like MFS and Teleport can win contracts by offering some local service more cheaply than Nynex are that they have fewer employees, which means lower costs, and they are not encumbered with the same obligation to provide universal service. "The new guys take the business-service cream and leave us with the job of providing telephone access to run-down areas and residential customers," a Nynex official points out, with very reasonable pique. This is not a new complaint, and an arrangement has been worked out by various governments so that these upstart companies must pay into a fund to partially reimburse Nynex for universal service; nonetheless, Nynex believes its big-dollar obligations far outweigh the pocket change it obtains from the fund. Moreover, New York State's Public Service Commission and the FCC are now mandating that, in order to foster competition, Nynex and other regional carriers reduce leased-line charges to the upstarts from $270 a circuit to only $5 a circuit. That's some deep discount!

One result of all this is that the Nynex skyscraper on our block is only half full.

Larry Forella, the building's property manager, also oversees another large Nynex facility on Second Avenue at 14th Street, and three ancillary buildings. Forella has the look of a man into whose lap all problems seem to get dumped. On the walls of his ground-floor office are photos of classic cars of the 1950s and 1960s, which he has restored by hand. In the beautiful Art Deco–embellished hallways, in the out-of-date elevators, people come up to Larry bearing various difficulties. His beeper is seldom silent.

This building is the focal point for 120,000 local phone lines, half residential and half commercial, in one of the most highly concentrated telephone usage areas of Manhattan. The service district is bounded by the Hudson River, Broadway on the east, 24th Street on the north, and Canal Street on the south, encompassing all of Chelsea and most of Greenwich Village and SoHo—an area that overlaps that served by the Old Chelsea Post Office, but that also extends a mile farther downtown.

The computer giveth and the computer taketh away. At the moment, three floors of the building are empty—one casualty is the ground-floor cafeteria, closed for lack of customers—but the upper floors have been converted to house a Computer Technical Learning Center. All those in the company who have touch with a computer, and many employees who work for Nynex's customers that use monitors that interface with Nynex's, are trained in these classrooms. The building's employees have a lot of respect for the CTLC; they understand it to be a lifesaving device for people in danger of losing their jobs. "We're doing a lot of retraining," Forella reports as we tour the CTLC, "giving computer skills to employees who'd otherwise be automated out of jobs." What he doesn't say, because it is obvious, is that those who can master the computer may survive in the company, but those who don't will almost certainly be ushered out the door. Across the country the use of video-display terminals, or VDTs, as they are called here, is growing. More than 7 million Americans already work in front of a computer-based VDT. The increase in VDTs (and the productivity gains from their use) particularly affect old-line clerical workers, who become vulnerable to being fired—or, at the very least, who are in need of quickly learning how to work with the machines, so they won't be fired.

The automation of telephone equipment is far advanced and can be seen on a grand scale in this building on the through-the-block floors, about 200 feet in length, that house the technical components of basic local service. These are very large spaces for an urban setting, warehouse-sized floors. One entire floor is taken up with switchers; these connect a caller to the other local line called in the 212 area code. Only one man is present in a room otherwise filled with computer-directed machines and kept at almost frigid temperatures to enable the machinery to function optimally. The absence of other attendants is standard for a slow day when there are no known system problems, but Forella asserts that "People do come running when there's a big glitch."

The feeling of automated systems being serviced by a few human beings carries over onto a third floor. There are a dozen people in this area, roaming among four banks of floor-to-ceiling electrical boards, which are composed of thousands of little Lego-piece units, two or three inches long and a half inch wide and thick, with protruding metal spikes. "The gray pieces are normal connectors," Forella explains; he spent years working in a similar room before getting into middle management. "The red or green indicate special arrangements, like internal phones in a company headquarters." On the back side of the boards, thousands of wires protrude. About a dozen people are changing connections, moving wire A so that it connects to B instead of to C. "When you order a new phone, the day before the installer comes to your apartment or office, somebody here physically sets up the connecting wires. The installer only connects the instrument at your end." The connecting of wires is partially automated, but some of it still has to be done by a knowledgeable human being.

Forella has been beeped thrice before entering the call-completion center, which is on another floor. "That means they really must want me," he says, and borrows a line from the supervisor's desk. As he listens, the furrow on his brow deepens.

"Call completion" is a welcome change, because it is a chamber that belongs to human beings. Located in a similar 17th-to-18th Street–wide room, it has an entirely different look, featuring cool purple decor, interesting pastel friezes and paintings of the city, along with a few windows. Here, in ergonometric chairs in front of individual cubicles with large monitors and keyboards, sit about two-dozen middle-aged women with headsets. Their supervisor, Sue, sits in the middle of the room, like a spider commanding her web, with a panel in front of her that allows her to patch in to any of the lines her workers are answering. The job here is to answer calls for directory assistance and assist people who dial 0 to seek an operator's help to complete a call.

These functions used to be at the heart of the phone business; every telephone company building had rows on rows of operators who completed calls for customers. Now, since more than 99 percent of local calls are completed automatically, there are only a half-dozen call-completion rooms scattered all through Nynex's territory. Ten years ago there were fifteen such centers in New York and New England, employing 20,000 operators; today only a few thousand people hold such jobs. To watch these women answer calls through their headsets is to be in the presence of a human transaction that is rapidly becoming obsolete and will shortly vanish into the mist of history. Near the door and on the walls are bulletin boards that feature "complaint call" and "thank-you call" materials: stick and carrot. On a bulletin board by the door, Sue has posted a shocked message saying that the two recent complaint calls could not possibly have been about operators at 18th Street, because hers are better behaved, but that any operator who did what these complainants allege—used offensive language or cut the caller off in midsentence—would be severely disciplined. The more unexpected display, in a lit box on a wall, are the thank-you cards. Occasionally, a grateful customer will call to say that a particular operator has been helpful. A card is made up that celebrates both the operator—her picture is posted—and the complimenting caller, whose name is given.

In the 1950s, about half of all clerical jobs in the country were held by women. During the past thirty years, as men moved more into management, women took over 80 percent of the clerical and records-processing jobs in business and government; in particular, in America's large cities, this expansion opened up employment in clerical positions to minority women. Behind-the-scenes New York is run by such women, and Nynex's call-completion services are almost exclusively so. The company seems to understand that these jobs require infinite patience and a special kind of employee, for it makes available many amenities to counterbalance the flak the operators have to endure. Operators are permitted frequent breaks, provided with a lounge and lockers on the floor, and so on. Of course call-completion operators have quotas—around 700 calls a day—and must not spend too much time on any one call. Of course the supervisor can patch in from her central desk and listen to how well or poorly this or that operator is serving a customer. Of course when an operator wants to go to the ladies' room or do anything other than be at her desk, she has to go to the central desk and sign out and then sign back in again; a little clock sits right by the signing sheet to remind her if she hasn't bothered to glance up to the one above the supervisor's desk.

Nonetheless, Forella maintains that "These women can more or less name their own hours, so long as the supervisor can get the right number of people to cover the jobs." Once the company has been able to successfully train a person for this sort of work and the operator has proved able to do it for a year, he insists, the company tries to do what it can to hold on to her, even to pamper her. Here is a neat paradox of modernization: In economic terms that weigh the women's output versus the cost of their labor, Nynex cannot afford to pay these call-completion operators high salaries—they make, on average, about $15 an hour; however, Nynex seems to have acknowledged that the call-completers provide an essential human connection between the company and its customers, and so while paying them moderate salaries it tries to make the other conditions of employment as comfortable as can be.

Given the evidence of the rest of this building, with its computer learning center and its floors of automated equipment, there seems little likelihood that this small outpost of dignity, the call-completion center with its middle-aged ladies, can hold out very much longer against the tides lapping at its edges, computerization and the need to cut costs in order to meet the new competition.

Forella has no information about that. He is busy readying the building for an influx of middle managers—several hundred sales and managerial people from Residence Marketing and Business Marketing. During the glory days, the need for managers and space to house them was so great that Nynex leased offices in commercial buildings for them; as the leases expire, and as the number of managerial employees shrinks, the remainder are being shifted into wholly owned facilities such as 18th Street.

The breakup of AT&T and the breakneck speed with which communications technologies are advancing have spawned a host of companies much smaller than Nynex but which travel along with it, or in its wake. Around our block, in a 17th Street building adjacent to the Art Deco Nynex skyscraper, is Birns Telecommunications, Inc., which also has offices in suburban New Jersey. In the dark ages before the phone company monopoly was broken up, virtually all telephone-related services for business or residential customers came from Ma Bell. For the past eighteen years, according to its Yellow Pages advertisement, Birns has been selling and servicing office telephone systems; today it claims that over a million times a day, a call is made through equipment installed by Birns. The company works mainly with Japanese equipment makers, such as NEC, SRX, Nitsuko, Toshiba, and Mitel; the NEC logo is featured on their trucks. And so is that of Nynex, because in addition to being a competitor of sorts with Nynex, Birns now works directly with Nynex, and this fall the combination is going quite far out into leading-edge territory by offering a hot, new, technologically very advanced service called ISDN.

Computer aficionados are very excited about ISDN (Integrated Services Digital Network) because an ISDN line enables a business or an individual to transmit voice, data, images, and video, simultaneously if desired, over regular telephone lines. Among the gee-whiz services that ISDN makes easier are working with computer on-line services and the Internet; desktop videoconferencing; and remote access to LANs (Local Area Networks) comprised of workstations in different places that are connected by telephone line.

Birns does not sell ISDN service but sells and services the equipment necessary for most business computer systems to hook up with ISDN. Why go to the expense of installing ISDN-compatible equipment? Nynex and Birns claim that, for instance, the access to on-line services ISDN provides is far better than can be obtained through a modem because transmittal can be much quicker, and in larger volume; that alone makes the $35-to-$50-a-month tab something essential for serious computer users. For businesses, the promise is far greater, because ISDN may be the service that finally makes the remote office and the virtual commuter more likely for the ordinary (rather than the occasional) office worker since it enables data to travel back and forth more readily to that remote office, gives the remote employee a visual link (via easy teleconference) with headquarters, and so on.

What this will do for the economy, for the number of jobs, or even for the ways future work is structured is currently unclear. Fifteen to twenty years ago, when teleconferencing via satellite first became technologically and economically feasible, there were predictions that it would seriously erode business travel, but it turned out that people go to conferences for the camaraderie, serendipitous meetings with clients and suppliers, handshaking, and other human interactions that videoconferencing can't replace, and so its great potential was never fully realized. The decentralization of the headquarters office, via ISDN and ordinary telephone lines, will have to overcome the same human yearning for personal, physical interaction, but it seems more likely to do so because the technology is easier and cheaper to use.

No manufacturing area as a whole has been more affected by technological innovation in the last quarter century than printing and publishing, which are heavily represented on our block. In the nineteenth century, printing and publishing were linked functions of a single business; as book and magazine publishing became profitable independent of a printing plant, the functions and industries separated. By the 1940s, the only major publishers remaining in the big cities who also printed their product themselves were the newspapers. In the past quarter century, the exodus of printing jobs from New York City has been staggering, with tens of thousands of printing positions moving out, generally to rural locations where real estate costs for the sprawling plants are low and where wages are also low. Not all the jobs have gone out of town, however; a great many were simply eliminated by a slew of technological innovations.

As a result of these splits in function and technological improvements, the pattern for publishing in New York became the same as it is for many other businesses that make a product you can hold in your hand—owners are willing to pay the relatively high wages of the city's highly skilled workforce (in publishing, that means editorial and graphic arts skills, as well as sales), but they do their actual manufacturing (printing) out of the city in locations that permit them to take advantage of lower costs. This is the same pattern adopted by Gear Holdings in furniture and home furnishings and by Alain-Guy Giraudon, whose shoes, designed on our block, are actually manufactured in Portugal. Such a pattern is likely to be the wave of the future for manufacturers who choose to continue to have a headquarters in New York.

But what of the manufacturing process itself? Will any of it remain in New York, or for that matter, elsewhere in urban America? Perhaps by examining the ways in which the printing and publishing entities on our block respond to technological innovation we can obtain some answers to the larger question.

The printing and publishing entities around the block represent a wide spectrum of responses to onrushing technological progress. Most companies are concentrated in what is still called the Midtown Graphics Center, at 216 West 18th Street. The building began life as the Monahan Express Company building, serving as a depot for manufacturers. Thirty years ago, a large real estate management firm, the Williams Company, renamed it and touted it to potential renters as having the large and solid floors, the abundant supply of electricity, and the several elevators that printers then deemed necessary. A perusal of out-of-date telephone directories and conversations with current tenants suggest that when this building was at full capacity it was home to two-dozen printers. Now there are six or seven businesses that have something to do with printing.

We've already seen what has been happening to a firm near one end of that spectrum, Guild Mailing, which has been unable (and somewhat unwilling) to buy new equipment and is rapidly becoming uncompetitive; conversations with old-timers in the building suggest that the firms that moved out over the past decade had even more antiquated equipment—and management.

Of those that remain, the occupant of the lowest floors, Downtown Offset, which has been in the building thirteen years, looks most like an old-fashioned printing business. It occupies a sizable amount of space, 20,000 square feet, most of it on the ground floor, which has its own internal loading dock. Signs legible from the street read "Annual Reports. Brochures. Book. Catalogs. Posters. Flyers. Stationery. Complete Prep & Binding. 24-hour service." The offices, up a narrow flight of stairs, are a printerly mess: paper all over the place, the air tinged with ink and oil, the lone desktop computer and a phone-paging system seeming like forced concessions to modernity. One almost expects to see Linotype machines, though there are none here, having been replaced by newer machines that perform similar functions. Cartoons and shopworn mottoes are pinned to the walls: "Do you want your rush job to be rushed ahead of the rush rush that we're rushing now?" and a price list that starts small and whose increases depend on whether the customer wants to wait for the job, watch, or help. The few employees visible are all orthodox Jews wearing yarmulkes, white shirts, and black pants held up by cords.

Manager Oscar Sabel is a portly, powerfully built man in his sixties, white-bearded, with faint cigarette stains on the parts of the beard near his mouth; he characterizes Downtown Offset as "a printer's printer." This means it does contract work for other firms in the printing field and is so well-known to printers that give them business that it has no need to advertise, not even in the Yellow Pages. Downtown also handles two Jewish monthly magazines, one in English. Other customers used to include some biweeklies, but DO gave them up because "they didn't pay their bills." Much of the firm's work is obtained for it by brokers, among them Carl Berman of Guild Mailing, and another man who once had a printing business in this building before it folded. The building's firms also trade business back and forth. "I could do envelopes," Oscar says, "but it would take me three days, and another guy who has the right kind of press can do it in three hours—so he does the envelopes, and I do what he can't do that well."

Downtown has twenty employees, mostly Hasidic Jews but some Hispanics. Oscar tells me that one of the latter "started at Downtown as a sweeper, was taught cutting, and on his own learned stripping [laying in graphics], and now makes $17 an hour."

Oscar has definite ideas on why printing business has moved out of New York. In his view, it has little to do with.advanced or nonadvanced technology and everything to do with cost. Customers who go out of town to get their printing done do so, he says, "because of one thing—price. And they come back because of two things—location and quality. When they print out of New York, they can't look at a proof or a blueprint before giving approval for final printing; or at least they can't put their hands on it quickly."

Sending materials by pouch to and from Europe takes time, Oscar points out; what purports to happen overnight actually takes three days, which is longer than some customers can bear. In the city, the quality is good and the interim stages of a printed product are more accessible for customer approval. Oscar also contends that it is mostly the unionized printing shops that have moved away or have gone out of business, driven out by what he says was union featherbedding, which caused labor costs to rise so high that customers found it advantageous to have their work done outside of New York. (The printing industry unions deny the charge of featherbedding.) Downtown Offset is a nonunion shop, and Oscar maintains that the firm's employees do not want to be unionized because the union cannot assure them of what the management already provides: steady work, some health-care benefits, and some semblance of job security. There are very few layoffs, even in bad times; most employees have been with the firm for many years. Currently, they work four ten-hour days a week. "If business picks up again, there'll be more overtime."

The sense is conveyed that if new equipment were available to Downtown, and the price was not outrageous, it would be bought, simply to enable the firm to maintain price parity in its field.

"We get what can't be sent out of town," says Vikram Patel, owner of Marvik Colour and Mira Graphics, two printing firms on a higher floor of the 216 Building. "We do things fast. And perfect." Patel is a thin, delicate-boned Indian-born man with long fingers and a shock of dark hair; he prides himself on his colloquialized American English, which he speaks with a faint, lilting accent, and on running a firm at the far end of the embrace-of-technology spectrum. His operation sprawls over many rooms and is testament to his acceptance of the power of the computer in printing, for many of the rooms are oriented around computerized machinery—one, a large device that resembles an accelerator. The corridor walls are lined with samples of the firms' work, mostly of color-corrected advertisements; the before-and-after scenes of a Victoria Principal ad for Jhirmack are striking, the latter showing her teeth more perfectly straight, her skin tones seamless. In Patel's office are a print of a *ganesh* (an Indian deity), an African wooden mask, the books of a Dale Carnegie speech course, and an advanced computer. The work of his firms is in the sector of the printing business known as "electronic pre-press," that is, color separations, stripping, and other technical ways of preparing materials for final printing. He has perfected and trademarked a computerized scanning and touch-up process called Pixeltone, whose slogan on Patel's business card is "Where art meets science." His customers are publishers, advertising agencies, and design studios—the sort of customers that want to have the latest in electronic wizardry at work on their products.

Patel's view of technological innovation, in consequence, is not just as a way to cut manufacturing costs—the reason usually advanced for the introduction of new technology—but as something that is revolutionizing printing as a craft as well as a business. "Once you had craftsmen with good eyes and sure knowledge and intuition born of experience," he explains. "What the machine has done is to break down all the tasks into minute segments, and to do them individually. Craftsmen—a dying breed—knew how to do more than one task. Now most firms have operators who do 'job-specific' work on the computer. We train each employee to do all the tasks here, but that is unusual."

Growing up in India, Vikram, the eldest of many children, began work in his father's paper business, and two years later started a packaging factory that by 1975 had about thirty employees. Then his wife, a physician, emigrated to New York and, after a year, pleaded for him to join her. "The family business was doing well, but I wanted to make my mark in the world—and one is always a child in the shadow of one's father." So he came to New York and while looking for work took reprographic courses. He could only find a low-paying job in packaging, but rose quickly through the ranks there, and then at a printing house. During the two and a half years that it took him to save $20,000, he continued to take courses at Columbia, NYU, the Pratt Institute, New York

City Community College, "whatever would be of importance for my business and my mind. One is forced to do that, to learn what equipment and techniques are coming through the pipeline." He also started the naturalization process: If he was going to be in the United States, he was going to do it right. He coaxed some brothers and sisters to emigrate; one sister is now an architect and another does technical work for a medical firm, while one brother is a polymer chemist and a second is a chemical engineer. "It is sad to leave India behind, but in the United States we are able to realize our potential based on our motivation rather than on some other factor."

In 1980, with the money he'd saved and a matching loan from a friend, he started his firm. At first he could find no one to give him a lease, because he had no credit history. Eventually he was able to locate on half a floor at 216, at a time when many other firms in the building were going belly-up. His previous employer also went bankrupt, and since Vikram knew precisely what equipment he needed, at the auction he was able to make wise use of his capital to pick up some bargains. A year later he incorporated Marvik Colour, which uses computerized scanning equipment. After that, his business grew steadily, to a gross of $1.8 million a year by the late 1980s. Needing more room, he expanded from a half floor to almost the entire floor.

Patel not only knew his technology, he understood the need to embrace its leading edge in order to stay ahead of his competitors. In March of 1989, in an attempt to lap the field, he purchased a state-of-the-art Siemens/Hell computerized scanning system. The price was high—payments were $11,000 a month. It was the first system of its kind in the United States, and it was going to enable him, Vikram estimated, to triple his business to $5 million a year. By 1990, he had two shifts working overtime. Then the roof caved in: The machine didn't work properly, and in his opinion its capacities had been misrepresented to him. He tried to force the distributor to attend to the problem, but nothing happened. At that time, Siemens was in the process of selling Hell Graphics to another firm; during this interim, the machine's problems were left in the lurch, and Vikram, unwilling to accept the machine as it was, went to court to force the distributor to take it back. From that day to this, a lawsuit against the distributor and Siemens has consumed a great deal of his time, energy, and money. Coupled with the general downturn in the economy at that time, the lawsuit hit Patel's business very hard. He has had to reduce his staff to a skeleton crew of six, "Some I am really carrying, now, out of my own pocket."

In buying his machine in the first place, Vikram was caught in a trap typical of the onrush of technology, especially of computer technology. The system he bought from Siemens was a proprietary one; nothing of an equivalent nature was available to other purchasers for less money, and that was partly why Vikram bought it, so he'd be miles ahead of the competition. But when he ran into problems with the hardware, his difficulties were compounded because computerized printing technology as a whole continued to advance while he was stalled. In that interim, for instance, software electronic publishing programs such as Adobe and Quark offered new versions that would do some of what his big machine could accomplish, with not quite as good quality but at a fraction of the price and available off-the-shelf. So in addition to having a machine that didn't work, Vikram was in a bind because his capital was tied up in nonworking technology at just the time when he would gladly have used that capital to supplement his existing equipment and software—as his competition was doing.

His legal costs mounted to a quarter million dollars. However, as with many new Americans, Vikram had faith in the judicial system, and he continued the suit, "a gnat fighting a giant," but a man determined that "no way would they stomp over me." What he sought was not vindication, but to be able to resume making the numbers on his five-year business plan.

In June of 1992, the court indicated that Patel had the right to return the machine and seek a resolution. Vikram was "just glad that he had survived." The nonworking machine was not removed until October, though, and it took until January of 1993 to have a new computer scanner installed.

With great pride, Vikram shows off the new machine, which is the device that impressed me on the way in—it looks something like a cyclotron or an MRI machine. Each run costs quite a bit of money. "We are just finishing the learning curve" on how to use it, he advises. Finally he is able to start the process of doing business again. Meanwhile, the suit goes on and on. The judge wants the parties to settle, but to date they have not been able to reach satisfactory agreement.

Vikram will not rest on the technology he has, however; he plans to use technology to enter a new business, to combine his graphics expertise with the computerized ability to generate audio-visuals in order to make CD-ROMs. "I will be able to work for the same clients, but in larger ways." Toward that end, he is already taking a computer-aided audiovisual design course at Pratt. His future plans are logical, but he will be hampered by the suit and its demands on his time and money; whether or not American justice may be blind, she is certainly slow.

Waldon Press occupies three high floors of the 216 Building and has been a tenant for twenty-five years. It is a firm that has kept up with changing technology and has absorbed several other firms once headquartered in the building—but its principal owner is not as enamored of technology as one might expect.

A young man has come to leave a badly copied résumé for the job of messenger; Bill Donat is kind to the youngster even as he says there is nothing available right now. Donat, president of the firm, is a man in his mid-fifties who resembles Dave Thomas of the Wendy's restaurants: stocky, graying, and with a similar engaging, long-suffering smile. He has just moved into a new office on an upper floor, and a favorite cartoon, currently on his desk, will soon hang again on his wall: It is a sly drawing of a king with an "uh-oh" look on his face, contemplating a nail in front of him on the palace floor and a horseshoe a bit farther along the corridor. "You know the poem, 'For want of a nail'? Eventually the whole kingdom is lost. The cartoon is the way I sometimes feel about the effort needed to keep Waldon Press going. Occasionally I wake up wondering what's gone wrong during the time I've been away from the office."

In the early days of this firm, its survival depended on specialized human knowledge. Bill's father, Alexander, formed the business in 1949, together with a partner named Wald. The elder Donat had been publisher of a daily newspaper in Warsaw before the war, much of which he spent in a concentration camp. Waldon began printing magazines and books, and quickly edged over into foreign-language publishing—Russian, German, Hebrew, Yiddish—which they were better able to do than other printers because many of the immigrant employees were multilingual. Based on his own and others' experiences, Alexander Donat wrote a book, *The Holocaust Kingdom*, which essentially linked the word "holocaust" to what the Nazis had done to the Jews of Europe. To keep the book in print and to sponsor others about the subject, the Donats formed a not-for-profit publishing umbrella called The Holocaust Library. "Over the years, we did fifty-six titles, such as *The Holocaust in Finland*, and kept them in print—no easy task in this era of publish, remainder, and shred." The achievement was possible, curiously, because the Donats as publishers were their own printers, a throwback to the way things had been done in the early days of publishing. Recently, Bill concluded an arrangement with the newly opened Holocaust Museum in Washington, D.C.—which had been the Library's largest competitor in obtaining operating funds. The museum is to take over the Library and he will sit on the museum's publishing committee. Although he knows that the Holocaust Museum is probably the right place for The Holocaust Library, he is a bit sad to relinquish the Library, for it has been a major part of his life and heritage. He also worries that the museum may not work as hard as he did to keep all its titles in print.

After graduating from Colgate University, Bill worked briefly for his father, but ran into the usual difficulties besetting a father and son in business together: issues of primacy, tradition, innovation, and control. Not wanting to fight his father for his turf, Bill became production manager of textbooks at Harcourt, Brace and World, until in the mid-1960s, his father importuned him to return. "If I didn't come in, Waldon Press was going to be sold." Father and son struck a bargain: Waldon Press would move to larger quarters, and Bill would have room and latitude enough to make it his own firm. Today, Waldon has thirty-eight employees, including Bill's son Gregory.

Many of the unionized employees formerly worked for other firms in the building, which Waldon has absorbed. According to Donat, "We're the last firm in the building that is really a printer." Since the 1970s, Waldon's mainstay has been the printing of quarterly and annual reports and mutual fund prospectuses. "We've continued in business by being flexible, taking whatever work we could find, shifting emphasis when we had to. We took in minor partners because they brought business with them." In Donat's determination to do whatever is necessary to keep his firm afloat, there are faint echoes of his father's struggle for survival in the concentration camps.

While Vikram Patel sees advanced technological wizardry as the way to obtain new business, Bill Donat sees it as just necessary to keep up with the competition: Everyone else is able to send information back and forth to clients by modem, so Waldon must do so, too. "The cutting edge for us," Donat says, "is understanding that what we provide isn't really manufacturing—it's a service. When a customer says they want something tomorrow, price isn't the controlling factor in their decision as to which printing company to use. That's one reason why labor costs aren't a problem for us—we pass them on, and up to a certain point the customer is willing to pay for them. Also, union printers are more skilled than nonunion ones, and this high level of skill is part of what we're selling."

There are a half-dozen publishing entities around the block, and this section will examine the responses to technology and ways of being in the world of four of them. In three of the four, and in different ways for each, new technology has increased their possibilities and expanded their businesses.

At the end of the summer of 1993, renovations began in Books of Wonder, the children's books store that sits on the southwest corner of 18th and Seventh Avenue. As with many renovations, it marked an end and a new beginning.

In 1980, when nineteen-year-old Peter Glassman opened a small children's books store on a Hudson Street corner in the far West Village, his enterprise seemed destined for disaster: an unpromising location in a gay district, an inordinately young entrepreneur, very little capital. But Glassman, an articulate, redheaded, chunky dynamo, had been fascinated by books all his life, had been a book buyer for stores since the age of fifteen, and had some well-formed notions of what to sell and how to sell it—notions that owed nothing to modern technology. He wanted the store laid out so people would see the books and put their hands on them. "Books are a physical experience," Peter opines, "You can't curl up with a good CD-ROM." He pledged to sell mainly hardcovers, the most beautiful books he could find, all the classics, and to "never offer a book to a parent that a kid would hate." In the neighborhood of the Hudson Street location were three nursery and grade schools, and the parents of children at those schools made Books of Wonder a frequent stopping place. Moreover, because Hudson Street was a major axis for people commuting from New Jersey, soon 20 percent of the store's customers were from across the Hudson River. Twenty-year-old James Carey, who had done some carpentry and renovation work on the store, joined Peter in its management; Jim's attention to detail and calmness were a good balance to Peter's exuberance.

Within a year of opening, the partners brought out a catalog of rare children's books they had collected, and by the mid-1980s they had edged over into a new business, becoming publishers. Building on their base of knowledge, in association with the William Morrow Company they republished some of the many books related to the "land of Oz" written by L. Frank Baum, including in them sets of classic illustrations, some of which had not been in circulation since the first part of the twentieth century. The technological capacity to reproduce the illustrations, and the head start on potential purchasers given them by their computer-generated newsletter, made this leap possible.

By 1986, they were successful enough to open a second store in an area that was "a crossroads that wasn't recognized as such," the mid-Chelsea blocks that seemed to be "convenient" for many people who passed through going uptown or downtown. They first bid on the corner opposite Barneys, at 16th Street and Seventh Avenue, but when negotiations took too long, they snapped up the premises vacated by a coffee shop in the apartment building on the corner of 18th. Larger than their first store, it had plenty of room for customers to walk about without bumping into one another, plenty of display space so that attractive book covers could be seen, plenty of windows in which to advertise featured books, readings, and personal appearances by authors or illustrators.

A children's books store industry shakeout began in 1987, and Peter and Jim survived it, partly because their publishing activities provided additional revenues, partly because of their innovative retail marketing. By 1990, Books of Wonder was among the most sturdy children's books stores in the nation. Its special catalogs were bringing in a profitable mail-order business, and the republishing venture was continuing to expand. With some financing from old customers in the California area, Peter and Jim opened a third store in Beverly Hills in the fall of 1991. "Talk about bad timing," Peter groans. What with riots, floods, and other environmental problems, the Beverly Hills store began to "bleed badly." A few months later, when Hudson Street started being torn up for road repairs, their first store, too, started to suffer. As with other Hudson Street merchants, Peter and Jim could do little more than hope that when the repairs were done, auto- and foot-traffic patterns would resume. By the late spring of 1993, the repair crews had gone north of Books of Wonder but the expected resurgence of customers did not materialize. "People who walk have patterns, and once they're interrupted, it's difficult to get them back on track," Peter explains. Beyond that, the New Jerseyans who had made up 20 percent of the store's customers were still avoiding Hudson Street even after it had been repaired.

Reluctantly, Peter and Jim decided that they could not sustain two money-losing ventures on the profits of their other endeavors. Beverly Hills's numbers were on the increase, and that store might soon edge into the black. But the Hudson Street shop "had served its purpose." They determined that in August, when the lease expired, they would close their first store and move its operations to the Seventh Avenue location. In order to do that, however, they would have to move the publishing operations from the makeshift quarters in the basement of the 18th Street store and into a real office space. It seemed time to do so, anyway, because their publishing activities—books, newsletters, catalogs—were rapidly overtaking the retail operation in importance and had greater potential for expansion. Accordingly, they rented an office in the 216 West 18th Street building as the headquarters of Ozma, their publishing arm.

They hope that their best customers from Hudson Street will find their way to the corner of 18th and Seventh, but they have no assurances. The September opening of the Madison Avenue Barneys store took away some customers who usually combined a trip from the Upper East Side to Barneys at 17th and Seventh with a trip to Books of Wonder. Next spring, a Barnes & Noble superstore will open a few blocks from here, at 22nd and Sixth, and may provide a great deal of new competition. To offset inroads by retail competitors, Ozma will have to become stronger, and possibly even the center of Peter and Jim's operation.

For Glassman and Carey, publishing technology is mainly an adjunct to their own innovative ideas about what children's books to manufacture and how and where to sell them. For Robert Cavalero of Catholic Book Publishers, on 17th Street, the new publishing technology is central to his company's ability to remain in business.

Most of the twenty-seven members in the industry group known as the Catholic Book Publishers Association are relatively small, parish-grown pamphleteers. An exception is the Catholic Book Publishing Company, which takes up a 90,000-square-foot building on West 17th Street; it is not the largest in its specialized field, but it is the most diverse: Its catalog lists over 300 titles, including Bibles, catechisms, missals, prayer books, children's books in English and Spanish; there's even a cookbook written by a "charismatic" Italian nun.

To reach the offices of the company, one enters the faded red ten-story warehouse known as the Steiner Building through its ground floor, now used as a loading area; it is empty enough that alongside the pallets of completed books ready for shipment sit some old presses awaiting the scrap heap, several cars, and a fifteen-foot wooden dinghy. A hand-operated elevator takes a visitor up to the fifth floor, where, beyond glass-paned enclosures that look like bank-teller areas, a small office overlooks 17th Street. The cubicle is overwhelmed by old trophies on the walls—mounted fish, a fisherman's prayer, and an oil painting of a big, smiling, many-jowled man, Howard Cavalero. This Cavalero is also the author of the message on an ornately lettered plaque, which begins "God grant that I may live to fish/Until my dying day...."

Owner Robert Cavalero bears a striking resemblance to the portrait of his father, Howard. He, too, loves to fish, and owns the boat parked downstairs. Bob is thirty-seven and reveals his attitude toward the firm when he says he has been with it "only fifteen years" and when in conversation he has the precise dates of his father's, grandfather's, and uncle's deaths on the tip of his tongue. Most of the fish on the wall were caught by his grandfather, who began the firm in 1911 and moved it to this building in the 1930s. Even then it was a classic, nineteenth-century-type publisher, that printed all of its own materials. At first the firm rented a few floors here, but as other tenants moved out, Catholic Book Publishing took over the space for its own expansion, and by the early 1960s had bought the building and was using all of its space. Three hundred employees designed, edited, printed, bound, warehoused, and shipped from this site. Today, most of the printing is done by outside contractors, though two presses still operate in the basement, and forty-five employees rattle around in this large building.

"Our business is inventing books," Cavalero explains. "We contract with authors, do our own artwork in-house, and check the contents—both text and pictures—with the National Conference of Catholic Bishops in Washington, so that the books are cleared for purchase by lay people and clergy. What we sell are basically 'black books,' that is, books whose contents are obvious when you see the cover. We work hard to keep our prices down so that everybody who needs them can buy them." The books are retailed in religious books stores only, and that is the difference between Cavalero's company and commercial publishers. While the latter do business on a consignment basis—the books they ship to a bookstore can be returned for credit if unsold, and from 30 to 40 percent of them usually are—Cavalero's firm ships only to stores or middlemen who purchase the books outright and are not permitted to return any merchandise. Accordingly, Catholic Book Publishing must design books to have a long shelf life and to remain attractive to potential buyers for many seasons.

The great change in Catholic publishing was not as a result of technology but as a consequence of the Vatican II Conference, in the early 1960s, which, according to Cavalero, "threw out everyone's backlists." At that time, other religious publishers went under, and all experienced hard times. Bob maintains that his father's leadership permitted the firm to survive, and then to prevail, by means of a big gamble he took in 1975, bringing out a four-volume breviary (a reading and prayer for every hour of the year) that no other religious publisher had been willing to try. It became the big seller, a set that had to be bought by every priest in the country, and it put the family business back in the black.

In college during the introduction of the breviary, Bob entered the firm in 1978 and by the time his father died in 1985 had enough experience to keep the company on track. His sister handles the shipping and transportation of materials and finished books. "One or the other of us is always on the premises," Cavalero says. As with many small-business owners, the Cavaleros put in six-day weeks. A brother had also been employed here; he now works for a direct-mail company that is doing an increasing amount of business for CBPC.

To meet the challenges of the 1990s, Bob Cavalero has embraced whatever technology he can find that will help him cut costs and speed and smooth operations, and he has also shifted the firm to the pattern of business that may well become the norm for twenty-first-century big-city manufacturing—using the city's base of highly skilled people for the complicated parts of the process and subcontracting for the actual manufacturing to out-of-town plants that operate at lower cost than are possible in the city.

Currently, books are conceived, detailed, art-directed, and edited here, printed elsewhere, and the completed pages are then shipped back to 17th Street, where covers and jackets are printed and the volumes are bound before being shipped to customers. Bob communicates with printing plants and customers by modem; he has a modem at home as well as in the office for such purposes. The design and editing operation, as well as the final shipping, is highly computerized. Moreover, for CBPC—as for Books of Wonder/Ozma—direct mail, itself almost entirely computerized these days, is taking on more and more of the burden of marketing books to their ultimate individual consumers.

In pursuit of even lower costs, CBPC has recently purchased a brand-new distribution center in Totowa, New Jersey, near Bob's home, and within a few months, he informs me, CBPC will move some of its shipping operations from 17th Street to that plant, and eventually may move much more of the business out of the city. Accordingly, he has put some of the floors of the Steiner Building up for rent or sale—as the reader may recall, Louis Nelson of the Chelsea Gym, next door, had been interested in one floor of it, but the negotiations petered out. Just as CBPC once expanded into the Steiner Building floor by floor, it is now contracting down in its use of space here. "In these days of faxes and modems and direct-mail sales, you really can do our sort of business from any-where," Cavalero points out, but he thinks he'll never entirely leave the big city: "I'll probably keep an office here, anyhow, to meet with customers and do the design work."

Next door to Catholic Book Publishing Company, and many times larger and more technologically advanced, is Cahners, in two linked buildings that were first erected as warehouses. On January 1, 1993, Reed International PLC, the British-based corporate parent of Cahners, amalgamated with the Dutch-based Elsevier NV to form one of the world's largest publishing and information conglomerates, a $5 billion-a-year giant. A principal reason for the merger was to realize synergy among the two companies' "prop-erties" that would spur Reed Elsevier to produce more products to take advantage of what is becoming known, in the buzzword of the decade, as the electronic superhighway. Reed Elsevier's current crop of magazines, newspapers, and other publishing ventures are already so numerous that displaying just a single copy of each of the conglomerate's properties would likely fill an entire newsstand. The hundreds of titles in a dozen languages range from fashion magazines to television-viewing guides, prestigious scientific and medical journals, sports publications, regional newspapers, the Bowker line of reference books, law and accounting journals and reference sets, textbooks, airline guides, and even a CD-ROM con-taining many versions of the Bible.

As an example of what is expected to happen as a result of the merger and the impetus to find new products, consider *Modern Bride*, which Cahners acquired in 1987 for $64 million, and then spun off *Wedding Gown Guide*, *Your Prom*, television specials, and the like. The seventy-person editorial staff of *Modern Bride* has only in the past few months moved to the 17th Street buildings, where they occupy most of one floor. There are more than a dozen other editorial floors, where editorial, production, and distribution staffs work on some of Cahners' other "consumer and entertainment division" publications, such as *Interior Design*; *School Library Journal*; *Home Textiles Today*; *TWICE—This Week in Consumer Electronics*; *Printing News*; *Graphic Arts Monthly*; as well as *Publishers Weekly* and part of the operations of the well-known entertainment industry publication, *Variety*. Cahners' half-dozen medical publications are edited at other buildings in Manhattan, and more than sixty other Cahners publications have headquarters at various sites around the country; for example, *Accessories/Today* and *Furniture Today* have offices in High Point.

One could argue that the 500 Cahners employees on this block, in addition to being the largest single contingent, are the most influential, since in the industries on which Cahners reports, its magazines and newspapers are essential regular reading. Not many people in entertainment can afford to miss *Variety*, nor can librarians be without *School Library Journal*; moreover, many professionals in these fields make decisions based upon information in these magazines.

Cahners is one of those entities in New York that has been providing new jobs on a regular basis as it expands. It began in the 1940s as a privately owned publisher of "business-to-business" magazines; it was bought by Reed in the 1980s, and by 1991 had become a billion-dollar operation.

The merger of Reed and Elsevier has given new impetus to the move of the Cahners group beyond traditional paper publishing, according to John Beni, chief of the Consumer and Entertainment Group of Cahners publications, that is, principally those located at 17th Street. He will be moving his office shortly to 17th Street, but is now still in a Park Avenue building. Yale and yacht memorabilia line the walls of this office, but Beni, a sixtyish man in owlish glasses, gives the impression of being so absorbed

and interested in his work that he has little time for either diver-
sion. Formerly president of the U.S. division of Gruner + Jahr, a
German publishing conglomerate, Beni came to Cahners/Reed in
1990 from the *New York Times* magazine group. In addition to
making deals to buy publications, he has been assessing precisely
how Cahners can use the information, expertise, and positions of
its properties to generate more income. "In ten years, the word
publishing won't have the same meaning as it does now," Beni
muses. "So we have to redefine our publications, to think of them
as more than what is being printed—to conceive of them as resource bases. We've got to slice and dice the information we
already have and get it out in new and different ways."

Here it is—the essence of the technologically induced revolution in the printing and publishing industry. Beni characterizes
the essential understandings as he ticks them off on his fingers:
"We're in the business of *accessing, packaging,* and *distributing* information, no matter what the format. And we will continue to be.
What we've got to figure out is how do we make money from
doing new things with that information."

One of the first tangible new information superhighway products to be produced after the merger, a joint venture between
Variety and Reuters, the British news service, came on-line in the
spring of 1993. It is an entertainment news wire offered to newspapers, radio and television stations, investment bankers—to anyone who needs up-to-the-minute information on the burgeoning
entertainment industry. Other products in the Cahners pipeline are
the creation of electronic databases and cyberspace bulletin boards.
"We have several publications that serve the printing and graphic
arts industry," Beni points out. "In one joint venture, we're creating a database for assessing bids in that industry. We're also starting a service for the industry that will allow someone who has
excess equipment to sell to post a notice in, say, the on-line version
of *Graphic Arts Monthly,* and reach a person who may be interested
in that equipment. Transactional is going to be a key word for us.
We'll be the medium that aids in the transaction, the medium that

brings buyer and seller together. We're already doing that in other forms of publishing."

Even with *Modern Bride?* "Sure. The buyer is the young woman about to get married who's going to spend between twenty and forty thousand dollars on her wedding and honeymoon and will make those buying decisions in a short period of time. We're partners with the advertiser, our customer." Such partnerships have been defining Cahners' expansion for some time and will increasingly do so in the future. *Your Prom* was spun off from *Modern Bride*, not because the same group of young women might be expected to buy both magazines, but rather because the idea of the new product was loved by key "partner" advertisers, specifically, the companies that manufacture ball gowns and party dresses. As an additional way of making a transaction between its consumer customers and one of the largest categories of advertisers in the bridal magazine, *Modern Bride* is also considering the production of a video on honeymoon destinations. It will be a natural for cable television travel channels.

Providing new products in this manner may be essential for large companies like Cahners/Reed Elsevier, but how will individuals deal with the imperative to slice, dice, and repackage information in new ways? "Our editorial and production employees must be constantly renewing themselves in order to keep up with the technology," Beni warns. "Editors and graphics people need new skills, not the old cut-and-paste knowledge; everybody's work is melding together, from the writer to the editor to the designer. Defining the boundaries between magazine personnel is getting harder to do because the computer makes it possible to perform many of the old, formerly separated tasks on one desk."

Something of that amalgamation seems reflected in the way the space is utilized inside the joined buildings at 245 and 249 West 17th Street, whose redesign was done by Jim Harb's firm. The atmosphere is extremely modern: functional, quiet, carpeted, and well lit, though a bit cold and impersonal. The 249 Building is twelve stories, the 245, six; walkways and stairways connect adjoining floors. There are blocks of cubicles, divided by five-foot-high partitions. Only the offices for higher-ranked executives, which are on the perimeters of the floors, have doors. One might presume that the atmosphere of the *Modern Bride* editorial area would be quite different from that of *This Week in Consumer Electronics*, but the only way to tell one publication's turf from another is by the illustrations pinned to inner office walls. "Publishing employees take up about 200 square feet each, including corridors and conference rooms and what-not," Beni calculates, "so we've got room for about a thousand people on 17th Street. We'll be consolidating our operations, moving more people in."

In casual conversations, the Cahners employees suggest they are excited by the changes and challenges, but fearful that the consolidation of two publishing giants and the imperatives of producing things by and for new technologies will put more pressure on them to produce profits rather than good products. They are concerned, if not yet worried, about maintaining editorial integrity because they know that megamergers are invariably accompanied by "economies" that mean lost jobs.

The building across from Cahners on 18th, visible out a window on that side of the Cahners offices, is the most mysterious building on the block, and few neighbors know what it contains. When a high-level Cahners executive was informed that in it was a man who had developed his own artistic ideas, published them, made a thriving business from them, and then sold that business to a conglomerate, he was impressed. "I don't know the guy," the Cahners man said, "but he's my idol."

The guy is also a man who has seen the information superhighway coming—and has decided not to ride on it.

The mysterious building is a few steps east of Authentiques and B. Schlesinger, a wide two-story edifice that goes through the block to 19th. The exterior at 18th exhibits no signs, only a swatch of artificial green carpet behind a closed, waist-high iron fence. An awning on the entrance at 19th calls it Hanlit Global, and a telephone directory listing exists for Hanlit Publications on 19th Street. The entrance, however, is on 18th, and occasionally some-one can be seen going in or out. Children from the Chelsea Day School next door occasionally knock balls onto Hanlit's roof, and a Hanlit employee periodically brings them back, but neither the people in the school nor other neighbors are sure what goes on inside the building; one believes that the business handles audio-tapes. A publishing directory yielded a number for purchases, but no hint of what sort of products Hanlit sells, and telephone calls were answered by a machine whose message-taking unit was out of kilter. Many phone calls were necessary to discover that the firm is a music publisher and that its principal owner is Ervin Litkei.

The interior of Hanlit is a dusty, old-fashioned warehouse, with desks in front, floor-to-double-height-ceiling stacks of shelves beyond, and a glass-paneled corridor along which the three visible employees move at an unhurried pace. They have a computer for tracking inventory and sales, but that's about it for modern tech-nology. A lobby waiting area features framed tear sheets, one from a Carnegie Hall concert of the music composed by Ervin Litkei, a second from another concert which featured the poetry of Andrea Fodor Litkei, a "National Book Award nominee," and a third from a Walt Disney production. An older male employee led the way upstairs toward what he calls "the inner sanctum," a wood-paneled office whose walls are covered with sheet music, awards, member-ship plaques, paintings, and other memorabilia.

Ervin Litkei is a smallish, nearly bald man in his early seventies who wears an old-fashioned suit and speaks with a thick Eastern European accent. He grew up in Hungary, where his early com-positions were praised by Franz Lehar, composer of the "Merry Widow Waltz." During World War II, Litkei wrote a march for President Roosevelt, and on the strength of it, came to this country in 1948. He wrote another march for Truman and has since writ-ten marches for every sitting president, including two this past year, one for Bill Clinton and another for Hillary. During the 1993 inaugural festivities, the marching band from Mrs. Clinton's old high school in Illinois performed Litkei's "A Salute to the First Lady March." The march for President Clinton, also performed then, featured a saxophone solo.

Litkei moved first to Hollywood, then came to New York, where he married Andrea Fodor, a ballerina, and started as a publisher of classical music. Two of Lehar's waltzes, which he arranged for marching band were Litkei's first best-sellers, but he also made money from publishing his own marches for presidents; Truman or Eisenhower was always appearing somewhere for a speech, and the local band would want to demonstrate their fealty and ingenuity by playing a march named for that person. Operating a business "was not a goal," he says, but "a defense against having to work for anybody else," a way of preserving his artistic independence. As he built Arovox, his music-publishing and recording business, he also produced a documentary film about the Hungarian uprising of 1956, invented and marketed a board game called ESP, and continued composing marches and classical suites. There was always some occasion in need of a post-Sousa patriotic extravagance, and no other composers boasted a track record in oompah. The Disneys commissioned a march to open Disney World. Woolworth needed one for an anniversary. The bicentennial committee wanted something for 1976. Or he would be inspired by world events. During the hostage crisis in Iran in 1979, he was sitting in the bathtub when he got an idea and jumped out in order to start writing down a march entitled "The Captured Fifty." "My wife was screaming because the carpet was wet, but I didn't want to lose the momentum," he later recalled. He takes his work seriously, but a July 4, 1991, profile in the *New York Times*, with tongue very firmly in cheek, says that his George Bush march "clomps resolutely across the musical page like a tuneful Presidential stump speech." Litkei lets such slights go because the marches are "my gift to my country," which he loves deeply for enabling him to fulfill the immigrant's dream of commercial and artistic success.

Part reason that his dream was fulfilled has to do with his innovative embrace of technology and marketing; to put it another way, Litkei has fulfilled the imperatives articulated by John Beni, to access, process, package, and distribute information. Litkei made an arrangement with Disney not only to write music for them but to distribute and publish Disney's movie music products as well as his own marches, Lehar's waltzes, and other pop classical compositions, in the stores of Sears and of Woolworth's. He went into the production of long-playing records and then audiotapes. The profitability of the business enabled him, twenty-five years ago, to buy this building on 18th Street, and during Arovox's peak period to gross $30 million a year and sustain 140 employees. "I don't even know the words *recession* or *depression*, because whatever the part of the cycle, I continued to do well." From time to time he was offered positions with other firms—to run the classical recordings division at CBS, for instance—but turned them all down.

What happened, then, that resulted in this almost-empty shell? For one thing, the sort of music that Litkei had sold for years has fallen into disfavor. For a second, Sears and Woolworth's encountered hard times. Third, the Disney company decided to handle its own publishing. Fourth, there was no familial reason for the enterprise to continue: Litkei's only child, a daughter, pursued a medical career. And fifth, the most likely direction in which to further expand the business—through electronic publishing—had as little appeal for him as did an electric guitar. At the inception of the age of compact discs, he refused to get into that business— putting in the equipment to manufacture discs would have cost a great deal of money. Recognizing, perhaps, that the CDs would eclipse audiotapes, in 1989 he sold most of Arovox to a British conglomerate, the Rank Organization.

Along with the Arovox licenses and such, Rank took the bulk of the employees, all but those who wanted to continue working directly for Litkei. Today, a handful of people roam the downstairs warehouse area where more than a hundred once worked. In an unhurried, not-particularly-busy manner, they fill orders for printed versions and audiotapes of Litkei's own music as well as for records and tapes of a jazz label, JazzMania; a classical label,

Aurora; and for books of Mrs. Litkei's poetry and essays. Upstairs in the inner sanctum, Ervin Litkei speaks with more enthusiasm than any other businessman around the block about the most visionary project in the area, the development of the sports-entertainment complex on the Chelsea piers, but evidences no further interest in making music-related products for the electronic superhighway.

Chapter 10

WHITE-COLLAR FUTURES

CHRISTMAS IN New York seems to begin just after Halloween and to end when it warms up enough in January to go outside and take down the lights. Our block becomes nicely festive during the season, with decorations everywhere, plus usually startling windows at Barneys and an extravaganza of lights at Authentiques. Heading into the Christmas season, Alan Gross, who owns the building above 18th Street News on Eighth Avenue, strings a set of colored lights outside the news store. He has given matching sets to the Gascogne restaurant to the north and to the P. Chanin boutique and the Blue Moon restaurant just south of his building, who will shortly hang theirs out. The lights are one of Alan's attempts to bring stylistic continuity to this section of the block; on his initiative, the stores also use matching blackboards to advertise daily specials and matching wire enclosures to protect the little trees that are bravely trying to grow in front.

Mostly at Alan's initiative, he and his business neighbors—

including the dry cleaner—have in recent years cooperated on getting rid of moths on their ailanthus trees, on making their backyards secure from those who had been using them as a place to sell drugs, on shoveling snow from each other's walks. Once, according to Alan, a travel customer of his in Korea attempted to evade payment for coupons, and Man Yohn Lee of the dry cleaners helped Alan track down the customer and obtain payment.

If there were a mayor of the block, Alan would be a leading candidate for the position, since he knows virtually every store owner and resident because of his long residence in the area, and because, as he puts it, "I'm a buttinsky." Alan is in his late fifties, slim, with a mostly gray beard of the academic/psychiatrist type; in fact, he holds a Ph.D. in psychology and was chairman of the psychology department at the University of Maryland. He also has a master's in business administration and is currently a part-time radio talk-show host on WVOX in Westchester, a volunteer in the New York City mayor's office, an arbitrator on American Arbitration Association panels, the Democratic committeeman for the block, operator of a travel-coupon agency, the relief manager of the newsstand, and is writing a book and often takes temporary jobs.

Back in 1979, while employed as a full-time college professor, he discovered that plenty of people had frequent-flyer coupons but were wasting them by not using them, so he more or less invented the secondary market for those coupons. Eventually, this business and its successors had offices in California, Hawaii, Alaska, and Washington in addition to New York. It was taking up so much of Alan's time that he extended a sabbatical into a two-year leave; at the end of that period he asked for more time off, the university said no, and he chose to resign. He sold the travel business to a competitor, Issy, who made a condition of the sale that Alan be a consultant to the business for three years. Now Alan and Issy, who also lives in New York, are close friends and partners in several ventures, including the ownership of the building above the newsstand, a building in which Alan and his wife maintain an apartment.

Currently, in addition to Alan's other tasks, he is taking a Spanish course in preparation for a trip to Argentina. He has become an interested investor in a "transponder" system, an alternative to branding cattle, which works via a capsule injected into a cow's earlobe. A reading device can note the cow's identification number and be used to obtain data on milk production and other useful information from the cattle on the pampas.

Last spring, Alan was offered an opportunity to buy a large number of heavily discounted airplane tickets to six different locations and willy-nilly turned his apartment into a travel office with a handful of employees, as many computers, and twice as many telephones ringing off their hooks. The business will last only as long as there are discounted tickets to sell.

Before the recent election, Alan had been doing volunteer work for the man who has just won the new post of public advocate, Mark Green, and also for the area's city councilman, Tom Duane (a study of the viability of the wholesale flower market), and spent considerable time as a volunteer working in Mayor David Dinkins's office, interceding with city agencies on behalf of complainants. "When you say you're calling from the mayor's office, you can get things done." He managed to clear up a few pension problems for individuals, have a street repaired, and—using his expertise as a psychologist—to dissuade a handful of chronic petitioners from their "long-term fantasy fixations." He won't be doing that anymore, since Dinkins has just been defeated by Republican Rudolph Giuliani.

Not content with his investments, travel service, and volunteer work, Alan occasionally takes temporary jobs. "I drove a taxi to learn the city. Worked as a bike messenger, a street vendor, did office work. I like these short-term things, especially the taxi and retail, because you have full control and it's brief. When I was an academic, it would take me years to complete something. But I can go to the temp agency, get a job, do it for a while, and I'm out. I haven't met my best friends while taxi driving, but it's interesting."

The existence of the newsstand downstairs is also a result of Alan's specific initiative. Six years ago, at the time Alan bought the building, the store on the first floor was Bumbleberry's, which carried children's clothing and toys; that folded, and the next tenant was a health-and-beauty-products store. When it got in difficulties, Alan took it over, a move that resulted in what he calls "the only significant business failure I've ever had," attributable to a larger beauty-products store with more deeply discounted prices opening two blocks north. Alan eventually sold his inventory to that store at a fraction of its worth, and then looked for a new tenant. He decided to place ads seeking tenants who would operate a newsstand. A Lebanese operator moved in, but he began to do questionable things—put in gambling machines, for instance—and Alan had to buy the lease back. He ran the newsstand himself for a period, then transferred the business to an Indian partnership that also operated other, similar shops. Recently, Chander "Doc" Nandal, related to the family of the manager by marriage, purchased the lease from the partners. Much to Alan's relief, Doc has stabilized the business.

Trained as a veterinarian in India, Nandal worked there for the state veterinary service until moving to the United States in 1985. His in-laws own newsstands in Greenwich Village, and he worked for them and as a bank teller until the opportunity for his own store came along. "The work is boring, and I don't have any sort of job satisfaction," he says with a shrug, but adds that he has few options, right now, other than to run the store and fulfill his obligations to his family. Once the children are old enough for his wife to be able to take a job of her own, he hopes to make enough time to return to veterinary studies. "The problem is that the store can only really support one person comfortably," he says, "so I can't shift the burden to partners or assistants." Alan, who wants his tenant to remain in place and viable, often spells Doc during the day and has decided to help Doc expand the business into selling books. Since the sale of books is Alan's idea, he has bankrolled it by buying the stock for the shelves. Both men treat the books as an experiment; if it works, they'll continue it, but if it doesn't, very little money will have been lost, and none of it Doc's.

Alan Gross's ability to obtain work, invent businesses, and make money, seemingly when the spirit or necessity moves him, is little short of remarkable, but the basic activity in which he is engaged is not unusual: His various enterprises, most of them operated from his home office or out of his hat, are examples of something important to the future that is going on at many points on this block, the creation of wealth through what can be called mental capital.

Capital, current theory holds, was not an important element in human economic affairs during the first several millennia of human history. But when the world's human population became sufficiently numerous and densely situated enough to produce regular scarcities of goods, there arose a need to use the world's resources in a more efficient manner; something was required that could act on resources in a way that would create more goods than would otherwise exist. Capital was able to do this. In the form of money or a money equivalent, it could produce income, which could not be done as readily by the other two elements of production, labor and land (or natural resources).

By the time Adam Smith published his *Wealth of Nations* in 1776, capital had come to mean more than money. The concept of physical capital came into being—physical in the sense of tangible things such as machinery. The person who owned the apparatus of production was the capitalist and thereby controlled the ability to make money. As the industrial revolution took hold, the definition of physical capital was expanded to include ownership or control of any materials used to extract, transport, create, or alter goods. Soon thereafter, the definition of capital broadened still further to include marketable intangibles such as patents and franchises. Ownership of a patent, whether that came about because the owner created the patent or because he purchased it, became the key to enormous wealth.

Daniel Bell suggested twenty years ago that the basic product of the postindustrial economy would be information. As that economy approaches maturity in the last decade of the twentieth century we have been expanding further the category of marketable intangibles. Leif Edvinsson of Sweden has been advocating that big businesses properly value their "intellectual capital," a concept that he defines as including intellectual property, management skills, and worker creativity. But capital itself must now be fully redefined in order to stress the relatively high value of the contribution of the human brain.

As augmented by the computer and such electronic communication devices as the telephone, fax, and modem, an individual today has more capacity than ever before in history to act on resources in ways that produce more goods than previously existed. This completes the shift among the factors of production: Mental capital, a concept broader than intellectual capital, is capital that at its extreme has the capacity to reduce the factors of labor and land to a minor part of the production process and even to bring into question the relative power of monetary capital.

Consider that one person, sitting in a room of his or her apartment or in an office cubicle with some electronic equipment, can produce a product—a piece of intellectual property, say a software program or a new media vehicle resulting from what John Beni of Cahners referred to as slicing and dicing previously acquired information—that when properly manufactured and marketed will result in sales in the millions of dollars. To this inventor, the cost of the land and resources is relatively low, since the space used is only a few hundred square feet and the electronic equipment is relatively inexpensive. And what labor is involved is that of the mental capitalist's. Karl Marx argued that profit in an enterprise always comes at the expense of the workers; according to Marx, capitalists do not simply employ labor but exploit it by paying less for labor than labor contributes to the making of the product, and it is this "surplus of value" from labor's brow, rather than the workings of the capitalist's money or other factors, that is the source of all profit. But in the last quarter century the exploitation equation has radically changed in the United States, in a way that contradicts Marx's explanation. The majority of labor in the United States, and certainly in New York City, is no longer manual in character; today, in the New York area, only one in sixteen employees labors on a factory floor, and a much higher fraction of the workforce is involved in operations that require considerably more brain power. This shift allows us to understand that the dichotomy between labor and capital, which Marx did more than anyone to point out, can be seen in retrospect as a distinguishing feature mainly of the manufacturing economy, which is rapidly being eclipsed.

In the new postindustrial economy it has become possible, and even usual, for an individual inventor to be able to sell his or her "intellectual property" product for millions of dollars. Marx might argue that such an invention is incapable of producing wealth unless and until a venture capitalist purchases the software program, replicates it for sale, and markets it—but we can counter that argument with the observed fact of today, which is that if an invention is good enough, there will be many people willing to back it, throw money at the inventor, and take the product through to production and marketing. This ready availability of monetary capital for certain mental-capital products suggests that the balance has shifted away from the traditional capitalist and toward the supremacy of the mental capitalist. Monetary capital is still essential and powerful, just not as scarce as it used to be.

Edvinsson's intellectual capital concept has been applied to sizable companies, mostly in the field of computer software programs. Mental capital, which reflects a greater grab bag of brain-power actions, has more resonance for smaller companies, and not only for those making computer software. Early observation of this block seemed to reveal it as a blue-collar place with a few white-collar outposts. Now it is clearer that a great many more of its businesses rely on mental capital. These fall into three major categories.

There are the *artists-entrepreneurs*, ranging at the small end of the scale from individual practitioners such as painter Richard Pitts and computer-game inventor Helen C. (though she hasn't produced anything tangible yet), to a middle rank occupied by the shoe designer Alain-Guy Giraudon and the clothing designer Raymond Dragon, whose products are sold nationwide, to composer Ervin Litkei, who turned his ideas into a multimillion-dollar merchandising operation, and to Raymond Waites and Bettye Martin Musham, who have done the same with Gear Holdings. The upper echelon of this category includes the Catholic Book Publishers firm, which uses the service of many mental capitalists, and the giant Cahners, which uses even more such services.

A thin line separates the artists-entrepreneurs from the *artistic service providers*. Among these are architects such as James Harb, Lee Mindel, and Bernard Tschumi, all of whom operate and staff offices on this block; Marina Yashina the art restorer; Bill Tansey, whose floral arrangements for events have caught on with big-party givers; and on a larger scale, the Madelyn Simon plantscaping company, which enlivens offices all over town. People like Vik Patel and Bill Donat might argue that their printing-trade establishments contribute artistically to the products that pass through their shops.

A third category comprises *merchandisers of taste*. This must include such traditional entrepreneurs of taste as galleries: The Chisholm Prats Gallery is a good example here because Robert Chisholm's ability to recognize and champion as art a previously neglected form—posters—has enabled him to make a good living and to employ several other people in the gallery. But in terms of innovation, we must also feature such tastemakers as Peter Glassman and Books of Wonder, with its newsletters making recommendations and its republishing ventures.

Adding such entrepreneurs to the list brings up some tantalizing questions, but before going more deeply into them, there is an aspect of mental capital that defies categorization but which seems relevant and deserves mention—the degree to which the American dream of "making it" and achieving economic success seems most greatly embodied around this block by immigrants from foreign lands. Marina Yashina, for instance, arrived in this country from Russia with nothing but her art-restorer's expertise, a knapsack on her back, a suitcase in her hand, and her seven-year-old daughter by her side; today, she and her partner are restoring one of the city's great treasures, a series of large-scale paintings of mammoths that have been gathering dust for forty years since they were taken off the walls at the Museum of Natural History. The reader has already been introduced to Pino Luongo, Jung-ok Hwang, Vikram Patel, Ervin Litkei, Jennifer Endersby, Chander Nandal, and Tim Cass, and there are several other notable immigrant entrepreneurs on the block, from the former airline steward Alain-Guy Giraudon, now a designer, manufacturer, and retailer of shoes, to dry cleaner Man Yohn Lee and woodworker Joe T. Abeijan. Vibrantly alive in this disparate group of people is the sense that the American dream remains worthy of being chased. To many native-born Americans, especially those born into the middle class, the dream has yielded to a sense of entitlement, as though a life of comfort and achievement is their birthright, rather than something to be won and savored, step by step. In business, it seems clear, the feeling of entitlement doesn't take you very far, while a sense of needing to make step-by-step progress is essential. All the successful entrepreneurs on this block understand this, though the immigrants appear to feel it most deeply.

That understanding has to do with how you portray yourself to yourself—and is the reason for this slight detour. Something of that aspect of mental capital comes through in certain merchandisers of taste. Many retail merchants on this block other than Robert Chisholm and Peter Glassman contend that what they, too, are selling is their taste, as reflected in what they buy and stock. The Authentiques partners, Robert Pusilo and Paul Lemma, certainly claim that it is their taste that makes their enterprise go— but a similar assertion is made by Ken Goldstein of CityKids, who must pick toys, clothing, and such that will appeal to customers, and by Roger Roth and Dave Samuels, whose ability to reject the

Hallmark salesman's card selections that characterize the usual card store's merchandise, and instead to choose their own mix of greeting cards, commission their own T-shirts, and stock quirky small gifts, has brought them a loyal repeat customer base. Camouflage, the men's boutique, satisfies its equally loyal customers in the same way, through providing them with a very tasteful selection of clothes. On a larger scale, Barneys would make the same claim: What they buy, or in some cases commission a designer to manufacture, is essential to their success. Are these merchants mental capitalists or just distributors whose sales edge is their taste? It can be argued either way. Americans are going to have to learn that the terms "artist" and "businessman" are not mutually incompatible because the categories are being combined more and more often into viable businesses. We have all fallen for the myth of the creative artist who is a lousy businessman, and the businessman who hasn't got an artistic bone in his or her body. Actually, many of the businesses on this block demonstrate that artistic sensibility is not only alive and well, it is intrinsically connected to making modern businesses go. In terms of the future, then, the emphasis needs to fall on the side of considering taste-merchandisers as mental capitalists and artists of sorts because that way lies more new business ventures.

That widening conception of self can be seen in operation in several changes taking place around the block in the last quarter of the year, as individuals try to become entrepreneurs and as small entrepreneurships try to enlarge their operations.

Last spring, Collette Whitney was the manager of the HomeWorks kitchen and bath furniture showroom. Adjacent to Solco and once a part of that enterprise, HomeWorks was directly competitive with LeeSam, around the corner on Seventh Avenue, in the sale of fixtures such as marble sinks, wood and Formica counters, and bathtubs. The atmosphere of each retail salesroom sharply differed from that of the other. LeeSam was so chock-full of fixtures that a visitor could hardly move through them, and its sales force was male, shirtsleeved, and tended to stay at a counter that backed onto a shipping area. HomeWorks was considerably less cluttered, with isolated fixtures individually spotlit, and the sales force, seated at managerial-type desks, consisted of three well-dressed, bejeweled, coiffed young women.

Manager Collette Whitney, a striking woman in her early forties, emphasized then that HomeWorks was different from LeeSam in that HomeWorks functioned as a design service as well as a seller of fixtures, hence its slogan, "We do the complete job from custom design to installation." In 1989, when the bottom fell out of the real estate market, affecting all businesses that were dependent on real estate, Collette, an interior designer, had begun work for HomeWorks' Brooklyn office, and had then been asked to design and manage this Manhattan showroom when the owners took it over from Solco. She and the other women in the store all worked on a draw-against-commission basis. In all, Collette reported, it had been a rough few years at HomeWorks because of real estate market conditions, but in mid-1993 prices for co-op apartments were trending up, signaling a recovery for real estate, and Collette hoped that would soon translate into more business.

In the fall, Collette resigned from HomeWorks and restarted her own interior design and consulting business, in an area of her SoHo loft set aside for that purpose. Relaxed and less bejeweled, she explains that as far as her work at HomeWorks had gone, "I did the managing and sales job well enough, but it was never for me. I'm not a shopgirl, I'm a designer." For the past two years, since the moment she had hired one particular woman as her associate at the office, she had been planning to leave to restart her own design service. "Even that woman didn't know it then, but I was training her to be my replacement. She's more suited to the position than I ever was." In addition to preferring it, Collette needs to work from her home because she is now taking care of her mother, who is recovering from a stroke.

As a design consultant and freelance salesperson in the kitchen-and-bath field, she sets her own hours and works on behalf of a large number of showrooms. "I present myself to architects, show them what I can do for them in kitchens." While most architects, she says, are "generalists" who can't take the time to microdesign space, she can and does, finding out from their homeowner clients what the various fixtures and cabinets are to be used for, and then matching the uses to the available hardware, budget, and space considerations. Her service costs the architect nothing because the showrooms give her a commission on products bought by the client. She now also selects and recommends decorative finishes. At HomeWorks, this had been an ancillary service. What she now does *not* do—a part of the job that had always annoyed her at HomeWorks—is allow anyone else to supervise the installation.

To sum up the evolution of the design service: Once upon a time, HomeWorks charged for it; then, because of a tightening market and more competitors, HomeWorks threw in the design service, without ostensible charge, to attract customers. The showroom emphasized the added value it gave the customer in terms of designing the whole kitchen or bath. Now what is happening is that Collette Whitney has split off this function and given the design part enhanced value. Instead of working solely for HomeWorks, she is able to draw from several different showrooms. These retailers gain something in the new configuration because they have less overhead (one less employee to provide health coverage for) and only have to pay a commission if Collette is successful in selling a job. The architects also benefit from a free design and client-hand-holding service. And the ultimate client, the end user, as Collette styles the homeowner or apartment dweller, seems to pay nothing because the charge is concealed in the price of the fixtures. Maybe in the future, new twists on split-off functions, à la Collette, will result in, say, car buyers/designers who will help a customer design a car, select among a growing assortment of options, and go with the customer to choose among competing manufacturers.

The most important factor spurring people like Collette to make the jump from employee to entrepreneur is the realization that as an employee in a small business one has little chance of ever becoming an owner of that business. The incapacity of a small firm to be able to offer good employees much beyond a salary constitutes a ceiling on ambitions, one that may become increasingly problematic in the future, both for the small firms and for their key employees. Rather than stay on and toil for someone else, employees with the imaginative power to go out on their own—to use their mental capital for their own purposes—look for opportunities to do just that. In the last hundred years, the defining goal of the American dream has been ownership of one's own home; in the future, the defining goal of the American dream may very well become owning part of an entrepreneurial business.

Bob Pereira found a similar though somewhat less risky opportunity to jump ship, if not entirely to set sail on his own, in the last quarter of 1993. As the manager of the Blue Moon restaurant, he was a valuable employee, but the lure of becoming the manager of a much larger new restaurant, one at which Bob's brother Cliff is the executive chef, has proved very attractive. Being manager of the Metronome, on Park Avenue at 21st Street, isn't quite going out on his own as owner and operator of a restaurant —something he's considered doing—but it seems the next best thing, and Bob has leaped at the chance. The restaurant will officially open in early 1994 but is taking reservations for Christmas-period private parties now. It is in demand because it is one of the few places that can seat more than a hundred people and not feel crowded.

The problem of retaining a key employee can be seen in a new light if that employee is understood as part of the business's mental capital, one who can be tied to the entrepreneurs and to the company's future by offering some form of participation in the profits. Such an understanding and arrangement with a key employee permitted the recent expansion of Food/Bar, where the new chef is a partner, and can even be said to be the understanding permitting the opening of the mad. 61 restaurant at the uptown Barneys, where partner Pino Luongo supplies the active management of the enterprise.

Knowing that a similar sort of restaurateur's mental capital was in place seems to have been the key to an even more recent expansion decision on the block. For at least a year, Bob Pereira and many other restaurateurs have been licking their chops over the expected demise of The Pasta Pot bar and grill on the southeast corner of 18th and Eighth. It finally shut its doors for good in the late fall, and near the end of the year, the lease for the premises has been bought by Niccola Accardi of Cola's, the other Italian restaurant on the block. Nick says that he has convinced his brother John to participate in this new enterprise. The presence of a trusted brother will permit Nick to run between managing two restaurants, something he might otherwise have been reluctant to do.

Everyone agrees that the former Pasta Pot location is a good one, and that the interior is well set up for a restaurant. Nick reports that he was offered the spot seven years ago, when he began Cola's, but it was too expensive for him at that time. Now he is ready for it, and he also knows its true value. Nick got what he characterized as a good deal, but he might have paid anything within reason to rent this particular space right now, not only because he has become so experienced in the business that he will be able to design a restaurant that will be profitable, but principally because he understands that as far as this new enterprise goes, the relationship among the factors of production have changed. He is providing the mental and monetary capital—and little else matters. That is because his mental capital includes his understanding that Eighth Avenue in Chelsea is becoming a "gay Broadway," and that gays have money and are particular about where (and in what company) they spend it. Knowing the trend and the proclivities of his target clientele, Nick is willing to bet heavily that an expensive and good-looking restaurant located on "gay Broadway" and known to be gay-friendly will prove a sure route to great profits. Cola's, Food/Bar, and Eighteenth and Eighth can compete for the $9.95 entrée crowd while Nick's new restaurant will occupy a niche one step higher in price and quality.

These examples underscore the idea that while monetary capital may be a fungible commodity, which means that a unit of it taken from one place is functionally equivalent to a unit of it from another place, mental capital is not fungible; rather, it is specific to the individual, a quality that makes it almost impossible to evaluate without taking into account the individual's personality.

This aspect becomes apparent when considering a half-dozen businesses on the block that are contemplating expansion. Many are the same ones that credit their business edge to their ability to choose among competing products and find just the right mix to display and sell in their stores. Each has conceived a yearning to open additional stores, postulating that what he or she has been successfully retailing on this block will prove attractive elsewhere. There is an element of need in their thinking, a need for personal satisfaction akin to that which they believe comes from being a successful artist. Perhaps that is why the presence or absence of monetary capital seems not to enter into the decision-making process.

In CityKids' current location there is hardly room for strollers since the store is packed with more than a thousand items—toys, socks, shoes, jumpers, pop-up books, virtually anything for a youngster from birth through the primary grades. Owner Ken Goldstein is in his forties, energetic, balding, though with a ponytail. He had worked with his family's children's clothing manufacturing business, then operated two retail stores during the 1970s, one for women's clothes and the other for shoes, before deciding to open CityKids. Victoria Goldstein, who also has a background in retail clothing, works with her husband in the store. "In 1982, Victoria and I had a three-year-old. Also, I'd lived in New York City all my life, so I knew the area. We decided that a kids' store was the best way to use a small space." Books of Wonder later moved in next door, Ken believes, in part because CityKids had shown the area to be viable for a store catering to children's needs.

CityKids had a slow start, with so little merchandise in the store that "it looked like a gallery or a museum," each outfit and toy perfectly displayed. Over the years, the store became more and more dense with merchandise. Now, Ken acknowledges, it appears overstuffed. "Actually, we have enough merchandise to stock a 2,500-square-foot store, and most of it is kept at our warehouse, a few blocks away." They carry so many items because Ken and Victoria love to buy, and they buy liberally because they believe that if they take a liking to a product, it will sell. They attend ten trade shows a year, most of them in New York City, and only recently stopped going annually to Europe to scout merchandise. "Europe has gotten too expensive to warrant a trip, and anybody who has something interesting to sell comes to New York with it anyway. That's the advantage of being here."

Goldstein's experience and success led him to want to do something more with his formula. His difficulty is the same one faced by every expansion-minded retailer: by what route to grow. Franchising? Branch stores? Mail order? Licensing? "What's there to franchise—the way I buy? The only way to make franchising work is to have private-label stock, and we're not manufacturers. I looked into mail order, did my homework, but just as we were ready to get in, the mail-order field took a nosedive, so we didn't do it." As for licensing, potential partners approached him to open stores in Chicago, Texas, and on the West Coast, but nothing happened. The Japanese wanted to do a chain of CityKids stores, but after flirting with the idea, Goldstein decided that "It would eventually have been taken away from us" because Japan is so distant, and he declined to go ahead. Finally, the direction that seemed most logical and appealing was a branch store. They opened one in a mall in Boca Raton, a Florida resort town north of Miami.

There were two problems associated with that store. First, the business climate, and second, the lack of an associate whom Ken could trust to run the store without his daily input. He tells the story in these terms: "Within a year of our opening in Boca Raton, the mall lost its anchor tenant, several stores became vacant, and you could almost smell disaster coming. We were running the place by sending the figures here daily by computer, having lots of faxes back and forth daily, and being constantly on the phones—it got to be too much. I felt I couldn't be in New York and maintain control in Florida at the same time, so we closed the Boca Raton store."

Goldstein continues to look for opportunities for expansion, but has found no new ones that he likes. This past spring, he considered expanding into the space next door to the north, which had held a women's clothing boutique, but the rent asked by the landlord was too high, so he did not do so. Now the storefront is occupied by Raymond Dragon—whose flagrantly gay window displays, according to manager Tim Cass, provoked neighboring merchants to make protests to that landlord, protests that have had no effect on the windows.

As for the Dragon boutique itself, Tim reports that the parent company has had inquiries for licensing from Paris and Tokyo, and is considering opening its own stores in Los Angeles and in the South Beach district of Miami, but will only open stores under the right conditions, which probably means obtaining premises for which the rent is not too high and where the district is considered favorable to a gay clientele. Tim has undertaken managing this first store until it is on its feet, and he says he will go to Los Angeles or South Beach to do the start-up of a second store, should that happen. The decision not to begin a second store without the direct involvement of a company principal underscores the high value placed on mental capital in this business.

On Eighth Avenue, the P. Chanin "unisex" boutique and the Giraudon shoe store, which sells fashion-forward footwear for both sexes, are neighbors. Considering a joint enterprise together in Florida, they, too, are faced with a similar mental-capital problem. The stores seem a good match to be partners in a new enterprise; frequently, customers from one of these two stores, recent purchase in hand, have been seen going into the other.

P. Chanin is filled with caps, watches, ties, a display of jewelry, a rack of cards, but mostly with T-shirts, vests, blouses, jackets, and accessories that are more-or-less unisex. A few items are stacked atop cute stools whose bottoms are feet covered with sneakers. "Pamela and I are such good pals that we don't tend the store together, or else all we'd do is talk to each other," says co-owner Elizabeth Greenberg, a chiropractor. Pamela Chanin, a former teacher and lobbyist for the New York State Public Benefit Corporation, had been one of Elizabeth's patients, and five years ago asked her to invest in a boutique; the investment soon became "more than either of us bargained for." Although Pamela is the main storekeeper, Elizabeth spells her now and then, and does some buying. Elizabeth finds it "addictive" to try and stay "a step ahead of the curve" of what customers want, and "addictive," too, to tinker with the mix of merchandise, the display, the pricing. Elizabeth is excited that P. Chanin is the only store in New York to carry the entire line of forty-two products of the Hypnotic company, which does wild watches and caps. That company takes ads in *Details* and other trendy mags, and carrying the line has resulted in some free publicity. CNN videotaped a feature on the Hypnotic products at P. Chanin, and the influential "Best Bets" column of *New York* magazine has featured the store and these watches. The store's eclectic mix of clothing and accessories reflects both of their tastes, Elizabeth says, but she and Pam are not the sort of retailers who have a lot of ego invested in their choice of stock. "In the first two years," Elizabeth says, "we made a few big wrong guesses, buying stuff that we liked but that wouldn't move, or too many multiples of one item—the usual beginner mistakes."

"I try to sell what I think people will buy," Pam Chanin echoes. Does the public want crazy T-shirts? She will stock imaginative ones, even if she herself would not want to wear them. In the beginning, the store stocked five baseball caps; now, she reports, they have fifty because people like them. Pam also seems to rate personal pleasure lower than the store's needs: She stays open many hours, especially on the weekends, because half the week's gross is done then. While Roger Roth and Dave Samuels have reached a level of sales where they are comfortable opening only six days, Pamela Chanin finds it necessary to "be here seven days a week," even though she laments that she hasn't had a vacation in five years.

During those five years, though, she has not always been able to tend the store because of illness: Multiple sclerosis has at various times rendered her unable to see, to speak, to walk. Episodes of MS come and go, and only complete rest seems to facilitate recovery. Elizabeth takes over when Pamela is incapacitated—but Elizabeth, too, has been ill, with chronic fatigue syndrome. Her robust physique and high energy seem to belie this illness, but she says that after only a few hours of work she must lie down for a while. "We joke about how lucky we've been that our episodes of being sick haven't overlapped," Pamela comments.

As part of Elizabeth's therapy, which requires quiet work, she began making jewelry; it is now sold in the store. Months in the sun were also prescribed, and it was Elizabeth's already having an apartment in the Miami area that got the partners thinking about opening a branch store in South Beach. Alain-Guy Giraudon, the proprietor of the shoe store next door, with whom they share customers as well as a common landlord, has many outlets for his shoes all over the country but only two stores of his own, both in Manhattan. Since P. Chanin clothing and Giraudon shoes have already proved compatible, the business neighbors were encouraged to think about a jointly owned store in the South Beach area. And since Elizabeth would be on the spot for a large proportion of the time, the prospective partners could be assured that things would be done to their specifications. Because of good business in the last year or so, the P. Chanin partners have accumulated a $10,000 reserve. This, they think, could be part of the down payment on leasing and stocking that new store. Though they have a business neighbor partner who can share the expense and the risk, opening a new store is not something to be entered into lightly because, Pam and Elizabeth know, the additional burden of maintaining a second store could very quickly sap the resources of the first one and lead to disaster. But it's an exciting possibility.

Roger Roth and Dave Samuels run a successful card shop business which is as much a result of their interesting and quirky choice of merchandise as P. Chanin and CityKids are the results of their owners' choices. The notion might well translate into another store, possibly in a similar neighborhood elsewhere, but Roger and Dave are not currently considering expansion. Their future plans involve translating the success of their store into hiring assistants to do some of the work so the principals can cadge more leisure hours for themselves. To open a second store would likely mean that the owners would have to split up, one to manage each location, and part of the fun and satisfaction for these two guys is tending store together.

Their business neighbor Paula Shirk, of Womens Workout Gear, has previously expressed the belief that expansion, at least in terms of opening another store, or even moving to larger quarters, is at present out of the question. As the reader may recall, Shirk must sometimes purchase stock for the store by use of her personal credit card. Despite her demurral about expansion, it still appears that Paula's concept for an enterprise—a sports-clothing store for women—is among those that could well be replicated or used as the basis for additional growth.

These examples make clear that mental capital is the very opposite of fungible and cannot be easily considered apart from the personality of the individual who possesses it. Which is to say that the health and expansion possibilities of enterprises that depend on mental capital, as so many of the block's businesses do, turn on the owner's health, on his or her sense of satisfaction, and on the business's capacity for adaptation to that person's preferred lifestyle at a particular time in his or her life cycle. Juvenal's phrase, *mens sana in corpore sano*, a sound mind in a sound body, needs only a little tinkering to bring it up to date. In terms of future small business, the ultimate goal is a sound mind—with that soundness being partially dependent on the individual's ability to reap an adequate amount of personal satisfaction from the entrepreneurship—in a sound corporate body.

In past years the Barneys Christmas holiday windows have featured famous people and what they might give or receive as gifts for Christmas. Those windows, at least, showed merchandise that might be for sale in the store, a necessary invitation, since many retail stores do as much as a quarter of their annual business during the holiday season. This year, installation artist Martha King has created for both the new uptown and the old downtown stores a series of windows that have nothing to do with the store's merchandise. Each "Seasons Eatings" buffet in a window has a different theme, but in all of them groaning tables are laden with plastic and other fake party foods, and their signs point up the verbal and visual puns. At the downtown store, the Hawaiian buffet features a dish named Poi George, while the Apeteezer has Paté Hearst, and a marine buffet has a Goldie Prawn. The windows exert a strong fascination; many passersby stop to look, read the labels, and grin or groan. Very few, however, then go on into the store. Around the corner on 17th Street are additional Barneys window installations by James Vance that look as if they were blasted out by fire or earthquake: the remnants of households torn to pieces, overturned furniture, detritus, and broken crockery, a sign warning to check for PCB contamination, and a frozen TV dinner splashed on the floor, all mingled with broken candy canes and Christmas ornaments. If the purpose of these windows is to shock, they are effective.

The most noticeable Christmas transformation among the smaller stores on the block is that of Authentiques, whose outside display boasts a profusion of lights, signs, and the like, and whose interior has been similarly festooned.

On a winter afternoon, several customers roam through Authentiques, all with the look of shoppers seriously behind in their gift-finding obligations. Michael Palmadessa, who owns the pet-grooming establishment a few steps away, searches for some tree ornaments among a sizable collection. Robert and Paul have recently opened yet another cubbyhole of a room, in back, for serious items, that is, those which cost proportionately more than the collectibles in the front rooms.

None of the customers leaves empty-handed, for the eclectic cornucopia contains so many things, a Christmas shopper almost can't fail to locate something there for someone on his or her list. As customers get ready to pay for their purchases, an interesting arrangement that Robert and Paul have evolved comes into play. Robert's items have green tags; Paul's have white. They each buy their own items to be put up for sale, and the sales are recorded in different books. For customers, this occasionally means signing two different credit-card slips. "Paul came up with the two-color idea," Robert reports. "We use the technique so that neither of us can ever say to the other, 'Why did you buy that? It's not moving.'" If a bit cumbersome, the green and white tags stratagem serves to keep the peace between partners—no small matter in a partnership of any size, and an aspect that reemphasizes the personal nature of all such enterprises.

Candies made by Liberty High students are for sale in Taylor's bakery alongside the pies and cookies and such but are tallied separately so that the proceeds from these sales can be returned to the school. The proposed expansion of the Hudson Street Taylor's into the storefront next to it has been forestalled because a chain of coffee bars has taken that space; this may put some pressure on the downtown store. On the other hand, the messenger service next to the 18th Street location wants to give up half of its two-store premises and wouldn't mind if Taylor's wanted to expand there and take up the remaining months of its lease.

At a quarter to five on a wintry late December afternoon, a glimpse in the windows of Le Madri reveals the staff having dinner, sitting around a few tables in freshly pressed white jackets, the ladies and gentlemen of the kitchen and dining room looking more decorous and proper than the few guests who have lingered long over lunch or have arrived early for dinner. Pino Luongo's two new Upper East Side restaurants, mad. 61 and Amarcord, have recently opened to two-star reviews in the *New York Times*, an almost certain guarantee that they will be filled with patrons for the next year. An equally respectful biographical article chronicling Pino's rise from busboy to restaurant-empire owner has also graced the pages of the *Times*. The public relations director who oversaw the summer film series is no longer with Pino's company, but a former long-term employee has returned to take over the position.

The block's other restaurants are enjoying a good season, they report. Bob Barbero of Food/Bar got a Christmas card from Joan Santini, with a return address somewhere in Connecticut, though no one is quite certain where GianCarlo is or whether Chelsea Place will reopen. The caged birds kept in the front of the former Chelsea Place have been removed, but on the other hand there are lights on, which means that some sort of arrangement with Con Edison has been made, a necessary prelude to any reopening. Competition is going to be increasing on this restaurant row, and not only from the new restaurant that Nick and John Accardi will open in the premises of the former Pasta Pot. Two newcomers located on the adjoining block, on the west side of the avenue between 16th and 17th, are expected to open within the next month or two, and a third restaurant is to open in an alley on 17th just west of the avenue; this latter one will utilize the building that once housed the kitchen facilities for Chelsea Place, so if that nightclub reopens, it will either have to do so without a kitchen or carve a new one from a smaller space.

At the St. Francis Residence III, one day tends to be just like another for the tenants, but even the residents are not completely immune to the excitement that permeates New York during the Christmas season, a holiday spirit that is almost impossible to escape. More so than other holidays, Christmas is associated with family gatherings, and that gives the holiday special meaning for the residents of St. Francis III, most of whom are isolated from their families. So the several Franciscans who oversee the mission plan a big holiday meal, with a ham intended for the Christian residents and a turkey for the Jewish ones. The Franciscans expect that as usual—just to show that they are alive and kicking—the Christians will eat the turkey and the Jews will eat the ham.

Chapter 11

RESTRAINTS ON BUSINESS

THE YEAR 1994 begins with an un-
usually cold January; the rapid drop in temperature is blamed for
numerous water-main breaks, one of them on Seventh Avenue just
below 17th Street. The recently elected city controller estimates
the cold spell will cost the city $57 million in snow removal, the
fixing of water-main breaks, and other repairs. New York's underground system for moving water is not only old, it is overburdened,
and for the past twenty years the city has cut budgets for municipal
repair and has put off upgrading the water mains. Con Ed and city
repair crews barricade Seventh Avenue between 17th and 14th,
rerouting traffic and thoroughly disrupting the flow of customers
to the stores, including Barneys.

This is sale season for most retailers; although much of the
merchandise in Barneys is not advertised in its windows as on sale,
some items inside are reduced in price. The block's smaller clothing boutiques are in the throes of what are variously billed as inventory clearance, January sales, or warehouse sales, the latter at

CityKids. Camouflage's sale is the best-advertised, with rotating lights and clearly marked prices on the merchandise in the window. Camouflage at 17th and Eighth is actually two stores, the larger on the southwest corner and a smaller one a few steps south, separated by a slice of real estate that was vacant for a long time but has recently been turned into the Paradise Muffin Company. This is not a bakery, per se—it imports muffins from Connecticut—but a well-lit coffee bar, part of a battalion of them that have steamed up the city in the past year. Perhaps in response, Camouflage's owners temporarily closed their second store, transferred the sale merchandise to the corner store, and began renovating the auxiliary premises. It remains to be seen whether the presence of the muffin man, with its high foot traffic, will help or hurt Camouflage. Taylor's, the bakery on 18th, reports that its business is not feeling any impact from Paradise Muffin.

The clothing retailers on the block have been grumbling that the only thing selling really well, these days, is food. Recent real estate activity on the block and its fringes seems to bear out this complaint. Beyond Paradise Muffin, farther south, though on the same side of Eighth Avenue between 16th and 17th, there soon will be a spacious wood-paneled café serving German food, pastries, and coffees. And, as mentioned in the last chapter, there is a new restaurant going in on 17th Street, west of Eighth, behind what was the Chelsea Place restaurant. A neighborhood newspaper reports on its "police blotter" page an unusual Saturday night robbery of 18th Street News: two men came into the storefront, took fifty copies each of *Glamour* and *Spy* magazines, worth about $270, and escaped.

An incident not reported to the police or newspaper but which I happened to witness: At around 6:30 in the evening on Tuesday, January 11, a white stretch limousine pulls up to Chelsea Place and four people get out, greet a man who is standing by the door, and go inside. The visitors wear determinedly flashy clothing, the three men sporting gold chains, open-necked shirts, and tight pants, the woman in an evening dress. Lights go on in the storefront, and since the street outside is rather dark, the action inside is quite visible to passersby. It seems like a scene from a gangster movie. The visitors systematically take the tie-dyed shirts and scarves and barrettes and everything else out of the window, remove all the other clothing and merchandise from the shelves of the front room, and stuff all of it into garbage bags. This process takes about fifteen minutes, because the visitors stop to try on a hat or two, hold up a sweater against a chest, match a scarf to a shirt. Then, as quickly as it began, the episode finishes—the four visitors with their now-full bags pile into the limousine and get ready to pull away from the curb.

George, left behind when the limo pulls away, is one of the brothers who bought the building at auction, and he says that the Chelsea Place nightclub will open sometime in the near future, but without Santini, who is "not involved." He doesn't say anything about the emptying-out operation just witnessed, but the merchandise in the drawers and window hardly seems worth the time or effort or money of people who travel about in stretch limos. The impression that the episode was about revenge, not about money, is later corroborated by neighbors, who suggest that the visitors were allied with Santini. According to neighbors, the new owners of the building and Santini had made an arrangement that would allow the nightclub to open and not pay rent; in lieu of rent, the building owners would share in the club's proceeds. Since the club has not reopened, the deal appears to have finally fallen apart, and Santini has been told to go away or has agreed to do so.

Nine months into a year of observation, it is clear that some businesses are bursting their seams while others are struggling. Accordingly, observation in the final three months concentrates on two matters having to do with growth: What sort of jobs are being created on the block? and also, What sort of restraints are holding back the block's businesses? For clarity, the emphasis in this chapter will be on restraints and in a later chapter on job creation—

but the reader is asked to remember that positive and negative signs show up in tandem and are not always mutually exclusive.

At the messenger services they have a saying that the worst business day of the year for couriers is a comfortably hot Wednesday in July because that is when the client's secretary or assistant says to the boss that he or she will take that parcel over to the customer themselves during an extended lunch-hour walk. Conversely, lousy weather means brisk trade for messengers; during the January 1994 cold snap, businesses are more willing than ever to pay someone else to move things around, and things are hopping at the two adjoining storefronts on 18th Street that are a depot for a courier service. Bike messengers usually deny they are affected by the cold because to admit it would be less than macho. However, frigid temperatures and snow and ice on the streets and in the air translate into an excruciating ride. Making speed creates more wind, exacerbating the wind-chill factor, and icy roads are more dangerous than usual for the bikers.

During a brief warm spell in the winter, Steven Bonfiglio, dispatcher for the messengers at the 18th Street Mercury depot of the WI Messenger Services, had time for a chat. Bonfiglio, born and raised in Woodhaven, is built wide and solid, with slightly protruding eyes and a stoved-in mouth, a turned-around cap on his head, he's an arm-waver with a gruff manner. After spending ten years as a foot messenger, for the last five he has been taking incoming phone calls and sending out messengers. He boasts that "I am the best phone operator in Manhattan," and proceeds to tell me why. "I do 230 calls a day, and I do two things good. I answer on the first ring, and I get you off the phone fast so I can get the next call. Most customers, I recognize their voices right away, so I'm typing before they tell me what they want." He holds the phone to his ear with one hand while using the other hand to punch at his computer with such force that it is a wonder the keys don't break. By the time he jumps on to another call, he either has a slip for a messenger coming out of the printer or has sent the information to one of the other locations that is either closer to the pickup point or less jammed up at the time. "Because I have a sense of who's busy and who's not, I can get the call to the right office," Steven says, and this, he believes, helps WI to offer better service than its competitors. Those who want to move up in the business, he says, have to be very good at this. "Ain't that right?" he asks of a confederate behind the wall that separates the operators from the messengers. His fellow operator, a tall Puerto Rican with glasses and a scholarly look, nods.

"I want to volunteer for Channel 13 [the educational television station] during their fund-raising," Bonfiglio says unexpectedly. "With my phone skills, I bet I could do a lot for them." The only problem is that he is uncertain of how, where, or when to volunteer.

A young black messenger whom we'll call John has lost several tickets, which is to say he has nothing to show that the recipient has signed for a delivered package; without signed receipts, the service may have a difficult time getting paid for those jobs. A customer might even claim that a package for which there is no receipt has been lost and that it contained items worth many thousands of dollars—and then WI would have a hassle with its insurance carrier to pay for the loss. Sending John out on his regular rounds, Steven enjoins him to try and retrieve the lost tickets or convince the people at those locations to sign something saying they did receive the packages. Since most of the customers are regulars, this should not be impossible to do. Later, John calls in and says he is having difficulty in obtaining the signatures. Steven orders him back to the depot; when he returns, there will probably be hell to pay.

"Although Steven is pretty good at what he does," says Dwane Illes, coproprietor of WI Messenger Services, in a later interview, "he represents the past of the messenger services, and the guy with the glasses—he's a computer whiz—represents the future. He'll likely go further into management than Bonfiglio will."

To explain this prediction, Illes cites the history of his company and industry. "In 1991—when the recession started—there were three hundred firms in the messenger business; now there are about a hundred. During the downturn we bought two smaller firms that were about to go out of business. We could have let these two fail completely and just picked up the pieces later, but we felt it was better to buy them out, take on some of the employees and the customer lists."

Illes founded the company with Reuben Weiss about twenty years ago. It survived the fax revolution, which sent many services under, and grew modestly but steadily. Today WI is the third-largest messenger service in Manhattan, employing about 150 foot, bike, and truck messengers. The 18th Street depot is one of three that the company maintains in Manhattan; another is in the Wall Street area and there is a third in midtown; a corporate office is also on 18th, closer to Fifth Avenue. Illes drops in to the 18th Street depot at least once a day, to keep his finger on the pulse of the business at street level. He is a very slim man with a trim gray mustache who wears stylish clothes that seem out of place in the midst of the bare-walls messenger depot with its piled-up bicycles, ringing phones, and young black men in skintight clothing and Walkmans getting ready to wheel out on their runs.

Competition is still cutthroat in this business, and margins are thin. What this means in practical terms is a different employment arrangement with each of three types of messenger-employees. The foot messengers, Illes says, are paid the minimum wage. While such foot soldiers were initially the nucleus of the messenger industry, Illes says that today he actually makes no profit from them, because he cannot charge a high price for sending a package by foot messenger, even though it is a time-consuming task. "Among the people who do the foot work are a few retarded men, long-term employees," Illes says. "Once a customer gets used to one of them, that same messenger is usually requested time after time."

The bike messengers, in contrast, are individual entrepreneurs—they are on commission. WI splits its fees with the bicyclists, fifty-fifty; since each messenger can handle sixty or seventy drops or pickups each day, bicyclists can earn about $500 to $600 per week. "Some of these guys are educated. But they're all rejects of society—they don't fit in, or don't care to. They don't want a nine-to-five job or being told what to do. They're not much suited for work elsewhere that would pay them as much as they can earn with us. Many are very steady workers, have been with us a long time, but they don't have ambitions in the usual sense; their dreams are outside the sphere of work."

The other entrepreneurs are the truck messengers. Trucks take material that weighs over ten pounds or that has to be delivered to far-flung or possibly unsafe destinations. Fees for this service are also split, with the truckers getting more than half what WI charges, since many of the truck messengers use their own vehicles.

Among the reasons that WI survived the recent recession is that the company invested heavily in computer, modem, and advanced telephone systems, which help it operate quite efficiently. Today, WI's largest customer is represented by the trucks that arrive each morning from Pennsylvania, carrying such things as the output of printing plants—the same sort of plants that were once down the block from the messenger depot but that have moved out of state; when the WI deliverers have completed their rounds with the one hundred or so trucked-in packages, copies of the signed waybills are sent to Pennsylvania by dedicated modem.

Even at the outset of 1994, WI continues to feel the results of the recession. "People are still paying late, from forty-one to fifty-one days," Illes says. "And we lost $100,000 when Macy's went bankrupt. That's a big hit for a company the size of ours. But then Macy's offered us more work. They're too big a customer to say no to, and they're OK on current bills. So I just read the papers every day and see how many cents on the dollar we may eventually get on what they owe us."

About six weeks later, Illes continues the discussion in a quieter environment, his corporate office, nearer to Fifth Avenue. In the interim, the company has made a significant change and taken a big hit from a direction they appear unable to do anything about. This was a 14.4 percent jump in the rates for workmen's compensation which took effect on October 1, 1993. The rates in New York State are 75 percent higher than in New Jersey, 59 percent higher than in Connecticut, and 57 percent higher than the nation's average. Businesses with employees in New York State pay into a fund that compensates workers for medical treatment and part of their lost wages if they suffer injuries on the job. The rates differ for various types of businesses, so with bike messengers continually exposed to danger on the streets, it makes sense for WI's rate to be high—but then, business owners all up and down New York State have been complaining about the rates, which have gone up by double-digit jumps in each of the past six years, for a combined rise of 153 percent.

For Illes and Weiss, such rates are a headache, one that directly cuts into the company's profitability, because rather than risk losing business by passing along these charges to customers in the form of higher tabs for services, WI simply absorbs the cost as part of its overhead. Illes implies that high workmen's comp rates act as a restraint on his company by sopping up money that might otherwise go into the partners' pockets or to expand the business.

But then, WI is no longer expanding, at least not at the rate it did in the past. Having reached the level of third-largest courier service in Manhattan, in the early spring of 1994, Illes and Weiss say that becoming larger is no longer of principal interest to them. They have recently added to their staff a president—a man, not incidentally, who began in the courier business as a foot messenger—and now have three top executives able to supervise their three depots. The result is not only lessened work burdens for Illes and Weiss, but a heightened ability to be more selective in taking and in keeping accounts. "Let somebody else do the downscale business," Illes says. "I want to do the best job possible for the right client." That customer may be an individual, a small company, or a giant organization, "so long as the relationship between us is good and the bills are paid on time." During the years when

WI was growing rapidly, they took "everything and everyone" and never gave a thought to turning down a client. Now, Illes says, they are happy with 1,500 jobs a day, because in addition to making good money from that level of activity, they have an enterprise that is comfortably manageable.

The issue of high workmen's compensation rates as a constraint on operating has been raised by various other businesses in the area. Though high rates out of proportion to those in neighboring states are a legitimate beef, and though such rates obviously cut into a company's profit, the notion that these constitute a genuine restraint to a business such as WI is less compelling. The same high rates apply to all companies in that field, which means that all the companies are, in the current phrase, on a level playing field. WI may even realize a bit of a competitive advantage from the higher rates because a smaller courier service, whose margins are presumably narrower, would feel a greater pinch from raised rates.

The same reasoning applies, in part, to the universal concern among business owners about high taxes. New York State's combined total of state and local taxes are the second highest in the nation—only Alaska's are higher—and significantly above those in neighboring New Jersey and Connecticut. In Manhattan the tax bill is even more elevated because of added special taxes associated with doing business in the center of the city. Businesses below 96th Street that pay more than $11,000 annually in rent—a category that includes nearly every storefront on the block as well as every company in the several office buildings—must pay a 6 percent surtax on that rent to the city. If the business is a corporation, it must pay 8.85 percent city corporate income tax on income realized before the deducting of compensation to owners and officers; if it is unincorporated, there is a 4 percent tax on the income of owners or partners. These taxes are a burden on the block's businesses, and even though they are a burden that is supposed to be shared by all in relative measure to the business's size, they sit more heavily on smaller businesses than on medium-sized and larger ones.

That is because smaller businesses tend to have fewer expenses that can be deducted before taxes are figured.

For example, Pam Chanin and Elizabeth Greenberg of the P. Chanin boutique have decided to spend their $10,000 in reserves for advertising rather than to open a second store in Miami; they agonize over where to place the ads so that they will get the most bang for their bucks—while Barneys, which carries some of the same merchandise as P. Chanin, spends prodigiously on daily ads in the newspapers, on television and radio, and in glossy magazines. Advertising expenses are equally deductible for both business entities but are likely to make up a larger fraction of the overhead for Barneys than for P. Chanin—with the result that the smaller store is likely to pay proportionately higher taxes on its income.

The burden of taxes could be more happily borne by the small businesses of the block, their owners say, if they could see a greater correspondence between the amounts they pay out and the services that the city and state render to them. They are willing to purchase with their tax dollars such things as fire and police protection, building and food service inspections, but believe that too great a fraction of the municipal budget ends up in social welfare services that are mainly of use to residents—schools, hospitals, public housing, and other welfare benefits—and not in services that might benefit individual businesses, such as good public transportation for customers and employees, assistance in obtaining loans, assistance in advertising to tourists or other definable groups of customers, or even a reduction in paperwork associated with government regulations. Several of the block's entrepreneurs cited the fact that most businesses must pay privately for garbage pickup while they also pay in taxes for a municipal garbage collection service that the city's rules bar businesses from using. They feel the municipal bureaucracy is overly bloated, with dozens and dozens of offices and city workers devoted to making life difficult for businesses by means of regulations. The dog groomer, for instance, must report to the city whether dogs brought in by their owners are wearing up-to-date city license tags.

Another matter considered a restraint on business is the rising cost of providing health care for employees. Throughout 1993 and on into 1994, a national and Congressional debate over health-care reform has been heating up. Republicans have charged that the Clinton format, which relies on forcing employers to provide coverage for their employees, will place an unbearable burden on small businesses. Currently, the national statistics are that in companies with fewer than ten employees, 32 percent of the employees are uninsured, 22 percent are covered by privately purchased insurance, 25 percent are covered by their spouse's employer, and only 23 percent are directly covered by the employer. Around the block, the issue of health care is not so much debated as dreaded, because business owners believe that no matter what the specific solution reached by the president and Congress, the cost of doing business will go up, and it will not be possible for a business to pass on the added expenses to its customers.

"Insuring my workers—that would put me out of business," insists Carl Berman of Guild Mailing. Very few among the employers and entrepreneurs disagree with the need to provide health care for all working people and to reform the present system. Employers on the block creep up piecemeal on the goal of providing health care for their employees. The Taylor's bakery and take-out foods business, which has two stores, provides health insurance for upper level employees but not for clerks. A similar split in coverage is the norm at the restaurants. Chefs and managers earn coverage as part of their remuneration. Waitpersons, busboys, and kitchen assistants must generally fend for themselves. The irony, of course, is that many among those latter sort of restaurant employees are recent immigrants, minimum-wage earners who cannot afford their own health insurance, so when they are ill, they seek treatment in municipal facilities—which ends up raising the tax bills for business entities.

The very largest employers on this block, Nynex, Barneys, and Cahners, have well-defined health-insurance plans that are part of the reason people go to work for such big firms. In large companies nationally, 71 percent of the employees are covered by the employer's insurance. Midsize employers, defined as those with from 24 to 99 employees, nationally cover slightly more than half of their employees, with the percentage rising to almost two-thirds when the number of employees goes over 100 but is less than 500. Middle-sized enterprises such as Catholic Book Publishers began covering their employees long ago when costs were lower and continue to do so. Other among the block's midsize employers, such as the WI Messenger Services, to save money have shifted away from more comprehensive plans to those that are less encompassing. Even GMHC has been caught in the bind between wanting to provide coverage and being nearly bankrupted by its cost; in fact, this AIDS-activist organization was recently accused by some employees of shortchanging them on health insurance.

Downtown Offset pays most of the premium for its employees and their families, but requires employees to contribute to the coverage. The firm spends what Oscar Sabel describes as an "astronomical" $600 a month per employee with family; he also is quick to note that even the $50 per month that each employee has to kick in represents a hardship for them. He acknowledges that costs might be lowered somewhat by switching to an HMO-type organization, but points out that this is unacceptable to many Hasidic Jewish employees, who want to be able to consult doctors with whom they are familiar and comfortable. Upstairs in the 216 Building, Bill Donat at Waldon Press covers management-level employees, while his unionized employees obtain a relatively low-cost but good "wraparound" benefits package through the printers' union. "In fact," Donat says, "when a new employee comes on, I usually urge him to join the union. They do a better job on health insurance than we do." Other employers who use union labor, such as Solco Plumbing Supplies, echo Donat's relief and admiration at what the union can offer.

As for individual employees on the block, a few look forward to having the sort of national health-care plan that would enable them to leave their present employers and go out on their own without losing basic health-insurance coverage. Some have contemplated becoming entrepreneurs on their own, but say they have not acted on their impulses because the current cost of independently obtained health coverage is prohibitively high, on the order of $5,000 to $8,000 per year for a family. Although employees staying put out of fear of losing coverage is not the nub of the health-care-reform debate, it may eventually prove to be a crucial aspect for American business. If it becomes possible for employees to float away from an employer, secure in the knowledge that their insurance coverage can be continued at an acceptable dollar cost to them, arrangements between employer and employee may substantially alter.

As with the payments for workmen's compensation, city and state taxes, and the cost of complying with government regulations, the money spent by small entrepreneurs for health insurance for their employees does crimp a business's profitability, but by itself does not constitute a real restraint on business growth. Put all of these profit-devouring elements together, however, and they have a considerable impact on expansion plans.

Not as much, though, as the factor cited by nearly every small business as a barrier to its growth: the cost of real estate.

Although the classical economists agreed that the three factors of production were labor, capital, and land or land-based resources, Henry George, a reformer and prophet of the late nineteenth century—and an unsuccessful candidate for mayor of New York City—claimed that land was the sole source of all wealth, including capital. He traced many fortunes back to owning land or reaping the bounty from it. There are many places in the world where Henry George's dictum of land as the basis of wealth is only partially applicable, but currently in Manhattan it seems all too true. That Manhattan is an island—a very finite piece of property, with fixed borders and divided into very small parcels—has always been the main reason why real estate is so expensive here. Scarcity drives up prices, and because there is only a limited quantity of prime

Manhattan land available, for the past hundred years both the average price and the average height of the buildings have been almost continually on the rise.

In 1975, experts trying to predict the shape of New York City after the year 2000 concluded that because of rising rents and declining job opportunities, in the next century Manhattan would lose its middle class almost entirely and New York as a whole would become a city of the very rich and the very poor. Evidence that New York has traveled in the direction envisioned by the experts is everywhere, and as we approach the turn of the century, it seems that the trend is accelerating. The shoemaker yields to the retailer of shoes, the low-cost diner to a restaurant with higher prices and presumably higher quality food, the bank with tellers to a cubicle with automatic teller machines. Modest-volume or modest-price retailers or service providers find themselves displaced by merchants who can pay higher rents because of their own high volume (Blockbuster) or high prices (the new restaurant, Viceroy, that will replace The Pasta Pot).

For a long time, when entrepreneurs considered obtaining premises for their businesses, they, like individuals, restricted themselves to paying only about a quarter of their monthly income for rent or a mortgage; in recent years, however, the percentage that generally has to be paid out to occupy premises has ballooned beyond any expectations to a third or even a larger fraction of income. For businesses that have only a few employees, rent has become the largest single business expense, and one that absorbs so much income that it deeply affects profits and possibilities of growth.

This is part of the problem for CityKids and other storefront retail concerns with good business concepts and personnel, and it also affects wholesalers and manufacturers. More than a few businesses know they are paying too high a rent, but feel they have no viable alternative. Carl Berman says that he could find space in other buildings where Guild Mailing Services could operate for half of what he pays in rent at 216 West 18th. However, since approximately 50 percent of his business comes by referral from other printers in 216, he feels it would be imprudent to relocate, even though the "extra" rent he currently pays represents the difference between being in the red and in the black. Upstairs, Bill Donat of Waldon Press considers relocating because the 216 Building, which has slow elevators and no loading dock serving the upper floors, no longer meets his needs—but his thoughts on moving are short-circuited when he factors in the quarter- to half-million dollars it would cost to move to lower-rent facilities.

In recent months a two-faced rental cost phenomenon has been operating in this particular neighborhood: Certain new businesses have been enfranchised by a downswing in local storefront real estate prices, while existing businesses have been limited by the generally rising prices throughout the midtown business area. As the reader may recall, for some time the ground-floor space of the Grand Chelsea Building on the southeast corner of 17th and Eighth has been mostly empty, except for Blockbuster Video, but the new owners of that space recently dropped the price of renting there and were quickly able to make deals with new-to-the-area businesses—the American Fitness gym, a drugstore, and a bookstore.

When the prices were dropped by the Grand Chelsea's owners, the owners of several spaces on the other side of Eighth Avenue between 16th and 17th were forced to drop their own prices or lose all potential customers to the bigger building—and the result has been the advent of Paradise Muffin, the Kaffeehaus, and on the 16th Street corner (opposite what is to be the new bookstore) a sports bar. Camouflage, the existing store whose long run at its current location is the envy of many neighborhood clothiers, had been unwilling to pay the price initially asked for occupancy of the tiny storefront in between its two current shops, but the new Paradise Muffin shop was willing to pay the price.

The real estate climate on Eighth between 17th and 18th has been affected by these lowered-price sales in the adjoining block, but also, and in the opposite direction, by the price Nick Accardi was willing to pay to snap up the corner-bar premises of the former Pasta Pot. (Nick has just paid an extra price for the acquisition: during the cold snap, pipes burst in the cellar, necessitating expensive repairs and cleanup.) Perhaps this is part of the reason why the premises of the former fish store continue to remain unrented.

On 18th Street, the Madelyn Simon plantscaping enterprise has finally moved into larger quarters near 34th Street, and the sign that advertised the entire building for sale is now gone. As the reader will recall, when Simon was unable to find a buyer for the bottom floor, she joined forces with Jean Rosenberg, the Chelsea Day School head who owns the upper half, in an attempt to have the entire building sold at once, preferably to a buyer who would then lease back the upper floor and roof to the school. The building has been sold, but not to Jean Rosenberg, who was unable to find the money either from banks, who were unwilling to accept the upper half of the building as collateral for a loan to buy the lower half, or from private lenders. The new owner is the famous photographer William Wegman, whose images of his weimaraner dogs dressed in costumes have been the stuff of best-selling books, advertisements, and calendars. Wegman has agreed to give Rosenberg and the Chelsea Day School a lease on the upstairs premises, but only for a shorter amount of time than Rosenberg desired. Accordingly, Jean will be unable to take in more students or commence the ambitious family and community resource center she had envisioned for the building, and within a few years will have to move the school.

The huge Steiner Building on 17th Street, in which Catholic Book Publishers is located, has similarly changed its For Sale sign: Now, instead of advertising the sale of individual floors, the whole building is categorized as for sale or net lease. The Cavaleros, with a new warehouse building in New Jersey, near the home of the firm's chief officer, are preparing to reduce the size of their operations in Manhattan and move some of them to that new facility. This big old building here is a major asset of the company, but it may become a major liability if they can't sell or net lease it, because the costs of carrying it—the taxes, for example—are high. That at least one similar warehouse building on same side of the 17th Street part of the block is also for sale makes the task of selling or renting the Steiner Building more difficult and less likely. The publisher's ability to expand further may well be constrained by the cost of carrying his now uneconomic real estate.

A third sign that spells real estate trouble for a business is the neon one above Joe Hwang's House of Cheers: the *u* and the *o* in LIQUORS are dark, while the other letters remain lit. Since Hwang is a careful man who pays attention to detail, he would not ordinarily leave such a distress signal unattended. However, the real estate that he owns has become a burden to him, and leaving the sign unfixed may be a reflection of that fact. Joe bought the corner building when prices were high, with a reasonable expectation that they would go even higher. Unfortunately, his purchase turned out to have been made at the height of the market, and the property has since fallen in value. Now, contemplating a change in his existence—retirement, or a position in a church, or a possible return to school—he finds that ownership of this property no longer meets his needs. He has listed it with a broker but so far has not had encouraging responses. He finds himself in the same bind as most homeowners in the country: His capital is largely tied up in his real estate at the very moment when he needs liquidity.

The first Saturday night in February is relatively warm, a welcome relief after weeks of arctic blasts. The restaurants of the Eighth Avenue strip are having a good night. Another new restaurant, called Alley's End, on 17th Street just west of Eighth Avenue, encompassing what used to be the kitchen for Chelsea Place, is having a private party prior to its official opening next week. The restaurant's only sign visible from the street is a neon crossed fork and knife, and the entrance is hidden in an alley, giving it a feeling of privacy.

A sign in the window of Flight 151 announces that this is the bar's second anniversary. Two-plus years ago, the bar's new owner managed to lease these premises for what was probably a fairly low price, because before that the space had been used as a dingy down-market bar, its insides almost invisible from the street. The front window is now so large that removing it during the summer months turns the front part of the bar into an outdoor café. The window is shut for winter, at the moment, but is decorated for Valentine's Day with a comical though crude cartoon of Bill Clinton leering at a Gennifer Flowers type, while above a cupid in a state trooper's uniform shoots arrows. At nine in the evening, the crowd inside is mainly in their twenties, heterosexual, and drinking beer, either Mexican bottled or bar drafts. The place is not yet jammed, though people continue to arrive all the time.

The customers don't look very polished, but neither are they in dungarees: attractive young men and women who probably live near this location. On the television screens, Nancy Kerrigan skates in her one-hour NBC special, and about a quarter of the bar's patrons watch. Kerrigan as a type, and her background, are similar to these patrons, who are white, lower-middle-class, young, and attractive. Their homogeneity is the result of the bar becoming known as a place where young singles can be comfortable in each other's company. As at Food/Bar, the crowd at Flight 151 is homogeneous on its own terms, and a patron can stay the evening for a modest amount of money. A young man or woman may spend $15 and take up the whole evening here talking to others his or her own age, making or fending off advances, forming friendships. After all, how many beers can one down at $2.50 or $3.00 a pop? Most patrons are nursing, not chugging, them.

Owner Roy comes in, goes behind the bar, rips off his sports jacket, revealing the same uniform of loose-fitting shirt and narrow tie worn by the bartender and female waitpersons, and yells for quiet. Having subdued the buzz, he announces what is ballyhooed on a third sign in the window, a contest for a second-anniversary prize, a several-day, all-expenses-paid trip to the Bahamas for two.

Tickets are $10, and the buyer must be present at the midnight drawing in order to win. "You can take the partner of your choice," Roy says, and adds, "I'm available."

In February, as well, there is a big brouhaha at Raymond Dragon, occasioned by the window display. This is a life-sized photo of two well-muscled young men, wearing the flimsiest of swimsuits—RD design—facing one another with arms at each other's waists. Tim Cass reports that this is actually a recognized photo in the gay community, previously published in *Out Magazine*, of a former Mr. Universe and a well-known model. Bob Paris and Rod Jackson, recently married in Hawaii, signed the photo with both names, hyphenated—Jackson-Paris. Stacks of the book they have written are also featured in the window display.

The photo has brought both wanted and unwanted publicity. What Tim styles as a "homophobic radio announcer" started taking potshots about "two men making out in underwear," and passersby regularly spat on the window. A cable television news program shot some videotape of the display. There has been some hate mail—a thing Tim has never before experienced. Someone called the landlord to complain, but wouldn't leave a name. Since the landlord has a clause forbidding pornography in the window, he called Tim, who explained what the picture shows and doesn't show; the landlord took no action. On the plus side, according to Tim, the window display has been drawing in a lot of customers who buy the swimsuits, the books, and smaller versions of the photo, which the couple has autographed. Usually the window displays are changed every two weeks; this one is being left in place for three.

Tim's bigger news is that the next display will show a Raymond Dragon catalog and an 800 number that customers can call to order the Dragon-designed merchandise. This represents an important decision by the company. They have determined not to open stores in Florida and Los Angeles just now, because the real estate prices in the "hot" areas have become too high. In that sense, real estate prices have become self-defeating, because instead of opening new stores Ray and Tim have decided to expand in a different direction, to put out a catalog and send it directly to their own mailing list and to a purchased list of an additional 4,000 names. The Raymond Dragon merchandise has previously been offered through the mail in other gay-oriented merchandise catalogs, but Ray and Tim did not like the way it had been handled, and so will do their own. If this spring line RD catalog produces as heavy a response as expected, there will be other catalogs later in the year.

The most sensible solution to premises-overhead problems in the area seems to be owning your real estate. For example, ownership of the premises has partially enabled the success of the Le Madri restaurant; a landlord other than Pino Luongo's partners, the Pressmans, might have demanded a greater share of the income from the dining establishment. In an even more straightforward way, ownership of the premises has been very good for Vic Sherman's Solco—the reader may recall that Sherman sought to buy the premises after he had purchased the old Solco enterprise—and for Marc Bernstein's Maxwell Lumber depot, next door. Actually, the other depots on the block, Leesam (bath and kitchen fixtures) and Eigen (plumbing supplies), also own their own premises. None of these enterprises would have been able to survive the drastic upswing in property values in this neighborhood had they occupied rented premises.

The need to own one's business premises struck Robert Chisholm of the Chisholm Prats Gallery so hard that he returned to New York from Germany prematurely, late last summer, to take part in a city-held auction for the building that houses his gallery. For a decade, Chisholm had been paying rent; the amount had started small, but by the end of his last year-by-year lease, the total was approaching $100,000 a year. The building, the oldest on Eighth Avenue, dating back to 1823, had been owned by Gian-Carlo Santini until it was seized by the city for nonpayment of taxes. Once before, Chisholm had tried to buy the building but had been outbid—by the man who turned around and sold it to

Santini. Chisholm thought Santini might try to buy it back once again at auction and also was wary of a bid from the owner of several properties on 17th Street west of Eighth Avenue, who had been trying to dissuade Chisholm from buying it with the promise that he would do so and give the gallery a long and favorable lease. So pleased was Chisholm that his own bid was accepted that immediately after obtaining title to the building he went to the expense of having the exterior stripped and repainted. Currently, he has to deal with a couple of resident tenants in the upstairs apartments who are refusing to pay rent, but even this headache cannot mar his relief at being able to control the current and future cost of his premises.

Small-business entrepreneurs owning their own premises, this study shows, is the wave of the future, and one of the surest routes to the continuity of middle-class neighborhoods. When areas of the city become gentrified, it is through a process of rents becoming ratcheted up to the point where businesses that make their money from lower-income residents can no longer afford to stay where they are and are replaced by businesses whose customers have more money to spend. Right now, New Yorkers are experiencing the dead end of a gentrification evolution in Soho, the former blue-collar warehouse and factory-loft neighborhood just below Houston Street: The prices for buildings and lofts and the rental rates for storefronts and gallery spaces have become so astronomical that the people who pioneered the area a quarter century ago are being pushed out, and only high-priced restaurants and shops can afford to remain. But is such a dead end inevitable, once the process has begun?

It need not be. The limiting factor to gentrification—and to maintaining the middle-class nature of a neighborhood—can be the level of ownership among small-business operators. On our block, premises are owned by such stable blue-collar-based businesses as Solco, Eigen, Maxwell Lumber, B. Schlesinger, and House of Cheers, and by such long-term middle-class establishments as Chisholm Prats Gallery, Authentiques, and Chelsea Gym/

Video Blitz. It is virtually certain that the day will come on which the renters among the lower-priced restaurants and clothing boutiques on Seventh and Eighth Avenues will be forced to make a difficult choice—to raise their own prices and cater to a more moneyed crowd or to move to an area with lower rents or to close their doors entirely; but even when that day comes, the entities that own their own premises on this block are unlikely to have to move or to radically alter their price scales or their clienteles.

What is more likely is that they will continue to thrive, as have most of the premises' owners, and also that if a difficulty arises, they will stay in place by some variation on the pattern set by Louis Nelson, who has sold his lesser business, Video Blitz, in order to realize some income from the property he owns by obtaining a rental income from the new owners, thereby helping maintain his core business, the Chelsea Gym. As winter turns to spring, on the block, another pioneer business owner, Robert Pusilo, does something similar. With his partner Paul Lemma, Bob decides to condense Authentiques into a smaller space on the ground floor of his building on 18th Street and to rent part of the remaining storefront space to a milliner. Among the reasons for doing so are that his property has appreciated greatly in value since he bought it many years ago, and in consequence, the taxes on it have risen to the point of being a greater burden than his business can readily bear.

Nelson and Pusilo have not exactly turned impediments into competitive advantages, but at least they are trying things to make sure they can stay in business doing what they have been doing.

In March, a sign is posted in the window of Womens Workout Gear: "Sixth Anniversary / We Made It!"

This sign seems evidence of the entrepreneur's anxiety about her boutique's staying power—doubts that many observers around the block believe unwarranted, given the solidity and novelty of her concept. But this is an entrepreneur who spoke about putting purchases of stock for her store on her personal credit card and of preferring a one-year-at-a-time lease on her premises—in contrast to the longer-term leases of her business neighbors who share the same landlord—even though shorter leases generally mean higher rents because of the annual renewals. Perhaps the anniversary sign is a totem of a business stalled in place.

As winter turns to spring that guess is proven delightfully wrong, for this small merchant begins to make a big play for growth. One of the gyms in the city approaches Paula Shirk with the notion of having a WWG mini-boutique on its premises, to sell workout clothing. She says yes, and then takes the ball in her own hand. She goes out and signs up several other gyms for similar enterprises. Then she makes a leap of understanding and faith: Now, she reasons, she will have several WWG outlets to sell women's workout clothing—and why shouldn't it be workout gear of her own design? She knows her main market, women who want to be athletic, and will go after them in venues where they are comfortable buying the clothing she will be offering. Her product is not so much the workout gear itself as what she calls the "attitude" of working out, which the clothing accentuates and enables. Since the clothing will not go out of style quickly, it will have a long shelf life, and since it is inexpensive to manufacture, it can be sold at a reasonable price for a profit.

Within a few months, sweatshirts and other items packaged under the label Workout Gear go on sale in these gym-based WWG locations as well as in the WWG boutique on Seventh Avenue.

It is mid-March, St. Patrick's Day in New York. The neon sign above Joe Hwang's House of Cheers has been fixed, and the broker's sign advertising the building for sale has also been removed. A customer displaying the map of Ireland on his face buys a pint of rum and a Lotto ticket. The day's newspaper headlines are full of the negotiations with North Korea over inspection of its nuclear facilities. Hwang believes that only a coalition consisting of the United States, Japan, and China threatening the North Koreans with a trade embargo will bring about compliance with inspection procedures in line with those of the rest of the world. He saw *Schindler's List* last week, and it knocked him out—such brutality, so tellingly portrayed. It makes one want to reexamine all feelings of bias, he suggests, because it reinforces the message that "all people are basically alike."

He confides that the For Sale sign has come down because although he could not find a buyer for the building who would lease him back his store, he has found one who wants to buy the building and his business, too. He has not decided whether to take the offer or not; after all, being unable to sell the building is something of a defeat, while receiving an offer for his business is at the very least a compliment, if not incontrovertible evidence of success. The possibility of such a sale has brought to the fore the need to make a decision. There needs to be a "summing up," a preparing for the remainder of his life. He is leaning toward staying here, but should he go back to school, or take that job as a minister?

The decision seems to hinge less on financial prospects than on more personal matters. For instance, Joe implies a worry that he will not be well-enough respected in his old age in the United States, as he could expect to be in Korea. He also is concerned that even though he has long since been naturalized, he will never be completely accepted here as an American. "The melting pot isn't so for people of color," he says flatly, and this bothers him not only for his own sake but also for the sake of his children, who have discovered this unfortunate racism while in college, and, he believes, may be hampered by it in the job market. Should he try to gather the children and all go back to Korea? The younger generation doesn't speak the Korean language very well, though they do so better than many other second-generation Korean immigrants because Joe and his wife pushed their children to learn it. So taking the family back to Korea seems out, too. Frankly, he says, he doesn't know what he is going to do next.

Chapter 12

UNWELCOME EVENTS

THE BIG NEWS IN big business on the block in the early months of 1994 has to do with Blockbuster and Nynex. In January, Paramount was all set to accept an offer from QVC when Blockbuster and Viacom announced a firm merger. Wayne Huizenga, chairman of Blockbuster, raised his stake in Viacom to $1.25 billion, an amount that permitted Viacom to make a renewed, higher bid for Paramount, $9.75 billion in cash and stock. On the strength of this counteroffer, the Paramount board put off its final decision until February. Of importance was that the Viacom bid included protections for stockholders if Viacom's stock price declined after the merger. In fact, all the stock prices of the largest players were falling: Paramount's, Viacom's, and QVC's. Viacom's stock has dropped so much that since September, Chairman Sumner Redstone's personal stake had deflated from $6.6 billion to $2.85 billion.

On the block, the higher Viacom bid was received by Nynex

and Blockbuster employees with resignation: The giants of the boardrooms were making a big deal and the little people would have no say in the outcome; not only that, the big deal would probably result in job losses. Nynex employees were more immediately concerned with the final stage of the name change initiated ten years earlier: Down from the archway entrance of the Art Deco skyscraper and from every other hiding place came the last New York Telephone signs. A comprehensive advertising campaign in newspapers, on television, on sidewalk telephones, and on repair vehicles announced that henceforth the company would be known only as Nynex. Few outsiders even remembered that the name derived from the company's bases in New York and New England.

In early February, only weeks after the Paramount board had virtually agreed to the QVC bid, the board reversed itself and recommended that shareholders accept the revised Viacom offer, thus going back to their first suitor, though at a price about 50 percent higher than initially offered. The deadline for tendering stock was midnight on Valentine's Day. Through the evening, proxy solicitors for the rival bidders for Paramount counted the tenders. By 9:30 P.M., unofficial reports put Viacom past the 50.1 percent mark needed to win the battle. Sumner Redstone received the news while at dinner at "21," and drank champagne toasts to the victory.

Immediately after the battle's end there are rumblings of discontent from Blockbuster and Nynex, who feel that the declining stock prices of Viacom and Paramount will translate into inadequate returns for the dollars the two companies have pledged to the takeover fight. Because of the magnitude and structure of Blockbuster's commitment, the video store chain has some leverage and seeks to renegotiate with Viacom, but Nynex, which has made its pledge in exchange for nonvoting stock, seems stuck. There are other complications, too. Blockbuster's Wayne Huizenga, part owner already of one National Hockey League team, will become part owner of another, the New York Rangers, which are in the Paramount stable, and by league rules will have to divest himself of one. Huizenga already owns three of Miami's four professional sports teams, so it will probably be the Rangers that will be sold. The Blockbuster chairman seems intent on matters other than the merger and takeover, announcing the start of a $1 billion sports and entertainment complex in central Florida to be called Block-buster Park, for which he has already spent $30 million to acquire land. "Wayne's World," as the project is becoming unofficially known, will contain a virtual-reality amusement park, golf course, shops, sports stadia, motion picture theaters and studios, and re-cording studios. On another front, Liberty Media, which had been part of the losing QVC team, now is reported ready to make an investment in Blockbuster that will in effect make a Blockbuster merger with Viacom more difficult by strengthening the stock price of Blockbuster. Topping off the rumors are stories that Via-com, to pay off the debt incurred in purchasing Paramount, will have to sell some Paramount assets, among them Madison Square Garden and the Knicks basketball team, in addition to the Rangers. Further support for the idea that the takeover is too costly is pro-vided when QVC's stock price goes upward while Viacom's and Paramount's continue to decline—evidence that Wall Street inves-tors believe QVC has done better by losing out on its bid than Viacom has done by winning.

On the block, there is a clear divergence of opinions about the final victory. Those who own stock in the victorious companies, including some Blockbuster and Nynex employees, view the merg-ers and investments as eventually good business, if not wholly pru-dent or entirely salutary for current employees in the short run. Those who don't own the stocks see the future approaching more quickly than it had prior to all the fuss. The likelihood is that the video rental enterprise itself will probably continue pretty much as it has been for a few more years, but that the mergers may hasten the ultimate demise of the rental business. Since Blockbuster will now be a partner in cable channels that will soon provide an al-ternative to renting through "video on demand" transmitted directly to homes, there will no longer be an incentive to open new rental stores.

Some Nynex employees on 18th Street believe that their company's investment signals a further attempt to decrease reliance on local service—the bailiwick of this group of employees—and that their unions will have to use whatever leverage they have left in forthcoming negotiations to wrest some sort of long-term job commitments from Nynex for local service employees.

On Wednesday, March 30, 1994, the manager of Eigen's supply depot in Brooklyn, Marvin Wildstein, is shot to death in the store by an intruder. The gunman also takes $60 from the cash register and robs a customer in the depot before fleeing. Descriptions of the gunman are vague, and he is not caught. Wildstein, a sixty-two-year-old Korean War veteran who had worked for Eigen for more than twenty years, had wanted to retire but had kept working because his wife was ill and the family needed the medical coverage that the company provided. Eigen coworkers and executives at the 17th Street headquarters of the company are shocked and angered at the killing. On the block the Eigen garage doors, usually kept open so that supplies can move in and out freely, are closed for several days, though the company remains open for business.

Wildstein is the 274th homicide-by-gunshot victim in New York City thus far in the still young year of 1994, and one among about 120 people murdered at work in New York City in the previous twelve months. A study by the Federal Bureau of Labor Statistics recently determined that New York City leads the nation in workplace killings, with a rate four times higher than the national average. Retail-store owners and cabdrivers have previously been known to be at particular risk, but this killing at Eigen emphasizes that even those in wholesale and distribution are vulnerable.

According to the BLS study, the second leading cause of death on the job is traffic accidents. Shortly after the murder at Eigen, one such traffic accident claims the life of a bicycle messenger when he is sideswiped by a bus at the intersection of Sixth Avenue and 22nd Street. Once more, the death does not occur on this block, but it affects people here. News of the accident spreads quickly among the couriers of the city, and the next day at rush hour, bicycle messengers from the 18th Street depot, many of whom pass by the 22nd Street corner every day, go to the site and are joined by a hundred other messengers from various other courier services. They all drop their bikes in the intersection, clasp hands in a circle, and hold a momentary memorial and protest service. Their action stops traffic and makes for a good photograph for the newspapers.

For years, drug-related killings, shootings, knifings, muggings, and robberies have taken place near the Fulton Houses at Ninth Avenue, just beyond the block, and now there is a notorious crack house on 17th Street near Sixth Avenue, in an almost-abandoned building only a hundred yards from Barneys. Addicts go there to smoke and shoot up, then sally forth to commit robberies to obtain money to support their habits. Effective work by the resident manager and tenant patrols at the Fulton Houses along Ninth Avenue and regular sweeps by the police patrols of the Tenth Precinct have made many pushers of higher-priced and harder drugs move away from that area. Similarly, the crack house on 17th is under fire from community groups and the courts, who want to shut it down completely and move remaining legitimate tenants elsewhere. Despite these advances, the corner of 17th and Eighth remains known to local residents as a place to score marijuana, crack, and other forms of cocaine. Patrons in business suits and those who look like derelicts hang around that corner at odd hours of the day and night.

The criminal activity that includes the sale of drugs and the robberies and other crimes committed in order to obtain money to buy drugs are a significant part of the underground economy. Most people confuse the off-the-books economy, whose main crime is tax evasion, with the more dastardly criminal enterprises of heroin dealers, muggers, and prostitutes. One recent scholarly book rates the underground economy among the fastest-growing sectors in New York, right up there with the rising importance of the city in international marketing and in the sale of luxury goods. Another suggests that off-the-books activity is more likely to take place in an area actively undergoing gentrification than in more settled neighborhoods. Our block is considered to be in the late stages of gentrification. The underground economy is not so visible here as it is in the ghettos, or so invisible as it is behind the walls of the apartment houses of the Upper East Side or inside the white-collar crime centers, but it exists.

It can be glimpsed in the early morning, in the form of a few of the delivery trucks that double-park near the restaurants. Most delivery trucks come from licensed, tax-paying entities who render bills that are paid by the restaurants' monthly or weekly checks. But here and there, on Eighth Avenue, principally where boxes of foodstuffs are exchanged for cash, the legitimacy level is lower. The COD delivery trucks are generally the ones with no markings, and their merchandise is handled by men whose salaries are paid in cash and go unreported because many of these employees are illegal aliens who work without green cards. Most restaurants who pay suppliers in cash keep their own records for accounting purposes, but they have no control over what happens to the cash at the other end. The questionable transactions tend to occur at the less expensive restaurants, because high-end restaurants are paid by customers' credit cards and don't usually have much cash on hand.

Throughout the school day, a handful of drug pushers hover about in the concrete playgrounds and on the fringes of the junior high, high school, and other public educational facilities on the block adjacent to this one, between Eighth and Ninth Avenues. For sale, according to the students, are marijuana, crack, angel dust, and various other drugs whose price per consumable unit is just a few dollars. In appearance the pushers are indistinguishable from the casually dressed, mostly black and Latino high-school students, and this camouflage is among the reasons the pushers are not easily identified. In the city, 60 percent of those arrested for selling drugs are under the age of twenty-five, and 35 percent are nineteen or younger. Liberty High keeps pushers away from its immediate vicinity by the tactic of not permitting its students to go out of the school unsupervised during classroom or lunch hours. Nonetheless, posters warning about the dangers of drugs or advertising detoxification and counseling programs are posted on the walls at Liberty, testimony to the fact that no high-school population in the city is immune to drugs.

Though New York trails Detroit and Washington in terms of overall crime, in 1994 it is still the mugging capital of the country. On the block there are occasional muggings and robberies, but not a distinct wave of them. The lack of conspicuous enclaves of the wealthy and the relative scarcity of foot traffic on the side streets make this a less than desirable hunting ground for muggers. On the other hand, shoplifting is a problem for the area's boutiques and stores. Several owners keep baseball bats behind the counter and go so far as to chase identified shoplifters down the street, on the possibly foolhardy presumption that the vast majority of them are unarmed. More disheartening to the boutique owners have been instances of employees stealing by means of such stratagems as not ringing up cash transactions. Store owners talk a lot about trusting their employees; those owners who cannot be present in their emporiums at all times must do so; when this trust is broken, the lesson learned is more bitter than the loss of money.

Although there is very little in the way of new construction on the block, there is a fair amount of interior rehabilitation work. Surveys taken within the last decade have found that as much as 90 percent of such work is done without the required city permits, and half of it by workers who are illegally paid. Storefront construction, in particular, is believed to have a large off-the-books quotient. In addition, many of the fixtures that are installed—cabinets, for instance—are fabricated by illegal aliens at furniture sweatshops in the outer boroughs.

In the tenements, an occasional family engages in home piecework associated with the outer fringes of the garment industry, work not covered by union contracts and which is compensated at prices below the minimum wage. Often, a worker in a garment factory will bring home piecework after a long day at the sewing machine, and while he or she sleeps, other members of the family will sew the parts of garments together, much as immigrants have done in New York since before the turn of the twentieth century.

Perhaps two-dozen residents on this block are houseworkers who are generally paid off the books. These workers, principally immigrant women, are paid in cash, with no deductions taken out, and prefer it that way, even though this keeps them out of the Social Security system and could deprive them of money in their old age; by that time, they figure, they'll have returned to their countries of origin, where it will cost them less to live. Most work for people who live in higher-rent districts uptown—people who in regular business circumstances would not consider paying anyone illegally, but who agree to off-the-books arrangements for their maids and nannies because the paperwork associated with paying household employees properly is too much of a headache.

As the neighborhood has gentrified, underground economy problems that had cropped up regularly in the past among the block's relatively poor population, such as illegal gambling in the confines of a club in the former Pasta Pot building and the sale of stolen goods, have moved elsewhere. There are no overt sex clubs here, and no peephole shows in stores that feature obscene videos; most of those enterprises are found in the 42nd Street area. Prostitutes ply the big crosstown streets, 14th and 23rd, and there are a few on Ninth Avenue, but in general streetwalkers do not roam side streets that have little foot traffic, which is the case along 17th and 18th in the evenings, as well as along Seventh Avenue at that time. The policemen of the Tenth Precinct do not believe any houses (or even penthouse apartments) of prostitution exist in the confines of the block. Two ladies of the evening do appear to live above the restaurants on Eighth, but evidently do not conduct business from their residences; they seem to be call girls, perhaps attached to an escort service. Most "johns" in the city, according to other prostitutes and to occasional surveys, tend to be middle-aged suburban married men, and this neighborhood does not have many customers of that sort, nor is it a place to which such potential customers would ordinarily go to find illicit paid heterosexual sex.

Several transvestites who frequent the block, and perhaps live nearby, reportedly make their living from the streets near the West Side Highway and its extensions in the evenings, completing their transactions in cars and trucks. The restaurants and bars on the block that cater principally to homosexuals, and which serve as places to meet potential partners, try to keep "professionals" out, and they say they manage to do so with varying degrees of success. The gay joints here have reputations of being relatively genteel; rougher trade is usually relegated to establishments farther west, also along the fringes of the West Side Highway.

At 2:30 on a Monday morning in late April, the bartender at Food/Bar locks up the restaurant and starts to walk home. Three teenage boys follow him, call him "faggot," and beat him up, breaking his nose and causing other injuries. In the weeks that follow, several other similar incidents occur, one to a gay man walking home from a gym, who is bashed over the head with a pipe, another to one of the electrician students who go to an after-work class at the Humanities High School on 18th. This young man was mistakenly believed to be gay and was beaten by six youths. In a fourth incident, a lesbian is hurt. There are also several other incidents that reach the level of harassment but not of injury.

Police reluctantly conclude that these are not individual or isolated incidents but evidence of renewed violence against the gay and lesbian community. In 1992, there had been many such incidents, but their level had dropped in 1993. Now, as evidenced by these incidents on and near our block, it is clear that violence is once more on the rise.

The series of attacks are one element that spurs a new organization into existence. The other goad is a street fair held along Eighth Avenue between 14th and 23rd Streets on a brisk but brightly sunny Saturday in late April. In all of 1993, there had been two fairs on Eighth in this area, each on a Saturday. This year, four fairs are scheduled. Such increased activity incenses many of the merchants, who do a hefty percentage of their weekly business on Saturdays. In the past, most of the fair vendors were transients—not from stores in the area—while merchants from the area who sought to take part were charged considerable vendor fees.

"What that means is paying double rents," Pamela Chanin says. "One for your regular space and another to get into the fair. On top of that, the merchant loses money because the street fair takes business away. The city and state also lose the tax dollars the store owners would collect, and they have to pay extra for clean-up costs afterwards." She charges that the fairs "are not really fairs, they're flea markets. The merchandise is second-rate garbage—you see the same stuff at every fair, schlepped from place to place." Chanin points out that the low-priced merchandise attracts to the area only the sort of shoppers unwilling to pay higher prices for the better merchandise in the regular shops along Eighth.

Chanin, a former Albany lobbyist, made these arguments to the local community board. Pushed by the board, the fair's sponsors agreed to let any merchant on the strip have a space on the street in front of their own facilities to sell whatever merchandise is usually sold in the store. Unlike other vendors, the store owners will not have to pay a fee for this privilege. There was a clash when one store on the block wanted to have nothing in front of it, and the fair organizers threatened to put another vendor there if he didn't fill the street space, but this has been resolved.

On fair day, the storefronts on the block that have displays in the street fair are two restaurants, Blue Moon and Flight 151, the latter with a setup that extends its open-window front into the street with table seating; P. Chanin and the neighboring 18th Street News; and, across the way, the hardware store, which mounts a display of inexpensive kitchenware. There are more units in the fair from this block than from any other block along Eighth

Avenue between 14th and 23rd. They are interspersed among the sellers of denims, Italian sausages, kitchen magnets, and low-cost jewelry.

Elizabeth Greenberg stands behind what in the store had been the sale racks of marked-down blouses and the like. The P. Chanin boutique's other merchandise is priced just high enough to be incompatible with the prices of the other merchandise being offered to the hordes of passersby, and so is kept inside the store. Alan Gross fills a table with items that he and Doc Nandal overbought and want to get rid of, Christmas trolls and other gifts. The sales tactics and degree of readiness of the block's merchants seem awkward in contrast with the practiced strategies of the fair regulars—but then, as Pam Chanin says, the units from this block are on the street this day not with an eye toward making money but just "to protect our turf."

Pam Chanin has tried for some time to get neighboring merchants to join with her in protest against increasing the number of fairs, and in the aftermath of the April fair a meeting is finally held. What brings the merchants together at this time is the conjunction of the danger from street fairs and the series of gay bashings. Chanin recalls that five years ago the idea of an association was bruited about but failed to take hold. "Some of us said then that what we needed was a cause. Now we have one."

On a Thursday morning, the owners of Food/Bar and several other restaurants, as well as Pam Chanin, Michael Palmadessa from Towne House Grooming, Robert Pusilo from Authentiques, and a dozen more merchants from along the Eighth Avenue strip between 14th and 23rd Streets meet at Food/Bar to form a merchants association. The store owners determine to meet every few weeks, and to lobby the police for more protection. At a second meeting, on May 5, the Tenth Precinct representative reports to them that the police are delighted to hear from them because the machinery of government responds best when there are definite, reasonably based requests from legitimate groups. Shortly, the police mount extra patrols on weekend evenings on Eighth Avenue, from dark until past closing time for the bars. Perhaps as important, the merchants who have been business neighbors for years begin to cohere as an association. "Now we know one another," Chanin says. The association could help the block counter the street fairs and work on other projects. Out of these unfortunate events, then, something positive may yet be made.

Chapter 13

EXPANSION, STABILITY, AND THE MIDDLE CLASS

WHEN THE PRICE of a stock climbs or when a publicly held company declares a dividend, some money is spread around, but the increase in the national wealth from these events seems of less moment than that added by the creation of jobs that will provide people with steady income over a longer period of time. To put just a slight twist on a biblical phrase, give a man a fish and he will have a dinner; teach a man the job of fishing and he will be able to provide many dinners for himself and others. In respect to the economy as a whole, then, one measure of the success of a business must be its ability to create jobs. While businesses can be quite healthy, remunerative, and long-lived with just the entrepreneur employed, or the proprietor plus an assistant or two, the growth, and usually the strength, of a business is intertwined with job creation.

The largest job creator on this block in the past year has been Barneys, which hired several hundred people to work in their Madison Avenue store. In general, though, the big businesses of this country, other than such retailers, have not been creating as many jobs as their relative weight in the economy would predict. Rather, large companies, especially publicly traded ones, have been destroying about as many jobs as they have been creating, eliminating along with blue-collar manufacturing jobs the sort of middle-management positions that for the last fifty years have been providing millions of people with secure middle-class incomes. As an example, when AT&T admitted to making $1 billion of mistakes in poorly conceived and executed business projects, rather than firing the high executives who were responsible for the "flops and fumbles," it announced plans to cut an additional 40,000 people from its countrywide payroll, among them a substantial number of middle managers.

According to one research report, in the fifteen-year period between 1973 and 1988, companies with more than 500 employees created more than half of the new manufacturing jobs—but then, manufacturing itself is on the decline. Since 1979, U.S. Labor Department figures show that a net of 36 million jobs have been eliminated from this country; the recent rate of job loss is about 3 million a year. On the other hand, a recent statistical abstract prepared by the Small Business Administration shows that companies with fewer than 500 employees created more than 13 million of the 19.3 million new jobs that emerged between 1980 and 1990, and that 10.75 million of those new jobs (82 percent) were generated by companies having fewer than twenty employees. Perhaps as important, most of these latter jobs are nonmanufacturing positions. Another study indicates that the number of people employed by small businesses just about doubled in the decade of the 1980s. Taken together, these statistics indicate a leading role for small businesses, especially in job creation, as we mature fully into a postindustrial, service-sector economy.

One sobering result of the eclipse of manufacturing and the flattening of management pyramids has been the elimination of previously assured routes into the middle class, and the substitution of new jobs that pay well below the $32,000 annual family income level that is the current national average. As a country, we need a strong middle class in order to keep the economy going; two-thirds of our economy depends on consumer spending. In the past twenty years, the fraction of net worth held by the top 1 percent of households increased by 16 percent to 36 percent, while the net worth percentage held by middle-class families declined almost as much. But a single family earning $3.2 million a year, which is a hundred times more than the average family earns, has no reason to consume a hundred living-room sets by Gear Holdings or a thousand cases of wine from Joe Hwang or a thousand baseball caps from P. Chanin, while a hundred middle-class families can be expected in the aggregate to buy that many things. Today, when people are laid off, only about one-third of them are able to find jobs that pay as well as their previous positions. In the postindustrial society, where will new jobs that support middle-class families come from? Can we realistically expect those jobs to be generated by small businesses?

With these questions in mind, as the year on the block draws toward a close, revisits to many of the smaller entities yield the information that, yes, job creation on the block is taking place, mostly among the smaller businesses, in small increments, and it is adhering mostly to three distinct patterns. The first is exemplified by the progress of Myron Michaels, the former high-school science teacher, at Sight on Seventh.

In the early spring, Michaels is more stylishly attired than on earlier visits, with a crisp gray shirt, modern-patterned tie, and braces—somewhat fashion-forward. Two well-dressed women in their late thirties enter the shop, and he attends to them. One lives in the neighborhood while her friend is a former resident who has moved to Canada but has come back during a vacation. The first woman has ordered some glasses and is bringing in her prescription, which she forgot on her last visit. As Michaels and this customer transact their business, her friend tries on several frames and seems inclined to buy something. Michaels is careful with the women, deferential but not fawning, giving good information, keeping any sales talk very low-key, trying to make things easy for them, and letting the neighborhood woman be the arbiter of taste for her friend. In effect, the first customer's market judgment on Michaels and his shop, which is favorable, enables her friend to consider buying here in the belief that Michaels's merchandise is tasteful, of proper quality, and properly priced. While the Canadian woman is looking, Michaels convinces the first customer to purchase in addition to frame and lenses a particular kind of glare-resistant lens coating, which costs $45; the total charge of around $450 for two pairs of glasses does not appear to make her blink. She hands her credit card to Michaels and tells her visiting friend, who is continuing to try on frames, that one horn-rimmed frame has a certain "attitude" while the other has a different one, so "It depends on what look you want." Michaels beams. He asks the friend if she has her prescription with her, and when she tells him she does not, he offers to put aside the two frames for her anyway, and encourages her to call or fax him the information when she returns to her home. They agree that the selection of frames is wider in New York than in Canada. The friend reserves two frames and seems likely to buy one of them when she obtains her prescription from Toronto. The total for the merchandise bought by both women will be $700 to $800, a very nice sale for a single fifteen-minute period.

After the women leave, Michaels expresses delight at them and at his customers in general: how polite and nice they are, how the transactions go on so smoothly, with no ugliness on either side of the counter. The customers, he says, understand that he is offering quality merchandise—his location, the look of the shop, and his own manner convey that idea—and that in this shop they may expect and will enjoy a civilized atmosphere for a sales transaction. "I suppose I could do more business with a location on Fifth Avenue, but it wouldn't be the same sort of refined customer as I get here, and I like this type."

In the past few months, Michaels has adjusted the merchandise he sells because he has become "more aware of having to stay one step ahead of fashion. It's a feel...takes time to get it." Having discovered that his customers "know what's out there and how much it costs," he has adjusted his prices to meet the approval of the comparison shopper and believes he is now providing more value. "But giving value isn't just cutting the price on an Armani frame; it's also making the customer aware that such an expensive frame is well made and will last and is a good value for the money you spend." He now sells more brand-name merchandise, such as Armani and Calvin Klein, than merchandise without designer labels.

"I'm learning a new fashion niche," he sums up, as opposed to "working with the geriatric crowd." In the terms used earlier in this book to explain how businesses work, Michaels has redefined and refocused his concept to better match the context of his business.

A month later, the sign on his window says that the optometrist is now available two days a week instead of just one—which means, Michaels says, that there are more customers to be served, and more demand for the optometrist's services. A pass by the store some weeks later reveals that Michaels has hired a part-time assistant.

Most of the small storefront businesses on the block that have been hiring are doing so in the part-time, one-at-a-time manner of Myron Michaels—extra help in the clothing boutiques and restaurants; extra design and architectural assistance, on a freelance or contract basis, in the professional partnerships. We must certainly classify as an expansion the opening of Gascogne, earlier each day, to serve lunch as well as dinner, because that means more hours worked by more people and higher income to the restaurant. A few businesses are hiring for full-time positions.

In the spring, Cindi Taylor and her family make a choice and create a handful of new jobs. They had already decided to expand—their two-store operation had become so successful that it began taking up more of Cindi's husband's and brother's time than originally intended, and so expansion of the business's money-making capacities became an important priority in order to justify the time the two men were spending. In addition, not only were the ovens at 18th Street large enough to handle more output, but there was capital that had not been completely absorbed in the construction and opening of the 18th Street operation. Cindi's first thought was to open a café. Coffee bars are becoming good businesses this year in New York, replicating their success in Seattle. But Cindi surveyed a few cafés and was annoyed to discover that "people linger far too long over $2.50's worth of coffee and a muffin." Running a bakery-with-café in a new location, she implies, might undercut the profitability of a prepared-foods emporium by clogging seats with too many people not paying enough rent for the time they occupy her chairs. Accordingly, the Taylor bunch made plans for an additional bakery and prepared-foods retail entity that would not have café seating. This decision effectively ruled out making a bid on the space next door on 18th Street, even though it would shortly become available because the messenger depot was giving up half of its space. During the winter, Cindi thought she had a perfect location, a storefront on West 72nd Street, but she finally decided that the lease there was too costly and turned her focus to a storefront in an entirely different area of the city, on First Avenue near 11th Street, in the East Village. Closer to the other two Taylor's facilities, and with a lower rent, this one makes more sense than something farther uptown, and the Taylor bunch have just signed a lease and begun renovations toward a late spring opening. Cindi is already thinking ahead and can imagine expanding at her current rate of one new facility a year for the next few years.

The new Taylor's location will require more staff, and while the people who tend the counter and do other sales and stock jobs will be mostly new employees, the managerial positions will be filled from within, following a pattern Cindi already established in opening the 18th Street store. The manager there had previously been the assistant manager at the original Hudson Street Taylor's, and the assistant manager had been a lower-ranked employee. Such steps up the ladder open the way for new hires to fill the positions being vacated by the promoted employees.

In a similar vein, Pino Luongo has promoted people from his existing restaurants (including Le Madri) to positions at his two new ones; the proprietors of Food/Bar, which is now a thriving establishment, are looking for another location in the city to establish a second "nice diner," which will require some hiring, too; Robert Chisholm has promoted an assistant and hired another; and the Raymond Dragon enterprise has expanded its manufacturing operation on 35th Street to meet the demand for its clothes that has blossomed in reaction to its first boutique and its first catalog. And Nick Accardi's Viceroy restaurant will be opening soon, on the southeast corner of 18th and Eighth, and will need to be staffed.

A third pattern of hiring is that being done by Vikram Patel. During a spring visit, he tells a story about his teenage daughter who had been trying out for her school's tennis team and believed that a new racket was essential. He questioned her need for it, recalling that when he was growing up in India, one of eight children, he had similarly asked his father for new sneakers with which to win a race. "My father told me, if you really want to win, you don't need new sneakers to do it. And he was right, because I did win the race." His daughter has also told him that she hates her homework. He can hardly comprehend this, he says, because the opportunities for learning that she is being afforded at her school are so much greater than they were for him and his brothers and sisters in India. He asked his daughter to describe her hatred for the homework, then picked at the inconsistencies in her response, and counseled her: "This is work to be done, not because you like it or dislike it, but because it is work that must be done."

He may have recounted this story in symbolic explanation for what he has been doing lately in business. His suit against the giant international company Siemens has ground on, held up in part because the judge assigned to the proceedings has had to deal with a much larger and more public matter—the trial and sentencing of those accused of bombing the World Trade Center in Manhattan. Vikram seems to have at last decided that he can no longer wait for full justice and must move ahead with or without validation or restitution from the courts. Accordingly, in recent months he has made a concerted search for new business, has found some, and has just rehired a few of the men he reluctantly laid off six and nine months earlier.

The other principal example in this category is a tale of two-steps-back, one-step-forward. In the late spring of 1994, Carl Berman's Guild Mailing Service finally runs out its string. Saddled with debts, hampered by outmoded equipment and by a long-term inability to broaden the basis of the enterprise, Guild Mailing Service goes out of business. It has clients, but not enough, and there seems to be no real future for the enterprise. Many bridges have been burned: It would take too much money to purchase the modern equipment necessary to compete with other mailers; the availability of home and small-business computer programs for low-multiple mailings continues to increase, thereby shrinking the pool of potential customers; and there is no longer any possibility that the foreman might buy the business, since the asking price is too high and so are the firm's debts. Carl Berman, who had long sought to get out, finally gives up the fight and moves himself to the upstate New York area that he mentioned, months earlier. When Guild Mailing Service had been a going entity, Berman would often contract with a client for both printing and mailing services, then subcontract the printing to Bill Donat's Waldon Press. Perhaps because the two men had known each other for many years, Donat had given Berman quite a bit of slack in paying for services rendered to Guild by Waldon Press; accordingly, when Guild closes, the firm that it owes the most money to is Bill Donat's. In an arrangement between the two men, Donat agrees to accept some of Guild's meager assets as partial payment and also to absorb key employees—as Waldon Press has done in the past with the employees and assets of other printing firms in the 216 Building that fell on hard times. In further response to this near-forced acquisition, Donat buys newer mailing equipment and, in essence, enlarges the capacities of Waldon Press by means of a mailing division.

Some other jobs are being destroyed outright. A For Rent sign goes up on the Kap's diner on the northeast corner of 17th and Seventh, opposite Barneys. For years, Teddy and Peter have complained to their patrons about the inadequacy of their business, complaints that the patrons have taken with a grain of salt, noting—sometimes aloud—that these stories share airtime with tales of the owners' children being sent to college from the hard-won proceeds of innumerable tuna-fish sandwiches and bowls of lentil soup. But now the landlords of the apartment building in which the diner is located (and which also houses Roger Roth & Dave, Womens Workout Gear, and Sight on Seventh) have evidently demanded a stiff hike in rent for a new lease, and Teddy and Peter appear to have refused to agree to it and must soon vacate the premises. Without a lease, the diner is unsalable, so they will shortly be going out of business and taking down with them the equivalent of eight to ten full-time jobs.

Then there is the fledgling computer-game enterprise of Helen C. At the close of 1993—six months behind her self-imposed schedule—Helen's prototype game, with its characters that alter their personalities along with their traits and tools, was finally deemed ready enough to be shown to potential buyers. Actually, Helen wanted to keep perfecting it, but her friends and husband insisted that it was far enough along for a manufacturer to make a decision, and Niko pointed out that their rainy-day fund had been almost entirely exhausted. There had been no money from investors because, as Helen puts it, "I didn't want my friends throwing money down what could be a rat hole." As an economy measure, she gave up the apartment in the nearby building that she had been using as an office, and from her own apartment's second bedroom made appointments to demonstrate the game at the offices of about a dozen computer-game manufacturers, most of them located on the West Coast. Personal appearances were necessary, she reasoned, because if she merely mailed a manufacturer a couple of disks, they could be copied and her ideas ripped off without payment.

So she used her personal credit to finance an extended trip to California, Oregon, and the state of Washington in order to demonstrate her game. "That's the part I hated most—being a saleswoman," Helen confides. Responses were varied. Some manufacturers gave her a flat no, outright, saying that they "had something similar in the works." Others said they would consider manufacturing the game for sale if she would invest, say, $50,000 for initial production and marketing expenses. Only one company offered to buy the game, and the terms were no money in advance and a royalty schedule that only kicked in after the manufacturer had deducted virtually all his expenses from the gross sales. Helen returned home to the block without a single offer for the game that she felt she could accept—but with two promises of employment. "After eighteen months and umpteen thousand dollars, what I effectively produced was a sample of work done on this machine," she sighs, tapping her forehead.

With her monetary capital tank on empty, and having exhausted the ranks of major potential purchasers, she has decided to stop spending all of her time trying to sell the prototype to manufacturers in the second tier—she'll still try them, but not as aggressively—and is considering accepting one of the jobs. The better offer is in Silicon Valley, and she is not sure whether to take it because it would mean commuting back and forth to New York (at considerable expense) until such time as Niko can also find a job in California. She may decide to wait for an offer from a New York–based company, but she doesn't have one now, and a bird in hand . . .

Last but not least, there is what is happening at House of Cheers. During the past year, in which Joe Hwang has been uncertain about his direction, he learned that he was unable to sell his major asset, the building on the northeast corner of 18th and Eighth, for what he thought it was worth and has now decided to also reject as inadequate an offer to take over the business itself. He has determined instead to sell another asset, the family home in Westchester, to move into Manhattan, to cut back somewhat on the amount of time he spends in the store, and to bring his wife in to assist him so they can spend more time together. He is also giving more responsibility and hours of work to his employees. The neighborhood that has sustained him and his enterprise for nearly twenty years cannot be left behind; Chelsea, which he has called "my second home," will become his only home. This immigrant will not go back to Korea nor eschew business altogether and take a paid position as a minister. Now, with his children all launched on lives of their own, and having taken the decision to remain in business, he and his wife can pore over college extension catalogs and in other ways set about the enterprise of what he styles "the rest of life."

It is difficult to figure the total number of jobs created on the block in the past year. When Authentiques condenses its selling area, reducing the need for part-time help to augment the owners, but at the same time opens up space for a milliner and her assistant, has there been a net job gain? When Solco does not replace Peter Miceli as manager but divides up his former responsibilities between two long-term employees and gives them each a raise, and paves the way for more hires at lower-paying positions, how much of a net gain can that be said to represent? Can we count as a plus for this block the added positions in the manufacturing loft of Raymond Dragon, up on 35th Street? The addition of Mrs. Hwang to the workings of House of Cheers? Or as a loss the dropping out of the entrepreneurial ranks of Helen C.? A guess is that the equivalent of 35 full-time positions have been added to the small businesses. This might seem a low percentage when compared to the block's total employment of 2,500, but if Nynex, Cahners, and Barneys with their combined 1,500 jobs are taken out of the mix, along with the post office's 250, the figure is somewhat more reassuring: 35 jobs to augment the 750 already provided by the block's small businesses, or an increase of nearly 5 percent. More-over, these jobs seem to be solid ones. Most have not been added in response to what could turn out to be temporary prosperity, but rather are the result of carefully taken clientele. The purpose of adding a job may be to service an expanded business, but just as often the aim is to reduce the entrepreneur's own workload or to free the entrepreneur from certain humdrum tasks in order to enable him or her to concentrate on finding new business or to otherwise enable expansion.

Does this added employment serve to stabilize or increase the middle class? It appears significant, even though most of the new positions are low paying and only a handful are on a managerial level, because of the following analogy: Suppose that on Eighth Avenue between 17th and 18th Streets there was only one restaurant, a cafeteria that served a thousand meals per evening. In such a place, there would be perhaps two or three owners, an equal number of head chefs, one or two managers, and the rest of the employees would be on a lower salary level. But that part of Eighth Avenue actually has five restaurants, dividing up among them that same thousand meals per evening, and it provides many more managerial-level jobs—six to eight owners, five head chefs, five managers, and several maîtres d'hôtel. The expansion in many fields taking place on the block and because of the block's enterprises is similar to substituting multiple restaurants for cafeterias and thereby expanding the number of entrepreneurships and mid-level managerial jobs.

This point needs further exploration, but first, other signs of health on the block beyond job creation must be noted. The taking-up of empty space, for example. As spring wears on, the next-to-last empty storefront on Eighth Avenue, the old fish store, which has remained stubbornly empty for several years, is rented to a new tenant, who will open yet another restaurant, one that serves Indian food. The former Chelsea Place remains boarded up, but there is news that GianCarlo Santini is about to open a new nightclub, five blocks north, that can be expected to be similar to the old Chelsea Place: Its advertisements stress the same attractions and promises. On 18th Street, the WI Messenger Service has given up one of the two storefronts its depot had occupied, and that storefront has now been rented to a health-foods bar. On 17th, one of the large buildings that has been closed all during the past year has also been rented, at least on the ground floor, to a furniture and furnishings emporium.

Other openings in the vicinity are affecting the block and threaten to do so more deeply in the future. On the northeast corner of 16th and Eighth, in the Grand Chelsea Building, there is now an eclectic bookstore with a coffee bar upstairs. A few weeks after it opens, the books come out of the window at 18th Street News; Alan Gross reports that before the new bookstore opened the newsstand was selling about forty books a week, and they are now down to three or four per week, which has made that aspect of the news store's operation uneconomic, and Alan and Doc have shut it down. Of greater significance for more people is the grand opening, in the spring, of a large Today's Man superstore opposite Bed Bath & Beyond on Sixth Avenue between 18th and 19th Streets. This large cut-price menswear store is an immediate hit, and means trouble not only for Barneys, but also for the smaller retailers like Camouflage. Later in the spring, a Barnes & Noble superstore is scheduled to open at 21st and Sixth, selling books, magazines, greeting cards, audiotapes, and CDs, and other superstores for women's clothing and for office supplies are expected to shortly join the Sixth Avenue crowd in the retail mansions of yesteryear.

As for the health of Barneys, there are contradictory indicators. In late February, two weeks in advance of opening its new store in Beverly Hills, Barneys took an unusual step. To counter speculation about its financial condition, the department store company decided to show some recent sales and earnings figures to the press. "It is painful for us to do this," Bob Pressman told the *New York Times*, "but we want to resolve any questions once and for all about our financial viability." The figures released showed that after the Madison Avenue store had been in operation only five months, the company had virtually doubled its New York City income of the previous year, to $150 million, and doubled its profits to $5.9 million. By fiscal year's end, Barneys expected sales for the company as a whole to be $326 million and earnings to be $11 million. The Pressmans and financial officers of the company attributed past problems to glitches in accounts payable that had grown more substantial while the executives were preoccupied with opening the Madison Avenue and Beverly Hills stores. Why these glitches had not shown up in previous years, when Barneys was opening a half-dozen suburban stores at a time, was not explained. Past bills were being paid, and high officers of the company were now actively placating suppliers and factors around the country (and around the world). This action was too late to save some small suppliers, and others swore they would never again sell to Barneys, but most, including the largest ones, now said that Barneys was no worse than its large-store competitors in paying its bills, and they would continue to do business with the Barneys chain. As for the Seventh Avenue store, according to a management spokesman there has been some falling off of business attributable to opening the uptown store, but not as much as anticipated.

A contrary indicator is that Barneys' favored architectural firm, Rosenblum/Harb, is still waiting for construction to begin on the gymnasium and spa floors of the new Barneys headquarters for which it is responsible. The green light is expected shortly. Meanwhile, Rosenblum/Harb isn't counting on new work from its former major patron. The firm continues to design retail stores, for Kenneth Cole and Dunhill, and is embarking on major department store commissions for Bloomingdale's as well as doing more private residential work. Another contrary indicator is the still-persistent rumor that the Seventh Avenue store is going to be downsized.

Gear Holdings, still a tenant in a Pressman-owned building, has undergone an important change this spring. Recently, the

Crown family of Chicago told Gear Holdings that it wanted to alter their relationship. A new generation of Crowns was taking over the reins of the family and wanted to get rid of its smaller investments and concentrate on larger ones. Bettye Martin Musham and Raymond Waites did not consider trying to find another investor to buy out the Crowns' portion of their capital, or even one who might put in additional money. Instead, they bought back the Crown investment, using Gear Holdings' retained earnings to do so. Now, once again, they own 100 percent of their company—which, in the interim between the time the Crowns made their investment and the present, has enlarged many times and become that much more stable. Such stability (and retained capital) are prerequisites for and precursors of expansion.

To return to the analogy of substituting restaurants for cafeterias, and thereby creating jobs: There is a myth in this country that a business, like a shark, must keep growing or it will die. Certainly this is true of publicly traded companies, whose stock prices rise or fall on the news that this quarter has been better or worse for them (in terms of sales, margins, size, market share) than last quarter. But growth is not the criterion of success or the basis on which executives are remunerated in most privately held companies, and certainly not in most smaller businesses. On this block, during the past year, about half of the business entities have not expanded or even considered doing so, but they have stayed even—survived—and for them, that has been good enough. Some are impacted by the flip side of the preference in our society for growth, a lack of dignity and respect accorded to straightforward service providers such as small shopkeeps. Such businesses would be better served by an understanding, if not an outright celebration, of the notion of owning, operating, or working for a small storefront retailer or wholesaler or manufacturer, and not less so if that business remains in a steady state for years and years.

But steady-state businesses will not provide enough middle-class jobs for the future, while expansion-minded businesses at least have the possibility of doing that. It is an excellent reflection of the contribution to the economy of this one square block that half of its small businesses are expanding or working toward that goal.

The future of small entrepreneurships and of middle-class jobs generated by those small businesses is, by the measure of this block over the course of a year, certainly different from original expectations and a bit better, yet not as good as might be hoped. Blocks like this one will survive and generate new employment by means of the quality of their goods and services—be that Taylor's baked goods, Gear Holdings' furniture and furnishings designs, Gascogne's lunch, Solco's plumbing supply expertise, or Vikram Patel's reprographic expertise. They will act as magnets for further growth in a way that may serve to balance the aggressive expansion of the chain retailers who are malling the nearby stretch of Sixth Avenue.

If the triumph of the United States in World War II was due to our ability to use our huge factories to turn out landing boats and other matériel that overwhelmed our enemies, the potential triumph of the United States today lies in our ability to fragment away from huge manufacturing enterprises into much smaller ones in which a larger percentage of the workforce participates in an entrepreneurial way rather than remaining simply as employees whose lack of skills leave them largely dependent on the employer. The limitations to achieving that goal are suggested as well by the experience of this block, not so much because these limitations weigh heavily on the individual units, which have demonstrated their hardiness and ability to innovate, but because they constrain the generating of new businesses and of middle-management positions in them.

Both the positive and negative experiences of businesses on the block suggest a handful of concrete responses to the limitations:

- We must encourage the newest formulation of the American dream, the owning of a business. The old American dream, of home ownership, was encouraged and underwritten by a combination of federally backed low-cost mortgages and a tax policy that permits a home owner to deduct interest payments; we need to find ways, perhaps through similar low-cost loans and generous tax deduction provisions, to encourage business ownership. If we believe in capitalism, we must back up this belief by programs that aid small business as much as, if not more than, we aid big businesses. The bailout of Chrysler was necessary and salutary, but a powerful argument can be made that monetarily equal assistance to a thousand troubled small businesses would likely produce far more wide-ranging positive consequences for our economy.

• As an important element in supporting small businesses, we as a society must find ways to assist or even directly underwrite the entrepreneur's ownership of his or her own business premises; the control of costs that ownership brings also provides a business with a stable platform for growth, and that growth, with attendant job creation, is desired by society. Responsibility for action here lies with municipal and state governments and their tax policies.

• To create more entrepreneurs in more niches, we must place increasing emphasis on putting the means of production—be that computers or the facilities to design workout clothes or expertise as a chef or a master's degree in teaching—into the hands of more people. The principal tool to accomplish this is education.

• To encourage entrepreneurship properly, our schools, especially our business schools, should teach the mustering and application of the artistic impulse alongside managerial ability and marketing. The experience of the businesses on the block demonstrates that the element of artistic imagination is as central to the entrepreneurial process as monetary capital or real estate location—especially so as we head more deeply into the postindustrial age and traditional manufacturing is done more and more by unassisted machinery.

• To further encourage individual entrepreneurship and small-business-employee participation in the enterprises in which they work, we need to make it easier for individuals to meet such personal obligations as the purchase of health insurance. This might be done through permitting individuals to buy it as members of a group, so as to lower their insurance costs. This doesn't have to be accomplished through a federal program; a neighborhood association or civic group could organize it.

• In order to build the middle class, we need to encourage ownership participation among the employees of small businesses, perhaps through the equivalent of the employee stock ownership plans that have saved many midsize businesses from going under. Such plans might ameliorate three chronic small-business problems, the lack of operating capital, succession planning, and the salability of the small enterprise. Employees buying into the business can bring capital for expansion, provide a way to pass on the business to a new generation of owners, or serve as informed purchasers at the time the original entrepreneur wants to move on. In addition, partial ownership would encourage employees to stick with a small company and link their lives with a profitable venture to which they contribute.

• To further encourage job creation, especially at managerial levels, we need to sponsor it by tax incentives or private subsidy. Maybe we could reward a company that creates a new managerial position, say, a year after that position has been in existence, by a tax code provision that would treat a fraction of the manager's salary as though it were a capital improvement—which would lower the company's taxes. This would result in no great loss to government revenues, as a middle-class job created is a tax base enhanced.

The current emphases on big business and on high technology as the routes to a stable economic future for this country seem now, after a year on the block, unfortunately narrow, wrong in emphasis, and perhaps misguided. Technology and standardization cannot bear all the burdens of growth, nor should they. If we insist that they do so, the personal scale of society will be lost; we will have a society in which decisions on the future of individuals will be made by corporations that are rewarded for rising stock prices and downsizing, not for job creation, and that ignore the health of the individuals who work for them and the neighborhoods in which they are located. If capitalism is to retain a human face, and to be viable in our cities, we must not permit it to be reduced to a creature of, or the product of, big business alone. The history of this block over the course of a single year demonstrates that small businesses, even in fields not overly reliant on advancing technology, are able to serve as engines of growth and also to provide their principals and key employees with the personal satisfaction, as well as the adequate income, that Americans desire. That is cause for celebration—and reason for support of similar enterprises.

THIS WILL
ONLY TAKE A MINUTE

Wednesday, June 15, 1994, is a blistering day, one more reminiscent of a hazy, hot, and humid August scorcher than of the late spring. At noon, the sun beats down as the teachers and students of Liberty High emerge from their facility on the block and file west on 18th Street. They cross the street to avoid the construction at the new Viceroy restaurant, which is still under way, and pass the Towne House Grooming, B. Scheslinger, and Authentiques stores, in front of which they often gather prior to school, and the House of Cheers, where Joe Hwang peers out curiously. Crossing the avenue, they glance at the coffee shop on the northeast corner, whose outside benches they sometimes occupy, and the deli-grocery where they buy soft drinks after school. The line stretches half a block farther west and then turns to enter the Bayard Rustin High School for the Humanities. This facility, named after a civil rights leader, has an auditorium, while Liberty's own building does not have a space that can comfortably hold all its students at one time.

The auditorium is a faded, peeling, un-air-conditioned, but nonetheless suitable setting for this ceremony: Wall panels depict civilizations of Egypt, Assyria, and Asia, as well as the Byzantine era, Middle Ages, and twentieth century, and there are murals of people of all colors, creeds, and races. Tables of trophies and awards are arranged on the stage by the staff as the 500 teenagers come into the well of the auditorium and take seats in homeroom order. From a balcony, a handful of parents and relatives look on. The students are noisy though not raucous. A few boys wear ties and jackets and a few girls wear dresses, but most students are casually outfitted and look just like all the other teenagers in this country—though perhaps a bit on the clean and neat side—despite being a very disparate, multihued group whose members were born in three-dozen different countries around the globe. There is excited chatter in several foreign languages as well as in diversely accented English.

Half the audience is composed of those about to graduate, and half of students who will finish the program next January. Very few parents are in attendance, but this is midday during the work week, and most parents cannot take time off for the ceremony.

With only modest difficulty, Principal Bruce Schnur calls the assembly to order. Jose Acevedo, a member of the staff, asks the audience to repeat the Pledge of Allegiance after him; they do, phrase by phrase, and when he finishes and says, "Please remain standing," they repeat that phrase as well, to some laughter. The national anthem is sung to guitar accompaniment. Deriphonse Delinois, to whom some of the words are still unfamiliar, brings a Caribbean accent to the song along with a good voice.

This is billed as an awards ceremony as well as a graduation, for although the graduates earn a certificate, they must still spend a few more years attending a regular high school in order to obtain a diploma. That is the reason coordinator Carol Yankay characterizes these proceedings as bittersweet, for while it is a passing onward, it does not have the full sense of achievement that goes with obtaining a real diploma. The principal's list, the honor roll, and the attendance honors are the main awards. "Mr. Bruce" announces the principal's list, which comprises those students who have above a 90 percent grade average. The top students are Nogbou Ahounou and Nikoleta Danicic at 97.2 percent, with Luis Martinez two-tenths of a point behind. About one-sixth of the graduating class is on this list; they are called to the stage individually and receive trophies, certificates, and T-shirts from Mr. Bruce, who beams as he hands out the loot. The names are Wang and Shin and Lu, Alvarez and Nunez and Reyes, along with Berecz and Sadowski and Suljovic: At least a dozen countries represented among thirty-five students. The honor roll is next, another forty or so students whose averages are between 85 and 90; no trophies for them, but they do receive certificates and T-shirts. These are clutched to bosoms and taken back to seats, amidst talk of going to "real" high schools next fall. There is a considerable amount of overlap between these two honor rolls and the roll of students with perfect attendance during the second semester. These are the children whom Schnur, Yankay, and other staff members expect will go on to distinguish themselves in regular high schools, which Liberty graduates have been doing for a half-dozen years.

As ceremonies go, this is a very relaxed assembly. The biggest applause and cheers are reserved for two transit police officers who work the subway platforms during the coming and going times of the student body. Officers Payne and Phillips receive plaques from Schnur and seem almost overwhelmed by the enthusiastic reception—after all, this is a city in which public-school kids and cops are often at odds, while in contrast this particular audience is most appreciative of the officers' work in protecting them.

"This will only take a minute, I promise," Bruce Schnur says in apologetic introduction to his principal's address. He knows the students are eager for the entertainment that will follow, performed by various singers and dancers from among the student body. Over the murmurs of the children, for whom the excitement peaked with the receiving of the sheepskins, Mr. Bruce retells one of the myriad stories that surfaced during the recent celebrations of the fiftieth anniversary of D-Day. It is of a GI who was put out of action that day by a "million-dollar" wound, serious enough to temporarily disable but not enough to permanently harm the soldier. A comrade in arms says, "Well, the war is over for you." The soldier demurs, maintaining that the war will only be over in fifty years, when they can come back and see that everything they fought for, and that their compatriots died for, has been accomplished and preserved. Liberty graduates, Schnur implies, must inculcate the same attitude. The story is prelude to his advice of the day: "Whatever the difficulties—and there will be many facing you out there when you leave Liberty High School—don't give up hope."

It is an appropriate and realistic message to these children who bear within them the promise of the American dream. For this ceremony is not a culmination, but a benediction and transition, a moment to remember, though just a way-stop on the road of a long life. May you come back in fifty years, Mr. Bruce says, and see how well it—and you—all turned out.

LATER ON

General Trends

Between the late spring of 1994 and the spring of 1997 the national economy grew steadily, and the recovery became complete enough to be considered full and healthy. New York's economy was considered quite strong, though it lagged behind the national average (national growth rate, 2.5 percent, New York region rate, 1.9 percent). New York's economy was also less healthy than the economies of many other major American cities, reporting higher unemployment and local rate of inflation and a lower rate of job creation. Growth in New York seemed at first glance to have been limited mostly to enterprises directly related to Wall Street.

Some commercial taxpayers received a few small local tax breaks: The commercial rent tax rate was reduced, and the threshhold at which the tax begins was raised to $40,000, with a sliding scale for rents between that and $60,000; this has been of assistance to the storefronts whose monthly rent is below $5,000. In addition, starting in July of 1996, small business corporations with low profits also received a break in the way compensation to small shareholders was treated for tax purposes. At the state level, work-men's compensation rates have also been slightly reduced, a boon to many businesses on the block.

In general terms, over the last three years the area surrounding our block has fared somewhat better than the city as a whole, though not as well as the Financial District. Notable in the na-tionwide recovery, for example, were the contribution of units from large retailers who used to locate principally in malls; the concen-tration of such retailers along Sixth Avenue between 14th and 23rd has increased, with units of Burlington Coat Factory and Old Navy joining the ranks of Today's Man, T. J. Maxx, Staples, Barnes & Noble, and Bed Bath & Beyond. Their success is one measure of how things are picking up in the surrounding area.

Around the block, the most noticeable changes have been those at street level: About 20 percent of the storefronts have changed hands. Most of the entities that went out of business or moved appear to have done so because they were faced with rent hikes. Another consequence of the upward trend in the economic climate is the addition of a few more new service enterprises, half-hidden in the below-stairs spaces of apartment buildings along 18th and in previously vacant buildings along 17th—places that in earlier years had not been rented for retail commercial purposes. All of this is consistent with latter-stage gentrification, when businesses replace residences and higher-income-generating business entities displace those that can only produce lower revenues.

Gentrification itself has been undergoing a redefinition, a wid-ening to include what happens to an area socially: In a nutshell, it is that more-gentrified neighborhoods are able to boast of popu-lations that have higher incomes, more advanced educational train-ing, smaller family sizes, and lighter-colored skins. As such, then, gentrification is considered a contributing factor to the increasing polarization of the city into rich and poor enclaves. These trends have become more pronounced around the block in the three years since the initial study was concluded.

Perhaps the most intriguing aspect of the changes is that the companies most deeply affected during this several-year period have been the largest entities on the block, while the midsize and smaller ones—at least those where the entrepreneurs own the premises or have long-term leases—have shown steadier courses. After a decade of independence, Nynex is on the verge of a merger; Cahners has become a card to trade in a large game; and Barneys has declared itself bankrupt.

As for the small businesses, they appear to have yielded to the imperative not to fix something if it doesn't appear broken; since they are profitable, they go on their way, catering mostly to the middle class and not embracing change. I wonder if their acceptance of the good-for-now status quo is an instance of ostriches burying their heads in the sand. That is because the other significant change on the block is one notable mainly by its absence: Very few of the established small businesses have pursued the new technology, specifically that which would enable them to sell products or services on the Internet. They appear to have been deterred by the generation gap that separates the current entrepreneurs of the block from the twenty-somethings who are more comfortable with such technology and by the expense of getting a web site and a catalog on-line. But their refusal to pursue the new technology seems to limit future large-scale expansion—to condemn many of these enterprises to a neighborhood clientele whom they can serve in face-to-face encounters and to one-generation ownership. One might envision an on-line men's tie shop, where potential customers could key in various combinations of shirts and jackets and receive advice on what ties might be purchased to complement them; or a printing establishment whose two-way communications enable it to have customers in faraway locations; or an interactive parenting course for parents to absorb after their little ones are asleep for the evening. But unless quantum leaps in imaginative marketing through new technology are made, it is not likely that such enhanced enterprises will be established by the block's current entrepreneurs.

While the area's banks seem more ready than in earlier years to make loans to small business entities, most of the smaller businesses around the block still lack capital for expansion, cannot afford to provide health care for their employees, and are still constrained in their ability to create more managerial-level positions. New York State seems willing to bail out the Chelsea Piers development, which has not been as successful as planned, at a cost of many millions of dollars to taxpayers, but not to do much for small businesses, leading to the inevitable conclusion that it is not only the squeaky wheel that gets the grease but the largest and loudest squeaker.

Barneys

The most convoluted story on the block involves Barneys, the large fish in this pond. In January of 1996, Barneys, Inc. filed for bankruptcy and simultaneously sued its Japanese partner, Isetan, for $50 million it had paid to Isetan in the previous two years. The story was front-page news in national as well as local newspapers, although the similar bankruptcy filing of retailer Today's Man, also in January, rated only a squib on the business pages. Isetan immediately countersued the Pressmans personally for $168 million that it said they owed in short-term loans that had been advanced to Barneys and guaranteed by the Pressman family. A statement accompanying the filing said that until November of 1995, Isetan had been unaware of financial problems at Barneys, an assertion hotly denied by Barneys, which also said that the $168 million had been part of Isetan's investment, not loans. Major suppliers to Barneys who stood to be hurt by the bankruptcy filing included Giorgio Armani, Hugo Boss, Hickey Freeman, and Donna Karan. In Japan, it was reported that Isetan might lose as much as $190 million in the bankruptcy as well as its position in the partnership.

Industry analysts believed that the bankruptcy filing was a strategic initiative in a fight for control between Barneys and Isetan. Most agreed that the problems for Barneys came from overrapid expansion, from its inability to convince customers beyond New

York City to buy its stylish clothing, and from the size of its debt load ($300 million) in relation to its annual sales ($400 million in 1994). Before filing for bankruptcy, the Pressmans had tried to convince Isetan to trade its stake in three new stores (New York, Beverly Hills, and Chicago) in exchange for stock equity in Barneys, Inc., so Barneys would no longer have to pay $2 million each month in "rent" to Isetan for those premises; Isetan refused to agree to that deal.

Things went quickly in court, at least on the smaller issues: The Pressmans agreed to pay Isetan $3.25 million in back rent, and Barneys agreed to buy Isetan's half of a credit-card-receivables business for another $20 million—so Barneys could gain access to those receivables, which Isetan had had the court freeze.

When the Isetan partnership came apart, it put intense pressure on the Pressmans' seven-year relationship with Pino Luongo. At the end of February 1996 a new deal was put in place in which the Pressmans agreed to sell their half interests in Le Madri and two other in-city restaurants to Luongo, while he would sell to them his interests in mad. 61 and the cafés attached to the suburban Barneys stores around the country. Pino told a reporter, "There was a major project that I wanted to do. And they managed to kill the deal. Since then, I choose to do it on my own." The two sides agreed, for the moment, that Luongo would continue to operate the mad. 61 restaurant inside the uptown Barneys. That temporary arrangement, too, broke down, and, in a move that smacked partly of revenge, Barneys closed mad. 61 and then made plans to reopen it under the direction of a man who had once worked for Pino as a chef and with whom he had publicly feuded for some time.

The bankruptcy proceedings careened on, with Isetan and Barneys angling for full control. In July 1996, Fred Pressman, father of Gene and Bob, died of pancreatic cancer. The following week, it was revealed that the Saks department stores, owned principally by a bank in Bahrain, were in serious talks with Isetan about henceforth running the Barneys stores together with the Japanese, as were two other companies, one from France and another from

Canada. Neiman Marcus, owned by Harcourt General, was also reported as in the hunt. The first bid, filed in February 1997 by Dickson Concepts (International) Ltd., of Hong Kong, fell far short of creditors' expectations. Barneys was reported as owing between $600 and $850 million, and Dickson's opening bid was $240 million. The low bid was attributed in part to Barneys' lower holiday sales figures for 1996–97, compared to those of 1995–96. In mid-June, the Pressmans announced that after 74 years, the 17th Street Barneys would close its doors forever in September. At press time, the viability and future ownership of the other Barneys stores remain uncertain.

Pino Luongo has come through the Barneys crisis reasonably well. He opened another new restaurant in New York recently and is talking of expanding his Cucina Tosca line laterally to packaged soups and other foods. He has already added a line of pasta sauces sold directly to restaurants in New York City.

Around the block, the most visible sign of Barneys' difficulties—other than the absence of Barneys executives from the lunch tables of Le Madri—is the revamping and scaling back of the flagship store. This is something that Barneys told local neighbors, as well as the press, that it would not do even after the Madison Avenue store was opened, but it has happened. The Barneys frontage along Seventh Avenue was reduced in the summer of 1996, and a notice went up that the southerly half would next be occupied by Loehmann's, a low-priced women's clothing retailer with a half-dozen outlets in the metropolitan area. Loehmann's opened in October 1996, in time to catch the Christmas season.

Gear Holdings is no longer a tenant in the Pressman-owned building next to Le Madri, having moved to a taller building farther up Seventh Avenue, but it reports that business is still thriving, and that it is still a corporate partner of Isetan. Architect James Harb has no further partnerships planned with Barneys or the Pressmans, but commissions from other retailers continue to be the backbone of his practice.

Along Seventh Avenue

A flurry of closings and some reopenings have taken place along the Seventh Avenue strip, less due, it seems, to initiative by the shop owners than to landlords seeking appreciably higher rents. Since Eighth Avenue is hot as "gay Broadway," and Sixth is hot as the home of the retail chains, it is not unreasonable for property owners and rental agents to think that Seventh will be the next to shine. CityKids unexpectedly closed its doors, and its space was immediately occupied by the Raymond Dragon boutique. Dragon then split its operations so the old storefront became Raymond Dragon for Women while the newer one became more specifically for men only. According to Ken Goldstein of CityKids, the rental agent for the apartment building in which these stores are located knew of Dragon's success and willingness to expand, and, with such a prospective tenant for the CityKids space in hand, asked Goldstein for a hefty increase at lease renewal time and would offer only a two-year lease. Goldstein, who had previously demonstrated a keen sense of when to hold'em and when to fold'em, declined to pay the higher rent and closed his store. "It was painful," he says, "but you regroup and go on." He and his wife have now opened Gift Baskets International, operating from an office a few blocks away and offering their wares (for adults and children) for sale through the mail, by telephone, and on the Internet.

The Raymond Dragon boutique was eager to expand, Tim Cass reports, because they had outgrown their first location and there was also demand from women for clothing that was made more precisely in their sizes. There are now RD stores in Los Angeles and Fire Island, and the principals have plans to establish an on-line web site. Recently, they helped introduce in the United States the "Billy" doll, the first such specifically gay doll, designed and manufactured by a London firm; Raymond Dragon even designed one of the doll's outfits.

After the switch from children's stuff to daring clothing in one store of the 200 West 18th Street building, another change took place in an adjoining storefront of that building: Books of Wonder closed its retail operation on the southwest corner and moved to what a sign in the old window described as larger and less expensive quarters, still on 18th Street but in the block between Fifth and Sixth Avenues. Glassman and Carey had told me that they were never afraid of being close to Barnes & Noble, because their clientele was not the same as that of the larger bookseller; now the guys have put their money behind that belief by moving even closer, to within a few dozen yards of the main B&N stores on two corners of Fifth and 18th, onto a block that is now heavily associated in the public mind with bookstores of several sorts. The former Books of Wonder storefront remained empty more than six months and was recently rented to New World Coffee, a chain of coffee bars. A few neighbors recall that prior to Books of Wonder that space had been occupied by a coffee shop. At press time, the new coffee bar has still not opened.

On the opposite side of Seventh Avenue, something similar is taking place. As the reader will recall, the Kap's diner on the northeast corner of 17th closed its doors in 1994. The space has remained vacant since that time. In the fall of 1996 the landlord of the larger building in which the Kap's space as well as several smaller storefronts are located declined to renew the year-to-year leases that Paula Shirk of Womens Workout Gear had held for most of the past decade. According to Shirk, the landlord did so to combine her storefront with the adjacent Kap's space, thereby making a larger and potentially more attractive spot for a new restaurant or other substantial tenant. Womens Workout Gear reopened on the southwest corner of 15th and Seventh Avenue in the fall of 1996. Shirk said then that the workout gear she had designed was doing quite nicely—but she obviously did not believe that occupying the entire 17th Street corner with the retail operation would have been a salutary move, even though she expected some added business from the opening of Loehmann's. The 15th Street corner location had an uninviting entranceway and a cramped feeling. Less than six months later, in February of 1997, the retail shop of Womens Workout Gear closed its doors. The combined Kap's-WWG space at the corner of 17th Street has still not been rented.

Of the other stores on Seventh, the most change in business has been that of Roger Roth & Dave, who have opened a second card store and gifts "outlet" on Eighth between 21st and 22nd. Roger says that he and his partner each manage one of the stores, and for variety switch stores often, but that the added responsibilities have made it no longer possible for both to tend the same store at the same time. Myron Michaels's Sight on Seventh continues in operation, with the optometrist now available three days a week and an assistant visible more of the time behind the front counter.

On the Eighth Avenue Strip

Around on the Eighth Avenue strip, there has also been some juggling about, though most of it has happened on the adjacent block of Eighth between 16th and 17th. The eclectic bookstore-cum-café that had once, and very quickly, caused 18th Street News to stop selling books gave up the ghost and was replaced by a real coffee bar, a unit of the Starbucks chain. (That may have given inspiration for New World to rent on the nearby corner of 18th and Seventh.) Several of the restaurants that opened on that 16th to 17th block in the spring of 1994 have changed character and ownership, from German to continental, sports bar to Irish pub, etc. If the Paradise Muffin bar is feeling any pain from the presence of Starbucks, no one is yet talking about it. Camouflage remains in its two stores, still a treasure trove of stylish menswear. Louis Nelson's Chelsea Gym continues in operation, as does Video Blitz under separate ownership, despite the presence of their hefty competitors, the American Fitness Centers gym and Blockbuster, respectively. The presence of counter assistants other than the owners in Video Blitz leads to a belief that the store is on a reasonably even keel.

The biggest change on the strip is at the former Chelsea Place, which has become—after another interim failure in the spot—a health foods emporium, Earth General. GianCarlo Santini's new nightclub, several blocks north, which opened in mid-1994, has since also shuttered its doors. Bob Pereira of Metronome, who worked for Santini for many years, reports that his former employer died in early 1997. The Chisholm poster gallery continues in operation, its quarterly window display changes eagerly awaited. Robert has taken in a new partner, Jerry Larsson, so that the gallery is now known as Chisholm-Larsson; the partners have also opened up a web site to sell their vintage posters and are pleased with browsers' interest in it. Years ago, when Robert Chisholm first bought his building, he had it stripped of paint to get rid of what he considered a loathsome color put on by the previous owner; the Earth General building, which also had been owned by the same man, has now been similarly stripped to match Chisholm's.

The restaurants Cola's, Blue Moon, Food/Bar, Gascogne, Eighteenth and Eighth, and Flight 151 all remain in healthy operation, joined by the Indian restaurant in the former fish store quarters, which has become the lowest-priced place on the block, and on the high-quality and higher-price end of the scale by Nick and John Accardi's Viceroy, which has become a spectacular overnight sensation. Bob Barbero and Pat Rogers of Food/Bar opened "g," a new bar on 19th Street, in January of 1997, and there are now two more Blue Moons in suburban New Jersey.

In another interesting switch, Alan Gross has sold his building, which contains the newsstand, to Roy, the owner of Flight 151, and has bought a residential brownstone in Chelsea that has no room for a store on its ground floor. The 18th Street News shop continues to operate, though Alan is less readily available as relief manager; it now features the lowest-cost public fax sending and receiving service in the area and is selling Lotto; Chander Nandal had to attend a school to learn how to operate the latter business. Doc is seconded at the newsstand, now and then, by his wife and by an assistant—evidence that business has expanded a bit.

Man Yohn Lee dry cleaners, P. Chanin, and Giraudon shoes
are still in business as is the hardware store across the avenue that
is everyone's resource. Pam Chanin has changed her store's stock
from "unisex" to a greater emphasis on the leather clothing and
accessories that appeal to gay men but still caters to women as well.
Dr. Elizabeth Greenberg has opened a new chiropractic office and
spends less time attending to the store. Patricia Evert has gone out
on her own as a fund raiser; the GMHC Special Events unit remains frequently busy with its several annual events. The St.
Francis Residence III continues on its unhurried way; Fr. John
Felice has been elected "provincial" of the Franciscan order in the
eastern part of the country, a post equivalent to that of a bishop.

Renovations and Relocations

A spate of renovation construction characterized the fall of 1996
on 17th and 18th Streets. The Catholic Book Publishing Company
entirely vacated the Steiner Building at the end of 1995, moving
its operations to the facility it had purchased in New Jersey. What
with modern communications technology and the potential of
quick commutes into Manhattan to see the occasional client or
freelance writer or designer, Robert Cavalero and his staff no
longer require any permanent space in the city. The Steiner
Building was converted into "residential loft condominiums" by a
real estate company; it was ready for occupancy by the end of 1996,
and three months later, thirty of the thirty-six residential units
were occupied and the ground-level area was being renovated for
retail use. The rapid sale of these condo units is perhaps the most
tangible measure of the accelerating gentrification of the area.
Several of the block's brownstones have also been put on the
market.

The transformation of the Steiner Building had been expected.
But the quick shuttering of the Chelsea Day School on 17th had
not; in 1994, it appeared that Jean Rosenberg had another few

years to go before the lease given to her by the building's new owner, photographer William Wegman, ran out. But during the summer of 1996 the upper floors were renovated to become a more integral part of the owner's complex, which a workman said was to include a studio for Wegman's work and other rooms for dogs. In the fall of 1996, the Day School moved to a larger building on West 14th between Eighth and Ninth, and Allan's Afterschool followed.

A third renovation was under way in the fall of 1996 at Hanlit—or, at least, on the 18th Street side of the building. This building, as well as the former Chelsea Day School, had been bought by photographer Wegman, who was in the process of renovating it. Ervin Litkei says that he had "grown tired" of the warehouse and sold it in 1995 and moved his operations to the associated buildings that front on 19th Street, a space he describes as smaller but more romantic. Its awnings, sporting the names of the Jade Gallery and Hanlit Publications, are newly painted but are still behind a high iron fence that does not invite visitors. By the spring of 1997, renovations on the 18th Street side were almost complete.

Liberty High's physical plant has undergone several million dollars' worth of renovations, which have brightened and modernized the interior space and also made its presence on the block more visible. Principal Bruce Schnur reports that the student body now has more Chinese- than Spanish-speakers and that bilingual classes are now also taught in Polish. Coordinator Carol Yankay is excited by a new internship program in which Liberty students work after classes at various nonprofit and community businesses, among them the neighboring Viceroy restaurant; this is the latest innovation in Liberty's comprehensive program to deal with the needs of newly arrived immigrants and ready them to take their places in American society.

As for relocation, Helen C. and husband, Niko, are now Silicon Valleyites, both working, though for different companies, and Helen is pregnant. Similar multiple-alteration-choice notions of the sort that Helen had built into her own computer game had also been developed simultaneously by a handful of other inventors, and hers fell by the wayside. But she has another game idea, for which she owes her employer only the right of first refusal and, if they pass on it, a small percentage of royalties if she sells it elsewhere. More knowledgeable about the marketplace and having better access to it, she thinks this one might go for big bucks.

The Other Big Boys

In early 1995, Reed Elsevier, the corporate parent of Cahners, bought the important on-line reference service Lexis-Nexis, and then announced that it would have to sell one of its other divisions in order to raise cash to help pay for the acquisition. In November of 1995, the company sold fourteen of its Cahners consumer magazines, including *American Baby* and several boat and yachting monthlies, to another media giant, K-III. Subsequently there were reports in the press that other Cahners publications were being shopped separately. Cahners itself, however, has denied these rumors, and at press time no further sales have been made. John Beni has left Cahners for a senior executive position at *Parade*.

Nynex, too, went on a spree of buying, selling, and looking to merge—mostly because of continued pressure on its profits, for instance in the form of competition for the local phone market from companies that formerly handled only cable television lines. Although Nynex has made midtown and downtown Manhattan the best-wired locations in the world for future communications-oriented businesses, the question remained as to how much of that traffic it would be able to carry without losing customers to other carriers. In the summer of 1996, a tentative combination with Bell Atlantic was announced, a merger that would put back together two of the largest pieces of the former Ma Bell monopoly. By the spring of 1997, after regulators had adjusted and agreed to the merger, it seemed likely that Nynex, after an existence of only fifteen years, would disappear as a separate entity.

In June 1997, Viacom-Paramount prepared to take a $1 billion charge for its "ailing" Blockbuster unit, which it acquired in 1994. Blockbuster's founder, Wayne Huizenga, has gone into a new business, Republic Industries, which is attempting to consolidate automobile usage (car rentals, used cars, new cars, car repairs) as Huizenga previously managed to do in two other industries, garbage hauling and home entertainment.

Steady State

Inside the 216 Building, such companies as Bill Donat's Waldon Press and Vikram Patel's Marvik Colour continue on as they have for years, as does Downtown Offset on the ground floor. Oscar Sabel reports that Downtown now has four computers used for printing and is contemplating the purchase of still more. The Microvideo Learning Systems assembly, packaging, and shipping department remains in a loft space there though the company has moved its main offices. MLS and Birns Telecommunications (on 17th) look more savvy than ever to have jumped into the forefront of the "new media" arena.

Across from 216, the Solco plumbing supply depot and Maxwell Lumber businesses are still in action behind their drab facades, as is the Eigen plumbing depot on 17th. Renewed demand for construction and renovation has augmented these enterprises. Marc Bernstein savors the irony of having neighborhood banks calling him, now, to offer loans.

The Old Chelsea Post Office has been modernized a bit, with a lift for wheelchair access, a quarterly newsletter, and the addition of such products as phone cards. The hours that the lobby and windows are open to the public have been extended. Ed Risdell continues as postmaster; he says his golf game is getting better.

Art restorer Marina Yashina was unable to win the contract to restore the murals at the Bayard Rustin High School farther west on 18th, but her talents and expertise remain in demand as artworks become more valuable and people perceive the need to restore and preserve them. Collette Whitney, formerly of HomeWorks, now has a thriving interior design business, with a specialty in kitchens and baths; she employs several assistants, and her work has been featured in national magazines.

Taylor's thrives; the lines for its bakery products seem longer and longer at every glance in the window and no matter what hour of the working day. It seemed in 1994 and 1995 that the enterprise might expand beyond three stores in three locations, but that has not happened. To become much larger would require additional trusted personnel, a larger capital investment, and so on—and meanwhile, there are solid profits to be made.

The messenger services depot, now reduced to half its former size—one storefront rather than two—still sends many messengers flying out on bikes each day. However, it is under new ownership; the parent company, WI, sold its business to a national chain, and WI owners, Dwane Illes and Reuben Weiss, have gone into a new field—telemarketing. Dispatcher Steven Bonfiglio now works for the national messenger services chain, at a downtown location, and at a better salary.

On the north side of 18th the enterprises in the half-dozen storefronts all remain as they were. Authentiques seems to coexist nicely, now, with the milliner; Robert Pusilo has continued the acting career that first brought him to New York long ago, appearing recently in a Chekhov revival and in his first feature film. The B. Schlesinger firm continues to sell uniforms to various municipal and private services, though uniform allowances have become a favorite target of managerial cost-cutters. Michael Palmadessa of Towne House Grooming, still going strong, says that the city is no longer requiring dog groomers to report to the authorities whether dogs coming in to be dipped have up-to-date license tags.

Joe Hwang's House of Cheers also remains in operation, with Mrs. Hwang now frequently present in the store. The Hwangs did sell their Westchester home, but rather than move into the city, they still rent in the suburbs. They have no plans at the moment to sell their liquor store and are awaiting the birth of their first grandchild. At the urging of his daughter, Joe has begun to attend a course to improve his English.

INDEX

clothing businesses
consolidation of, 14–17, 50,
110–11
department stores, 93
pricing, 139–40
specialized, 52–55
vs. food business, 237
CNN (Cable News Network), 173,
229
Coach Stores, The, 102
Cocopazzo (restaurants), 106–7
Cola's restaurant
concept and description of, 98,
134–35, 139, 225
location, 20, 137, 168
viability of, 304
Colgate University, 196
Colonnade Row, 119
Columbia University, 191
companies, large
advertising, 91–92, 121, 245
buying power of, 116–18
choices offered to customers,
113–14
health insurance, 246–47
and innovative concepts, 54
mergers between, 125–27, 203–7,
260–63
partnerships between, 95–96
small business relationships, 2, 5,
87, 99
See also Barneys, Inc.; Businesses,
small; Cahners Publishing
Company; Nynex; Technology
competition
franchise operations vs.
independents, 112, 116–18
large companies vs. small
businesses, 122–24
between large stores, 97, 284
in local phone service, 179–86
between messenger services,
241–42

Postal Service vs. private
companies, 149
Computer Technical Learning
Center (CTLC), 181
computers
databases, 205
direct marketing, 200–202
electronic superhighway, 203, 211
E-mail, 149
game design, 32–34, 50, 77,
280–81
general use of, 176–77
Internet, 186, 297
and mental capital, 217–18
on-line publication, 206
printing, 190–94
small businesses, 176
See also Technology
Con Edison (Consolidated Edison),
5, 7, 48, 146, 234, 236
Coudouy, Carol, 77–80
Coudouy, Pascal, 77–80
Cox Enterprises, Inc., 127
crime
drug related, 264–66
gay bashing, 268–70
homicide, 263
muggings, 266
prostitution, 267–68
robbery, 53, 237
shoplifting, 130
tax evasion, 267
traffic accidents, 263–64
Crown family of Chicago, 30,
286
Cuomo, Mario, 168, 172
customers
anticipating needs of, 13, 116, 140,
275–76
at Barneys annual warehouse sale,
92
and choices, 113–14
gay men, 15–17